CIVIL RIGHTS IN THE UNITED STATES

Issues in Policy History
General Editor: Donald T. Critchlow

CIVIL RIGHTS IN THE UNITED STATES

Edited by
Hugh Davis Graham

The Pennsylvania State University Press
University Park, Pennsylvania

This work was originally published as a special issue of *Journal of Policy History* (vol. 6, no. 1, 1994). This is its first separate paperback publication.

Library of Congress Cataloging-in-Publication Data

Civil rights in the United States / edited by Hugh Davis Graham.

      p.   cm. — (Issues in policy history; #4)
    "Originally published as a special issue of Journal of policy history (vol. 6, no. 1, 1994)"—T.p. verso.
    Includes bibliographical references.
    ISBN 0-271-01343-5 (paper)
    1. Civil rights—United States. I. Graham, Hugh Davis. II. Series.
KF4749.A2C54 1994
342.73'085—dc20
[347.30285]   94-33065
                                             CIP

Published by The Pennsylvania State University Press,
University Park, Pennsylvania 16802-1003

Contents

Editor's Preface

Thirty years ago, Martin Luther King Jr., in his poignant "Letter from a Birmingham Jail" (April 1963), called for the American people to support the militant nonviolent struggle for racial integration in America. In this letter King appealed to the nation to support a "constructive nonviolent" struggle to create an integrated society that would allow 20 million African Americans to live with dignity.

Today legal segregation has been outlawed. Yet America seems even more racially divided than in the early 1960s. The passage of civil rights legislation in 1964 made it illegal to discriminate on the basis of race, gender, religion, or age. Nevertheless, the issue of civil rights appears even more contentious than it was in the 1960s. The congressional authors of the Civil Rights Act (1964), as Hugh Graham tells us, explicitly stated that this legislation was not intended as a "quota bill," but the issue of affirmative action and quotas remains as politically charged as ever. While positive racial quotas were first employed in New Deal public works programs in the 1930s, Americans seem even more deeply undecided over the meaning of affirmative action. The extension of civil rights to "new" groups including the disabled has only created further dispute in American politics and the courts.

This collection of essays, edited by Professor Graham, places the issue of civil rights in America into a historical and comparative perspective. While American society remains uncertain, economically insecure, politically querulous, and profoundly divided over the justice of awarding benefits according to a schema of citizen attributes, Graham assures us, civil rights policy is not a "Pandora's box, which should never have been opened in the first place." He observes that progress has been made in the struggle for civil rights for ethnic minorities and women.

This collection, however, seeks more than simply to measure the success of civil rights policy in America. Instead, contributors to this volume assess the problems as well as the accomplishments of civil rights policy in America. This collection of essays, written from diverse disciplinary, topical, and cultural perspectives, offers the reader a broad and informed perspective of civil rights policy that should foster reasoned discussion, academic debate, and further research.

Donald T. Critchlow
General Editor

HUGH DAVIS GRAHAM

Introduction

Since 1960 the literature on American civil rights policy has grown massive in volume, comprehensive in scope, and increasingly sophisticated in its technical applications. In sheer bulk, the volume of books and articles addressed to civil rights in the fields of law, social science, and history has more than doubled since the 1960s.[1] Our personal, public, and research libraries are filled with description and commentary about civil rights issues and policy since the Kennedy administration. Yet to students of American society and government who regard historical analysis as essential to understanding the policy process, this vast accumulation of writing has been disappointing. The literature has been so fragmented by discipline, method, audience, purpose, ideological predisposition, and intellectual fashion that surprisingly little of it offers a coherent historical analysis of policymaking. Historical writing about civil rights has been abundant, but the historical component in policy analysis has generally grown weaker, not stronger, since the passage of the Civil Rights Act of 1964. As a consequence, our understanding of the development of American civil rights policy since the breakthrough reforms of the 1960s has remained immature. In what way has the civil rights literature in law, social science, and history been inadequate as policy history and why? I will suggest six deficiencies.

First, in the field of law, the books and law-review articles written by lawyers and legal scholars have grown so numerous and technically specialized in response to the waves of legislation, federal court rulings, and regulation by expanding enforcement agencies since 1964 that the continuity has been lost. During the 1960s the national reforms forced by the African American civil rights movement provided a core of developing doctrine that drew coherence from the narrative of its own drama. The nation's attention was first riveted to school desegregation, then to sit-ins and civil disobedience, the breakthrough laws of 1964 and 1965, the urban riots of 1965–68, and the accompanying shift of federal enforcement policy toward affirmative-action remedies. Because the historical continuity of the civil rights story was both self-evident and fresh in memory, the connections between social forces, political response, and policy change were reasonably linear and coherent. Moreover, because Anglo-American law has built on precedent and developed incrementally over time, legal scholars have appreciated the power of the past in shaping contemporary law and policy.

Both the legal community's residual respect for history and the continuity of policy change, however, were overwhelmed after the 1960s by the explosion of rights-based social movements and their attendant policy changes. Whereas the drama of black civil rights by the mid-1960s had engaged all three branches of the federal government in a policymaking process that was unified by its attack on the racial caste system in the South, by the mid-1970s the focus of civil rights attention had both split and polarized. In the area of race discrimination, lawyers and legal scholars concentrated on federal court-watching, as justices and judges appointed by Republican presidents altered in unpredictable and often surprising ways the precedents of the Warren Court. In the area of sex discrimination, attention during the 1970s was split between the federal courts, where feminists began to win unprecedented constitutional protections, and the heated campaigns in the states to ratify the Equal Rights Amendment. Court-watching is inherently a forward-looking game, mindful of historical precedent but concentrating on new rulings and speculating on their future impact. On the whole, however, lawyers and legal scholars have been more attentive to historical factors since 1960 than have been social scientists and policy analysts.[2]

The decline of historical analysis in the social sciences since the 1950s has provided a second weakness in the modern civil rights literature. The behavioralist movement of the 1960s swept historical analysis into the dustbin of old-fashioned institutionalism for most social science disciplines. Social scientists instead adopted the theoretical orientation and experimental methods of the physical and natural sciences, basing their studies on contemporary data and attempting to predict future outcomes. Some social scientists continued to use historical data to establish trend lines, especially demographers and institutional economists and sociologists, for example in understanding the development of the "underclass" in postwar America.[3] But most social scientists have sought the most

recent data sets available for their statistical manipulations and mathe-
matical modeling. In political science and political sociology the behavioralist persuasion dominated the disciplines at least until the 1980s,
when historical determinants of political and institutional culture made a
comeback under the rubric of the "new institutionalism."[4] Similarly, the
new schools of public policy that were established at leading universities
beginning in the 1960s have paid little attention to history. Most have
concentrated methodologically on maximizing the marginal utility of policy outcomes through cost-benefit analysis and operations research. History has remained virtually invisible in the curricula of the policy schools
and historical analysis has been absent from their methodology.[5]

Third, historians in America and elsewhere after the 1960s did not
move to fill the vacuum created by the behavioralist shift away from
historical reasoning. Few historians acquainted themselves with the
rapidly-developing skills of the "policy sciences" or selectively incorporated the stage-based model of the policy process into a historical method
of policy analysis. Instead, a new generation of American historians responded to the shockwaves of the 1960s largely by turning away from the
study of politics, and especially the study of political elites and policymaking institutions, which lies at the heart of the policymaking process. The
baby-boom generation of historians, swollen from 364 new Ph.D.s in
1960 to more than a thousand a year by the early 1970s, shifted as a
cohort toward a vibrant new genre of social history. It emphasized not the
top-down policymaking of political leaders but rather the workaday lives
and grassroots strivings of the common folk—of wage-workers, racial and
ethnic minorities, women. The "bottom-up" social history added an important dimension to policy understanding. By giving voice to the
nonelite masses who do not leave archival records, it drew new attention
to the impact of social policy at the level of local communities. Furthermore, it forced a more balanced and sympathetic understanding of social
movements, especially the two great social movements of the 1960s: the
African American civil rights movement and the feminist movement.
Paradoxically, however, these new sources of policy understanding by
historians were purchased at a great price. Just as political scientists and
policy analysts were developing a staged-based paradigm of the policy
process that emphasized contingency and timing, and also just as the
Great Society legislation of the 1960s was transforming and expanding
civil rights policy in the American administrative state, American historians in their enthusiasm for the new social history virtually abandoned
political history and the study of the state.[6]

Fourth, civil rights policy since the 1960s has been so emotionally volatile as a topic of policy debate that the literature has been ideologically polarized. The chief source of dispute has been affirmative-action policy.[7] Although the shift in federal requirements from nondiscrimination or "color-blind" policies to affirmative-action or minority-preference policies occurred during the Nixon presidency, the polarization began in the late 1960s in response to urban racial violence, campus turmoil, and war resistance. The election of Richard Nixon in 1968 brought a new era of divided government, which generally pitted conservative Republican presidents and their judicial appointees against a liberal Democratic coalition controlling Congress. Passions over civil rights policy were intensified during the 1970s by congressional approval of the Equal Rights Amendment (ERA) in 1972 and the Supreme Court's 1973 decision in *Roe v. Wade* to grant constitutional protection to abortion rights. In response, conservatives launched a counterattack based on a coalition of established Republican leaders and a new social movement combining rural and small-town Protestants, urban Catholics, and western Mormons. The constitutional legitimacy of affirmative action was challenged by the "reverse discrimination" lawsuits leading to the *Bakke* decision in 1978.

By the 1980s, when the Reagan-Bush administration attacked minority-preference policies and applauded the defeat of the ERA, the polarization had become so intense that the scholarly literature on civil rights became adversarial and academic writings read increasingly like lawyers' briefs. Arguably the most tendentious examples of politicized social science came from the running dispute during the 1980s over the effectiveness of bilingual/bicultural education. Like forensic psychiatrists testifying for the prosecution and the defense in criminal trials, the social science experts studying the effectiveness of bilingual education programs applied the scientific method to the same problem while arriving at opposite conclusions.[8]

Historians themselves tended to be at best a generation behind events in their writing and interpretations, primarily because they had so little evidence or perspective to bring to bear on the years since the Great Society (for political historians, the presidential papers of the Nixon, Ford, and Carter administrations were not opened for research until the late 1980s). Social historians, identifying with the insurgencies of the 1960s in which many of them had participated, produced grassroots histories of activist movements by African Americans, student and antiwar protesters, feminists, Latinos, Native Americans, gays and lesbians, and other groups that were textually rich at the community level. But the grassroots and social movement histories were difficult to mesh as case studies of a national policy process of expanding rights regulation, where federal requirements were ultimately dispositive.[9] Moreover, the historical monographs tended to reinforce the fragmentation of civil rights policy by concentrating on separate constituencies. This had not been a problem prior to 1964, when civil rights policy was understood to mean *black* civil rights policy, and "The Movement" was the African American struggle against racial segregation in the South. The subsequent chain reaction of the "Rights Revolution," however, brought under the umbrella of civil rights policy an expanding array of groups whose historical experience with discrimination differed in significant ways from that of African Americans and whose rights claims and remedies did not fit the model of black civil rights.

This is the fifth source of difficulty in the extant literature: the expanding definitions of civil rights policy since the 1960s. The African American analogy, rooted in a unique history of chattel slavery and racial segregation, shaped remedies in law and policy that became increasingly problematic when they were applied to new groups. After 1965, as the benefits of protected-class status that African Americans had won in the 1960s were sought by other groups—working women, the elderly, Spanish-speakers, the physically and mentally handicapped, homosexuals—the appropriateness of the black civil rights model was strained. Feminists, whose constituency had been discriminated against longer and more universally than any group in human history, pushed through Congress an amendment guaranteeing a sex-blind Constitution just as African American leaders were shifting away from the ideal of a color-blind Constitution that had united the black liberation agenda since abolitionist days. At about the same time, elderly Americans brought compelling rights claims against historic discrimination (as did petitioners for children's rights). But unlike claims of discrimination based on immutable characteristics like race and sex, age-based claims for protected-class status varied with the life cycle and hence were universally shared. Further, the three attributes associated with national-origin discrimination—ethnicity, religion, and language—were troublesome classifications for civil rights law. Historically a source of routine discrimination in American life, these attributes nonetheless were murkily defined concepts for classifying citizens and assigning benefits. Languages were learned, religions were changed, and ethnicity was a part-cultural and part-genetic concept of confounding complexity in a nation of intermarrying immigrants. In addition, the handicaps of the physically and mentally disabled, a source of discrimination and exclusion in all societies, created a quite different range of policy alternatives. Unlike the category of race, where public policy since 1964 permitted no *per se* restrictions on racial minorities, and the category of sex, where the ERA campaign reflected the liberal-feminist vision of a sex-blind Constitution, disability policy presented a complex spectrum of possibilities. What criteria should policymakers adduce to balance the rights of the disabled to be free of discrimination, and the hopes of the disabled to lead more productive and independent lives, against the public interest in avoiding hearing-impaired nurses, physically disabled firemen, mentally handicapped truck drivers?

As civil rights claims proliferated after the 1960s, the claimants were drawn increasingly into conflicts where the positive-sum solutions of the 1960s—unfettered access to schools, public transportation and recreation, hotels and restaurants, the voting booth, professional education— yielded to the zero-sum conflicts of the post-1960s. These were the dilemmas of rights claims in collision: the rights of women impregnated by rape against the rights of innocent fetal life; the rights of minority groups to compensation for past discrimination against the rights of nonminorities not to be harmed by the state or by employers on account of their race or other immutable attributes; the rights of African American public employees in Los Angeles to job security versus the right of Latino applicants to proportional representation in the public workforce; the right of Asian applicants to competitive college admission over the claims of African Americans, or Latinos, or impoverished whites.

In the face of such complexities, one is pulled nostalgically toward the moral clarity and policy simplicity of 1964. Yet for all the conflicts and controversies of the post-1960s era, it is important to acknowledge the vast improvements forced by policy interventions since 1964 in the choices and lives of most African Americans, women, ethnic minorities, and other claimant groups. Civil rights policy is not Pandora's box, which should never have been opened in the first place, and it is not Humpty Dumpty, fragmented beyond repair. As recently as 1960 in America, most African Americans lived under segregation law and fewer than 10 percent were middle class; most American women could aspire to paid careers no loftier than airline stewardess; exposure of homosexuality was ruinous. Yet the 1990s finds American society uncertain, economically insecure, politically in a querulous and distrusting mood, and profoundly divided over the justice of awarding benefits according to a schema of citizen attributes that grows ever more complex, like the tax code, in response to the normal coalition-building and legislative bargaining among interest groups.

Sixth, and finally, how can we draw conclusions about civil rights policy in the United States without comparing the American experience more systematically with that of other countries? The literature on American domestic policy has a deep tradition of parochialism. American historians, arguably the worst offenders in this regard, may have the most to learn from the comparativists in the social sciences and, more recently, in the world's legal and constitutional systems. In the 1960s the civil rights drama in the United States seemed unique in all the world. In the 1990s, however, with the collapse of the communist empire, the dislocations of global market forces, the flight of distressed peoples across borders, the spread of ethnocultural violence, and the disintegration of national entities themselves, the problems and accomplishments of civil rights policy in America must be assessed in comparison with similar problems and policies elsewhere.

In response to the complexities discussed above, practitioners of policy history have not developed a common approach or methodology. Given our different training and methods in law, social science disciplines, and history, we are unlikely soon to do so. In the interest of simplicity, I suggest that there are two basic tasks at the heart of policy history. First, we need to reconstruct the story of policy development over time—as, for example, Edward Berkowitz has done in his essay in this volume on disability policy. This taps history's narrative strength by emphasizing the temporal sequence and hence the causal relationship of events. Second, we should ask *what difference* this particular history has made, and therefore will likely continue to make, in the way policy initiatives have worked out. In public policy, this task requires us to concentrate on the historical determinants of American political culture and institutions as they apply to specific arenas—the Madisonian constitutional structure, the market economy, federalism, the system of party competition, institutional cultures in the branches and agencies of government, interest-group pluralism among the associations of civil society, public opinion, patterns of political leadership. At the broadest level, these elements help explain, for example, why national prohibition of alcohol failed, why the Republican party did not dismantle the New Deal, why Social Security has grown popular among American voters and welfare has grown unpopular (during the New Deal it was the other way around), why the U.S. Forest Service and the National Park Service have been bureaucratic enemies, why the newly established Equal Employment Opportunity Commission was hostile to feminist demands, why reform proposals to restrict gun sales, agricultural subsidies, and immigration draw wide public support but tend to get buried in Congress. Such institutionally rooted historical forces by themselves are uncertain predictors, because history constantly changes in response to new circumstances—like the African-American liberation movement, the feminist movement, the right-to-life and antiratificationist movements, the end of the Cold War. But they give historical scholarship its chief authority in policy analysis.

In the six essays that follow, the first three are written by historians who approach their topic by reconstructing the narrative of rights policy development in relation to a particular constituency. In the first essay, on African Americans and the pioneering of civil rights policy in the 1960s, I concentrate on the formative years 1964–72, when a national policy of nondiscrimination was enacted and then within a short and tumultuous period the emphasis of policy shifted to affirmative action. Subsequent developments in racial policy, such as the spread of minority set-asides in government contracting, intensified national divisions over minority-preference policies. These trends benefited conservative Republicans in presidential elections and federal court appointments but did not diminish the effectiveness of the civil rights coalition in Congress or fundamentally alter the federal commitment to compensatory policies.

In the second essay, Jane Sherron De Hart concentrates on the dialogue among feminists over the "equality-difference dilemma." Historically American women had disagreed over the conflicting goals of equal treatment of the sexes or special treatment for women based on inherent differences. From 1968 to 1982 feminist leaders waged a unified, bipartisan campaign for the ERA. But during the 1980s the failure of ratification, the hostility of the Reagan and Bush administrations to the feminist agenda, especially abortion rights and birth control, and the debate occasioned by Supreme Court decisions like the *Sears* case, led feminist legal scholars to a rigorous critique of liberal orthodoxies that had underpinned the ERA. Divisions between liberal, radical, and cultural or relational feminists deepened a debate that, in grappling with policy alternatives involving pregnancy, abortion, motherhood, and biological differences, engaged fundamental questions of philosophy, morality, and science far more searchingly than had the race-centered disputes over affirmative action.

Historian Edward Berkowitz, in the third essay, poses a paradox: Why did conservative Republicans in the Reagan-Bush years take the lead in passing the Americans with Disabilities Act of 1990, a law that vastly expanded the reach of civil rights regulation by granting broad new disability rights to 43 million Americans? To find an answer, Berkowitz reconstructs the story of federal disability policy since 1950, emphasizing political and bureaucratic forces and the changing rationale of federal programs. Beginning with Truman's rationale for adding disability benefits under the Social Security program (welfare support for non-wage earners), policy shifted toward vocational rehabilitation under Eisenhower (training the disabled to become productive workers and taxpayers), mental retardation under Kennedy (disabled children's rights), special education and antipoverty under Johnson (equal educational and employment opportunity), and reached a full civil rights rationale during 1973–77 under Ford and Carter. This remarkable record of sustained expansion under shifting rationales was possible because Congress, the courts, and participating agencies followed the expanding logic of the civil rights model in disability policy, while avoiding the partisan and ideological controversy that characterized the parallel rights-based movements of African Americans (affirmative action) and feminists (ERA and reproductive rights).

Political scientist Peter Skerry, in his case study of voting-rights policy and Mexican Americans in Los Angeles, uses historical analysis to define two conflicting models of political strategy. One, the traditional strategy of ethnic immigrants that was pioneered by the urban Irish in the nineteenth century, is community mobilization through neighborhood political organizations. The other is the black civil rights model, pioneered by the NAACP and adopted in the 1970s by the Mexican American Legal Defense and Education Fund (MALDEF), which emphasizes racial discrimination and litigation in the federal courts. Skerry examines the role of MALDEF in the redistricting suits in Los Angeles during the 1980s. He observes that the Justice Department under the Reagan and Bush administrations discovered the partisan virtues of aggressively enforcing the Voting Rights Act; by forcing urban blacks and Latinos into "minority-majority" districts, voting-rights suits drained surrounding districts of Democratic voters and thereby helped elect more Republicans. To Skerry, Mexican Americans are the "ambivalent minority" because their history provides some support for both traditions, and the choice they make will carry fateful consequences. The community-based political organizations of the traditional model, he concludes, offer organic representation and social mobility, while the race discrimination and litigation model reinforces insular leadership and the politics of victimhood.

The essays by Gérard Noiriel, a French historian, and Mary Ann Glendon, a legal scholar, both compare American patterns of civil rights policy with the experience of other democratic nations, especially since the 1960s. Noiriel concentrates on the dozen nations of the European Economic Community, and emphasizes historical differences between Western Europe and the United States. European nations rebuilt themselves after World War II as social democracies with long traditions of welfare provision for citizens. The American tradition, on the other hand, limited state power, provided many social welfare functions through the private organizations of civil society, and emphasized rights-based litigation in federal courts. The American constitution conferred full citizenship on all persons born in the United States, whereas in Europe foreigners enjoyed social welfare benefits but not equal civil and political rights. Europe lacked America's historic dilemma of African American slavery and discrimination. On the other hand, the surge of immigration to Europe, drawn first by jobs and prosperity and then accelerated by the collapse of communist regimes, has created growing civil rights problems in Europe that, unlike the United States, are exacerbated by European distinctions between citizens and foreigners.

In the concluding essay, Mary Ann Glendon compares constitutional traditions in the United States and the industrial democracies, including Japan. She notes that unlike America's eighteenth-century charter, the constitutions of most modern democratic nations were adopted within the past thirty years. These nations, with long national traditions of providing welfare-state benefits to their citizens, routinely incorporated such positive obligations in their new constitutions. In the United States, by contrast, the sequence was reversed: the constitution long ago protected the political and civil liberties of individuals, but legislative policies to provide welfare benefits developed only recently and, by European standards, haltingly. When the New Deal and its successors created welfare programs that left wide disparities in social provision, Americans turned by habit to litigation. The federal courts since the 1960s have greatly expanded civil rights protection and benefits for groups discriminated against on account of race, sex, national origin, and handicap, but they have resisted constitutional claims to general welfare rights (jobs, housing, education, medical care). To Glendon, the emphasis in recent years on pursuing personal and civil rights through lawsuits has reduced the efficacy of political and legislative institutions and weakened the ability of the mediating institutions in civil society—the family, church, local community organizations, and voluntary associations—to nurture our reciprocal obligations and responsibilities as well as our rights.

Notes

1. According to Bowker's *Books in Print*, between 1968 and 1993 the number of books about civil rights in the United States increased by 107 percent, books specifically about African Americans and civil rights increased by 80 percent, and the number of books addressing the rights of women more than tripled.

2. For two recent examples of historically-minded legal scholarship, see Herman Belz, *Equality Transformed* (New York, 1990); and Alfred W. Blumrosen, *Modern Law: The Law*

Transmission System and Equal Employment Opportunity (Madison, Wis., 1993). The historical shift to affirmative-action policy is criticized by Belz, a legal historian, and is supported by Blumrosen, a law professor.

3. William Julius Wilson, *The Truly Disadvantaged: The Inner City, the Underclass, and Public Policy* (Chicago, 1987); John J. Donohue III and Joseph Heckman, "Continuous Versus Episodic Change: The Impact of Civil Rights Policy on the Economic Status of Blacks," *Journal of Economic Literature* 29 (December 1991): 1603–43.

4. James G. March and Johan P. Olsen, "The New Institutionalism: Organizational Factors in Political Life," *American Political Science Review* 78 (1984): 734–49; David Brian Robertson, "The Return to History and the New Institutionalism in American Political Science," *Social Science History* 17 (Spring 1993): 1–36.

5. Peter deLeon, *Advice and Consent: The Development of the Policy Sciences* (New York, 1988).

6. Hugh Davis Graham, "The Stunted Career of Policy History: A Critique and an Agenda," *Public Historian* 15 (Spring 1993): 5–26.

7. Edward G. Carmines and James A. Stimson, *Issue Evolution: Race and the Transformation of American Politics* (Princeton, 1989); Thomas Edsall with Mary D. Edsall, *Chain Reaction: The Impact of Race, Rights, and Taxes on American Politics* (New York, 1992). See also the special issue on affirmative action, edited by Harold Orlans and June O'Neill, of *The Annals of the American Academy of Political and Social Science* 523 (September 1993).

8. See Coleman Brez Stein, Jr., *Sink or Swim: The Politics of Bilingual Education* (New York, 1986); Kenji Hakuta, *Mirror of Language: The Debate on Bilingualism* (New York, 1987); Rosalie Pedalino Porter, *Forked Tongue: The Politics of Bilingual Education* (New York, 1990); Gary Imhoff, ed., *Learning in Two Languages: From Conflict to Consensus in the Reorganization of Schools* (New Brunswick, N.J., 1990).

9. See Stewart Burns, *Social Movements of the 1960s: Searching for Democracy* (Boston, Twayne, 1990); David Chalmers, *And the Crooked Places Made Straight: The Struggle for Social Change* (Baltimore, 1991).

HUGH DAVIS GRAHAM

Race, History, and Policy: African Americans and Civil Rights Since 1964

The Enduring Controversy over Affirmative Action

Dwarfing all debates over civil rights policy and race relations during the three decades since 1964 has been the storm over affirmative action. Critics have argued that affirmative action in practice has meant requiring racial quotas, and hence practicing "reverse discrimination" against innocent (usually white male) third parties. This has been done, critics contend, in the name of a law, the Civil Rights Act of 1964, that explicitly prohibited racial preferences. Proponents have countered that racism is so deeply rooted in American culture and institutions that mere nondiscrimination will perpetuate the injustice of the past. There is abundant evidence to support both contentions. The purpose of this essay is not to weigh the evidence and determine which side is correct. Ultimately such profound disagreements are not resolvable by logic and evidence alone, because they hinge on divergent assumptions about human nature and the purpose and limits of government. My more modest goal in this essay is to use the insights of history to understand why civil rights policy evolved in this dual fashion following the breakthrough legislation of 1964–68, and to try to assess the consequences.

Policy history is a young and hybrid field of scholarly analysis without settled definitions of theory and method.[1] But the literature on race relations and civil rights policy in the United States since 1960 is rich enough to provide plausible answers to several puzzles and disputed questions. What was the legislative intent of the civil rights statutes of 1964–68, which required nondiscrimination but included recourse to "affirmative action"? Why and how did the federal enforcement agencies and courts interpret this and subsequent legislation during the years 1969–72 to permit or require minority preferences? How have these programs worked in the decades since the Nixon presidency, and what have been their consequences in accommodating racial issues in American public life? Finally, in what ways has *history* played not only a recording and background role but also a new shaping role in the policymaking process?

This essay begins by summarizing the content and meaning of the breakthrough legislation of 1964–68, emphasizing the roots of that achievement in the classic liberal tradition. The second section describes the implementation of those statutes, concentrating on the development of affirmative-action policies during the period 1969–72, and attempting to explain the rapid shift in some enforcement areas, but not in all, from nondiscrimination to minority preference. The third section deals in three areas with the consequences of this shift in the years since 1972. First, what were the chief structural, bureaucratic, and programmatic consequences as measured by the spread of affirmative-action remedies? This discussion follows events since the Public Works Act of 1977, in which Congress created a model of minority set-asides in government contracts that was widely emulated by state and local governments. Second, what have been the socioeconomic consequences of affirmative-action enforcement as measured by the growth of both the black middle class and the black underclass? Third, what were the political consequences for the Democratic–New Deal coalition that enacted the civil rights laws and cemented the loyalty of African American voters as the Democrats' most steadfast constituency? The final section addresses the growing tensions between history's more traditional and optimistic legacy, as expressed in the liberal accord of 1964–68, and newer uses of history that emphasize the tenacity of institutionalized racism and the historical justification for affirmative-action remedies?

I
The Liberal Accord of 1964–1968

Nineteen-sixty-eight was an apocalyptic year. It began with the Tet Offensive and witnessed the political retirement of President Lyndon Johnson, the assassination of Martin Luther King and Robert Kennedy, the burning and looting of large sections of the nation's capital and other major cities by rioting blacks, violent antiwar protest and radical insurgency on university campuses and at the Democratic national convention in Chicago, and the presidential election of Richard M. Nixon. Almost lost in the turmoil was passage of the Open Housing Act of 1968. It capped a comprehensive, four-year burst of social reform that was grounded in the liberal principle of nondiscrimination and that drew symbolic inspiration from the concept of the color-blind Constitution. In 1964 the Civil Rights Act outlawed discrimination on account of race in employment and public accommodations; one year later the Voting Rights Act banned racial discrimination in registration and voting. Together with the fair housing legislation of 1968, they constituted the liberal accord of 1964–68, a social compact forged from the fires of the black civil rights mobilization and hammered into law under the unlikely hand of Lyndon Johnson. The first two laws, in particular, forced changes in American society that were radical and rapid. The bedrock 1964 law destroyed the legal and economic foundation of Jim Crow segregation in the South, and the 1965 law empowered a formerly defenseless majority of African Americans who lived in the South to bargain politically with their ballots for protection and benefits.[2]

The great legislative accord of the mid-1960s was a climax, long delayed by the hypocrisy of American racism, of the precepts of classical liberalism. It rested on six principles, and in at least five of them it enjoyed philosophical coherence and historical legitimacy. One foundation principle was *individualism*. Rights inhered in individuals, not in tribes or clans or races, or in corporatist groups like royalty or aristocracy, capital, labor, the professions, churches, or ethnic organizations. A second principle was *universalism*. An inherently global value drawn from the Enlightenment, universalism in practice was qualified by the legal reality of national boundaries. By consequence the fundamental rights of American citizens, once discovered and proclaimed, were everywhere and for everyone the same. A third principle was *timelessness*. The equal rights of mankind were inherent in the human condition and were socially discovered through the unfolding of history. Because our fundamental rights were not socially constructed, they were not socially variable (except perhaps in time of war). Once such immutable equal rights were proclaimed for Americans in the Constitution, the Bill of Rights, and subsequent amendments, they became permanent. It was conceded that some ancillary rights claims, derived from statutes and administrative regulations, were properly variable (age limits for driving or voting, residency requirements, spousal and parental obligations). But fundamental rights could not be temporary. Fourth, rights were best protected *negatively* in the liberal tradition, by prohibitions against violations. The statutes of legislators and the decrees of judges banned discrimination; they commanded "Thou Shalt Not." They thereby avoided many dangers of ambiguity. Fifth, the essential guarantees of equal rights were *procedural*. They required equal treatment, not equal results. Equal opportunity meant freedom to demonstrate merit, not an entitlement to equal achievement.

A final principle of the liberal accord was modern, not classical. This was *centralization*. Like the New Deal, the accord of the 1960s required enforcement from Washington because federalism had failed for too many generations to honor the first five principles. The states-rights tradition in the South had always defended white supremacy. As late as 1960, 60 percent of the nation's black citizens lived in the South under the humiliations of a racial caste system, and only 28.7 percent of the South's voting-age blacks were registered. Thus in its core policies the accord provided for national enforcement of individual, universal, and timeless rights (as of 1964–68) through Washington-based negative procedures.[3]

Five Core Policies of Nondiscrimination

There were five core policies of nondiscrimination, all of them new in the 1960s. Three were contained in the Civil Rights Act of 1964, one in the Voting Rights Act of 1965, and one in the Open Housing Act of 1968. First, Title II of the Civil Rights Act banned discrimination by race in hotels, stores, restaurants, and similar places of public accommodation. Second, Title IV of the same law aligned the elected branches of the national government behind the Supreme Court's ruling against school segregation. Third, Titles VI and VII banned job discrimination by public and private employers (schools and local governments were exempted in 1964 for political reasons, but were included in 1972).[4] Fourth, the Voting Rights Act, primarily through its Section 4, banned racial discrimination in registering and casting ballots.[5] Finally, the Open Housing Act of 1968 added a fifth core requirement, nondiscrimination in the sale and rental of private housing.[6]

To enforce the core provisions, the Justice Department policed the first and fourth prohibitions (against racial discrimination in public accommodations and voting), which focused on the South.[7] The third prohibition, the nationwide ban against job discrimination (which included sex discrimination as well), was enforced from Washington by a clutch of new regulatory offices and agencies. The Equal Employment Opportunity Commission (EEOC), an independent regulatory commission like the National Labor Relations Board, was created by Title VII to ajudicate job discrimination complaints against all private employers except the very smallest. Title VI banned job discrimination by private employers who received federal contracts or financial aid (the overlap between Title VI and VII coverage for private employers was considerable and confusing). Title VI was policed by newly created offices in the main contracting departments—the Office of Federal Contract Compliance (OFCC) in the Labor Department, the Office of Civil Rights (OCR) in Health, Education, and Welfare, and similar offices in the departments of Defense, Housing and Urban Development, Transportation, and by 1972 in all federal agencies.[8]

It is important to recognize that during the initial implementing phase of the civil rights accord, the negative and race-neutral policing of discrimination produced striking results in some areas. Indeed, two of the five core provisions of the accord were enforced by bans on discrimination that worked spectacularly. The first, desegregation of public accommodations under Title II, had triggered a fierce defense of property rights by conservatives and was backed by the federal government's weakest enforcement club: lawsuits brought by private individuals or by the U.S. attorney general. This approach had characterized voting-rights enforcement under the Civil Rights Act of 1957 and it had proven slow, expensive, and ineffective. Yet in 1964 Title II toppled Jim Crow virtually overnight. The South's commercial establishment, weary of the turmoil over segregation, had quietly welcomed its abandonment.[9]

The second success for nondiscrimination, the Voting Rights Act, contained in Section 4 an automatic statistical trigger that removed procedural and institutional barriers between disfranchised southern blacks (most of them Democrats) and enforcement officials in the Justice Department (most of them also Democrats). As a consequence 930,000 new black voters had been added to the registration rolls in the South by 1970. During the 1970s the historical novelty of mass enfranchisement for southern blacks (and working-class whites as well) replaced the old one-party politics of racial demagoguery with a competitive two-party system and sent to the southern statehouses racially liberal Democrats like Reubin Askew of Florida, Jimmy Carter of Georgia, Bill Clinton of Arkansas, James Hunt of North Carolina, and Richard Wiley of South Carolina.[10]

In two other areas, school and housing desegregation, nondiscrimination worked poorly. In the first, Congress was careful in Title IV of the Civil Rights Act to specify that " 'desegregation' shall not mean the assignment of students to public schools in order to overcome racial imbalance." Shortly thereafter, however, the Supreme Court, in a series of decisions running from *Green v. County Board of New Kent County* (1968) to *Swann v. Charlotte-Mecklenburg Board of Education* (1971), rejected nondiscrimination in school assignments as insufficient to "undo" the effects of past discrimination.[11] Trumping a statute (Title IV) with the Constitution (the fourteenth amendment's equal-protection clause), the Supreme Court ordered widespread school busing to correct racial imbalance in the South. Color-blindness in assigning pupils and teachers to schools was rendered obsolete (or even unconstitutional) by the federal courts after 1968, at least in the formerly segregated states. On the other hand, 1968 marked the beginning of nondiscrimination as national policy in housing. Discrimination in housing, however, was weakly policed from Washington. For more than two decades Congress refused to give significant enforcement authority over the private housing market to agency bureaucrats in Washington.[12]

The enforcement results for the remaining core provision, on job discrimination, were more mixed. Success was dramatic in the South, where strict nondiscrimination destroyed the omnipresent barriers of segregated jobs and unions and soon opened hundreds of thousands of jobs and promotions to African Americans. Outside the South, however, the heightened expectations of the civil rights movement had not been met with such a visible payoff. The Watts riot of 1965 triggered a wave of long hot summers in the nation's industrial cities, most of them outside the South. The racial rioting, coinciding with the rhetoric of Black Power, antiwar turmoil, and political assassinations, frightened the nation's policy establishment.[13] In the judgment of the Kerner Commission report, issued in the wake of the Detroit riot of 1967, America was becoming "two nations, separate, and unequal."[14] The search for a faster and more positive job payoff than nondiscrimination, especially outside the South, led federal officials to experiment with more radical methods in four riot-scarred cities—San Francisco, St. Louis, Cleveland, and Philadelphia—and to forge in Philadelphia an affirmative-action plan that required racial quotas in construction employment.

II
The Shift to Affirmative Action, 1969–1972

That affirmative action took hold as enforcement policy during the Nixon administration is less paradoxical than it appears. Faced with growing urban violence, government leaders sought to fend off social chaos by launching benefit programs with quick and visible payoffs.[15] The goal of the new programs was roughly proportional representation of minorities in metropolitan workforces, where African Americans were underrepresented in most skilled trades and in white-collar jobs. Black unemployment remained double the white rate even in northern industrial states, where fair employment commissions had policed job discrimination for up to twenty years.[16] Moreover, Daniel P. Moynihan's study of the black family had concluded in 1965 that "the Negro family structure is crumbling," with illegitimacy rates soaring past one-quarter of all black births (the white rate was 3 percent).[17] Federal agencies were charged by President Johnson's executive order of 1965 to "take affirmative action to insure that applicants are employed, and that employees are treated during employment, without regard to their race, creed, color, or national origin."[18] To federal officials, the chief economic leverage for speeding job growth among blacks was federal contract dollars. In the late 1960s, 250,000 firms held federal contracts greater than $50,000 and together with their subcontracts they employed almost 20 million workers.

The result was the Philadelphia Plan, spawned during 1967–68 under the auspices of the Labor Department's new OFCC. The plan required construction firms receiving federal funds to submit hiring schedules that produced minority employees in numbers roughly equal to their proportion in the local labor force. Few builders were untouched by the Great Society's grant-in-aid programs, which helped states and local communities build roads, bridges, hospitals, airports, schools, libraries, government buildings, and urban renewal projects; few could risk being found "out of compliance" with federal hiring requirements. Conservative critics called such plans "racial quotas" that were prohibited by the very provisions of the Civil Rights Act used to require them.[19] The first sentence of Title VI stipulated that "no person in the United States shall, on the ground of race, color, or national origin, be excluded from participation in, be denied the benefits of, or be subject to discrimination under any program or activity receiving federal financial assistance."[20] During the last years of the Johnson administration the Philadelphia Plan was rejected by the U.S. Comptroller General, who cited both the nondiscrimination requirements of Title VI and the statutory obligation of the Government Accounting Office to award competitive contracts to low bidders. Following the election of Richard Nixon in 1968, however, the Philadelphia Plan was resurrected by the new Republican administration.

With the surprising support of the Nixon White House, by 1972 the plan's minority preference requirements had overcome opposition in Congress and the courts and had been extended beyond the construction industry to apply to more than 300,000 firms doing business with the government. This covered approximately half of the entire nonfarm private-sector workforce. How can we explain this dramatic change of direction under a Republican president who won overwhelming reelection in 1972 while denouncing racial quotas and calling for a constitutional amendment to ban racial busing?

Converging Forces for Minority Preferences

During the Nixon presidency three new and institutionally distinct streams of thought and behavior converged to shift the focus of civil rights policy from nondiscrimination to minority preference. The first was bureaucratic. It followed a traditional pattern in the politics of regulation that students of public administration called "clientele capture." The capture model was developed from studies of the independent regulatory agencies created by the progressives and the New Dealers. In its original formulation capture took the form of the regulated industry—railroads, shippers, airlines, broadcasters, power companies—capturing effective control of the commission or board designed to regulate economic behavior in the public interest. In the new civil rights regulation of the 1960s, however, capture took a different twist: dominance in the newly created regulatory offices not by the employers being regulated but by representatives of organized minority constituencies.. Redistributionist policies enforced by the new regulatory agencies for civil rights would benefit the protected-class designees, especially African Americans and, in the 1970s, Hispanics.

By time-honored practice in American government, interest groups have sought a dominant voice in programs and agencies that affect their welfare—farmers in the Department of Agriculture, veterans in the Veterans Bureau, ranching and mining and timber interests in Interior, unions in Labor, small business in Commerce. What was new about the social regulation of the 1960s and 1970s, however, was that the benefits of affirmative action affected the entire economy and hence all government departments, not just targeted program sectors. The legislation of 1964–68 had made civil rights enforcement a rapid growth field. In 1969 the civil rights bureaucracies included the Civil Rights Division in the Justice Department (created in 1957); one new independent regulatory commission, the EEOC (created by Title VII in 1964); and twenty-seven new contract-compliance offices established in the line agencies. The new compliance offices, created throughout the subpresidency in response to Johnson's executive order of 1965, were modeled on the OFCC in Labor and the Office of Civil Rights in HEW. To this array, the Nixon administration added the Office of Minority Business Enterprise (OMBE) in the Department of Commerce and a Voting Rights Section in the Justice Department.

The second source of pressure for more aggressive affirmative-action enforcement was theoretical. During the late 1960s intellectuals in the civil rights movement fashioned a new body of theory that would justify and indeed morally require the displacement of color-blind policies by minority preferences. The theoreticians of affirmative action, most of them based outside government, were affiliated with universities (especially law schools), foundations (most notably the Ford and Rockefeller foundations), think tanks (the Joint Center for Political and Economic Studies), public-interest law firms (the American Civil Liberties Union), and single-interest lobbying groups (the Minority Business Enterprise Legal Defense and Education Fund).[21] The social force that justified the new doctrine of affirmative action was *history itself,* in the form of past discrimination. As Lyndon Johnson told the graduating class at Howard University in June 1965:

> But freedom is not enough. You do not wipe away the scars of centuries by saying: Now you are free to go where you want, do as you desire, choose the leaders you please.
>
> You do not take a person who for years has been hobbled by chains and liberate him, bring him up to the starting line of a race and then say, "You are free to compete with all the others," and still justly believe you have been completely fair.[22]

The crippling legacy of history took the modern form of "institutional racism." The theory held that generations of racist thought and behavior had shaped institutional cultures and standards so profoundly that discriminatory results were perpetuated even in the subsequent absence of racial prejudice or discriminatory intent by individuals.[23] Whereas discriminatory behavior was relatively easy to identify, but its prejudicial intent was difficult to prove, institutional racism was subtle and difficult to identify in action but was easy to demonstrate by its consequences. The results of institutionalized bias were measurable by the statistical disparity between minority potential in the applicant pool (for jobs, promotions, appointments, awards, school admissions) and minority presence on the institutional rolls. Evidence of discriminatory intent, though required by the traditional code of color-blindness that had shaped the Civil Rights Act, was held to be largely irrelevant.

Compensatory justice was thus results-centered. What counted was not discriminatory intent but "disparate impact," the technical term for pro-portionately unequal results. The new results-oriented model for affir-mative-action enforcement did not fit the violation-remedy paradigm of Anglo-American law, which had governed the structure of the civil rights legislation of 1964–68 and which conformed to the negative and proce-dural principles of liberal nondiscrimination that lay at the heart of the accord. Instead, the preferred model for affirmative-action enforcement was the "new social regulation" of the 1960s.[24] Unlike the traditional economic regulation of the Progressive—New Deal tradition, which pro-tected citizens from economic injury (price-fixing, restraint of trade, fraudulent securities, unfair labor practices) through "cease-and-desist" orders and make-whole relief, social regulation was forward-looking, seek-ing to reduce citizen risk of future harm. Its goal was to protect citizens from the hazards of polluted air and water, toxic food and drugs, unsafe transportation and workplaces. By analogy, civil rights regulation would remain ineffective so long as enforcement agencies followed the old, quasi-judicial, "retail" approach—investigating individual complaints through courtlike hearings into discriminatory intent. Instead, civil rights regulators should set broad standards of compliance (like the Philadelphia Plan) through an administrative process of notice-and-comment rule mak-ing (like the Environmental Protection Agency).[25]

The third new stream of thought and behavior favoring affirmative action was judicial. Approval from the federal bench was essential to protect the new minority preference policies in the enforcement agencies from conservative charges that they violated the Civil Rights Act itself. Here the pathbreaking shift from nondiscrimination to positive obliga-tions in civil rights enforcement followed the drama of school desegrega-tion. The federal courts, embarrassed by a decade of tokenism following *Brown v. Board of Education* and encouraged by support from Congress and the executive branch in the Civil Rights Act, began in 1966 to demand from southern school officials not mere race-neutral behavior but rather "the organized undoing of the effects of past discrimination."[26] To redress the damage inflicted on an entire race down through the generations, the Supreme Court approved increasingly detailed school policies that stipu-lated the racial assignment of pupils, teachers, administrative staff, and the color-conscious construction of school budgets—judicial interven-tions that were similar to the minority hiring requirements of the Philadel-phia Plan.

When a contractor lawsuit charged that the Philadelphia Plan violated titles VI and VII of the Civil Rights Act by requiring racial preferences in hiring, federal courts in 1970 and 1971 upheld the plan's "colorconscious" hiring goals as a legitimate remedy under the president's contract-compliance program to compensate for past discrimination. When a North Carolina power company after 1964 instituted tougher but race-neutral employment and promotion standards and tests that weeded out far more blacks than whites, the Supreme Court in *Griggs v. Duke Power Company* (1971) ruled that the history of Jim Crow schooling in North Carolina had made the tests unfair even though the Civil Rights Act had specifically approved their use. In *Griggs* the Supreme Court, holding that the regulatory rulings of the EEOC expressed the intent of Congress, formally upheld the "disparate impact" theory of civil rights enforcement.[27]

The Odd Couple: Richard M. Nixon and Affirmative Action

These three streams of affirmative-action pressure appear in hindsight to converge in the late 1960s in a deterministic fashion, prefiguring the sea change that occurred during the Nixon administration. Powerful social forces, however, were arrayed against them and their success was by no means inevitable. In the presidential election of 1968, 57 percent of the voters supported either Nixon or George Wallace. Polls during the Nixon presidency showed growing national support for color-blindness and strong opposition to minority preferences.[28] Yet we know that Nixon, despite the "Southern Strategy" and his conservative appeal to the "Silent Majority" of middle- and working-class whites, encouraged his secretary of labor, George P. Shultz, to resurrect the Philadelphia Plan early in 1969. To defend this surprising initiative against attacks in Congress, Nixon in the autumn of 1969 formed an unusual alliance with civil rights liberals and defeated an equally unusual coalition of labor forces and southern Democrats who attempted to bar the Philadelphia Plan. On the heels of this victory, the Nixon administration quickly extended the plan's proportional hiring requirements to cover all federal agencies and virtually all significant employers in the United States.

Why this, from a Republican president? Most evidence and insider accounts agree (including Nixon's own, in general terms) that Nixon wanted to achieve four goals. First and most immediate, he wanted to punish organized labor, especially the AFL-CIO, for its successful congressional lobbying to defeat his Supreme Court nominee from the South, Clement F. Haynsworth. The AFL-CIO, long a major player in the civil rights coalition, nonetheless despised the Philadelphia Plan because it attacked the seniority principle and undermined long-established hiring-hall contracts. Second, Nixon wanted to drive a wedge between blacks and organized labor—between the Democrats' social activists of the 1960s and the party's traditional economic liberals—that would fragment the New Deal coalition. Third, Nixon wanted to build up the black middle class and cement its loyalty to market capitalism. This would expand a naturally Republican constituency and maximize its class interests while reducing its racial solidarity. Finally, and most important, Nixon the strategic thinker wanted to force a fundamental realignment in American politics. Black-capitalist Republicans were a minor component of this transformation; the major targets of Nixon's appeal were southern whites and urban ethnics. Their defection from the New Deal coalition would leave the presidency, potentially the Congress, and ultimately the federal judiciary under Republican control.[29]

By 1972, when Nixon crushed George McGovern at the polls, winning more than 60 percent of the popular vote while McGovern won electoral votes only in Massachusetts and the District of Columbia, the federal government was committed to an enforcement policy of affirmative action that conflicted with the accord of 1964–68 in five of its six principles. First, affirmative action placed primacy on group rights rather than on individual rights. Second, under affirmative action the rights of American citizens were not everywhere the same, because members of protected-class minorities held priority claims. Third, fundamental rights were not timeless; they were contingent. Affirmative-action preferences were justified as accelerated remedies to compensate for past discrimination. The unfair hand of history was thus palpable in the present; current and future rights were shaped in part by ancestor behavior. The fourth and fifth principles of classic liberalism, negative enforcement of race-neutral procedures, were thus supplanted by positive requirements for race-conscious compensations.

The liberal accord's sixth, newer principle, centralization of policymaking and enforcement, was strengthened by the spread of affirmative-action regulators throughout the federal government. Beginning in the late 1970s, however, the same forces produced a proliferation of decentralized state and local programs that were neither coordinated nor controlled by Washington authorities. During the Carter administration Congress enacted a set-aside program for minority business enterprises (MBEs) that excluded white contractors from bidding for designated public-works projects. The spread of the minority set-aside model illustrates in a new form the traditional American pattern of interest-group pluralism that historically has converted temporary remedies and relief projects into permanent benefits programs.

III

The Growth of Minority Set-Aside Programs

In 1977 Congress passed the Public Works Employment Act, an antirecession measure that mandated expenditures of $4 billion to stimulate a sluggish economy, particularly in the construction industry. The statute contained a set-aside provision—"ten per centum of . . . each grant shall be expended for minority enterprises"—offered as a floor amendment in the House by an African American Democrat from Baltimore, Rep. Parren Mitchell. Thus without committee hearings or a report offering findings about discrimination in the construction industry or elsewhere, and without attempting to offer a rationale for selecting a 10 percent figure, Congress in 1977 enacted the first statute in modern American history adopting a racial classification. Drew S. Days III, a Yale law professor and former assistant attorney general for civil rights in the Carter administration, remarked ten years later in the *Yale Law Journal*:

> One can only marvel at the fact that the minority set-aside provision was enacted into law without having a committee report and with only token opposition. . . .
> Without a careful examination of the facts and alternatives, the legislation may be misdirected and fail to assist those most deserving of aid, may harm others unjustifiably, and may operate . . . longer than necessary.[30]

The token quality of the opposition reflected an apparent consensus among the Democratic majority in Congress that contract set-asides offered blacks and Hispanics "a fair share of the action" in public-works contracting. Congress dealt with the measure as a conventional interest-group demand, not as a remedy for past discrimination that required hearings and findings.[31]

The 1977 set-aside law opened the door for the expansion of government programs in two directions. First, mandates for set-aside programs were added to the authorizing legislation for federal agencies with significant contracting responsibilities. In 1978 Congress furnished a statutory basis for the Small Business Administration's earmark program for business enterprises owned by "socially and economically disadvantaged persons" (DBEs). Initiated administratively by the SBA in 1967 in response to the urban riots, the DBE set-asides theoretically could benefit persons of any race or ethnicity. But in practice DBEs and MBEs were the same; in

1978 more than 96 percent of the firms in the SBA program were owned by members of "presumptively eligible" groups (African Americans, Hispanics, Asians, American Indians, Eskimos, and Aleuts), and two-thirds of the participating firms were owned by blacks. The 1978 law also required large prime contractors with federal contracts over $500,000 to set percentage goals for DBE subcontractors. [32]

The set-aside model for federal grants and contracts proved attractive during the 1980s not just to liberal Democrats in Congress but also to Republican presidents Ronald Reagan and George Bush. Like President Nixon, they attacked racial quotas but supported affirmative-action programs that encouraged entrepreneurship. The Surface Transportation Assistance Act of 1982, for example, required that at least 10 percent of all Federal Highway Administration expenditures go to DBEs. The 1987 National Defense Authorization Act set a 5 percent goal for defense procurement and research-and-development contracts, and by fiscal 1989 $5.3 billion was set aside by the Pentagon for exclusive bidding by DBEs. By 1990 the set-aside pattern for minority firms was common throughout the federal government: 10 percent of international development grants, 8 percent of National Aeronautics and Space Administration contracts, 10 percent of the construction value of U.S. embassies abroad, 10 percent of the construction and operating costs of the Superconducting Super Collider. By 1990, federal agencies were awarding $8.65 billion in minority set-aside contracts. [33]

The second expansion of government programs, more extensive and yet more diffuse, occurred at the state and local level. It was encouraged by a cluster of Supreme Court decisions during the late 1970s and by the growth of minority political power, especially by African Americans, in legislative coalitions and city governments. In 1980 the Supreme Court, in a 6–3 decision, upheld the constitutionality of the minority set-aside provision enacted by Congress in 1977. *Fullilove v. Klutznick*, which acknowledged broad congressional authority to implement the Civil War amendments, was the third of the controversial reverse-discrimination cases decided by the Supreme Court during the Carter administration. [34] The first case, *University of California Regents v. Bakke* (1978), produced a schizophrenic decision engineered by centrist Justice Louis Powell. [35] On the one hand, the Court ruled 5–4 that a quota-based admissions program for medical school violated Allan Bakke's right to compete because he was white. But more important, in light of subsequent developments, a different five-justice majority in *Bakke* (only Powell voted for both majorities) constitutionally approved racial preferences (as a "plus" factor in seeking diversity in higher education admissions) without the requirement of a finding of unlawful discrimination. In the second decision, *United Steelworkers of America v. Weber* (1979), a majority of five justices again upheld a racial exclusion.[36] The Court ruled that white steelworker Brian Weber's Title VII protection against racial discrimination was not violated even though his race disqualified him from a training program that his seniority otherwise had earned. The craft training program that Kaiser Aluminum Company had negotiated in 1974 with the steelworkers union admitted trainees on a 1:1 ratio between white and black workers until the proportion of blacks in Kaiser's skilled craft jobs equaled the black percentage in the area workforce (39 percent) near Gramercy, Louisiana, where the Kaiser plant was located. The Court in *Weber* held that Kaiser's training program was private and voluntary and was sufficiently justified by a history of segregation in Louisiana.

The burden of past discrimination, especially in the South, had weighed so heavily for so long against African Americans that the affirmative-action programs of the 1970s enjoyed a powerful moral edge. In the *Griggs* case (1971), the Duke Power Company, forced by Title VII in 1965 to stop segregating its fourteen black workers (all of them in the lowest-paid labor department) and its ninety-five white workers (all in the four higher-paid operating departments), instituted a new transfer and promotion policy that required either a high school diploma (only 12 percent of black students in North Carolina had graduated from high school according to the 1960 census) or a passing score on two tests (which none of Duke's black workers passed). In *United States vs. Phillip Paradise* (1972), where federal courts ordered the Alabama Department of Public Safety to hire black and white state troopers on a 1:1 ratio until African Americans constituted 25 percent of the trooper force (26.2 percent of Alabama's population was black in 1970), the Alabama state police prior to the court order has hired *no* black troopers.[37] In *Weber* (1979), blacks constituted 39 percent of the area workforce for the Kaiser plant but only 1.83 percent of the skilled craft workers in 1974. Briefs in the *Bakke* case reported that in 1970 there were 2,779 blacks per black physician in the United States as opposed to 599 whites for every white doctor, and blacks comprised only 2.2 percent of the nation's doctors and 2.8 percent of the medical students. In 1976 the U.S. House Committee on Small Business reported that only one percent of federal funds allocated to state and local governments had reached minority contractors.[38]

Against this background, the Supreme Court decisions in *Bakke*, *Weber*, and especially *Fullilove* gave a green light both to Congress and to state and local governments to establish set-aside programs. The Court's affirmative-action decisions coincided with the emergence of black political power in the nation's major cities, including by 1990 black mayors elected in Atlanta, Baltimore, Birmingham, Charlotte, Chicago, Cleveland, Denver, Detroit, Los Angeles, Memphis, Newark, New Orleans, New York, Richmond, Philadelphia, Seattle, and Washington. By 1989, at least 234 jurisdictions—states, cities, counties, and special districts—had established set-aside programs. Not surprisingly the political patronage surrounding such arrangements formed patterns long familiar in the history of ethnic city machines in the United States,[39] and during the 1980s the print and broadcast media were filled with stories of fraud and corruption. One steady source was Mayor Marion Barry's large government bureaucracy in Washington, D.C., where blacks constituted a majority of the district population and where the set-aside requirement for minority contractors was 50 percent. The problem of mixed descent and proof of claim for sufficiently ethnic bloodlines was illustrated by the $19 million in MBE contracts awarded by Los Angeles to a firm whose owner claimed to be 1/64th Cherokee.[40] The most spectacular political scandal was Wedtech, which began as a Latino-owned company in the SBA program and ultimately enmeshed cabinet-level officials in the Reagan administration.[41] There are no reliable estimates of the total funds expended by federal, state, and local governments on contract set-asides and other affirmative-action programs,[42] but the rapid growth of these programs and their budgets since the early 1970s, together with the persisting controversy surrounding them, raises not only legal and philosophical questions but also practical questions of effectiveness. How well have they worked to improve the socioeconomic status of African Americans?

The Economic Consequences of Affirmative Action

Early assessments of the economic effect of compensatory preferences in the job market reflected a general shift among economists during the 1970s against regulatory intervention in markets. Early critics, most notably free-market economist Thomas Sowell, argued that African Americans had benefited most from antidiscrimination policies during the 1960s, which freed labor markets from the economic impediments of racial discrimination.[43] The affirmative-action policies of the early 1970s, Sowell said, introduced new forms of regulatory distortion and harmed both the intended beneficiaries and the larger economy. Recent empirical studies affirm that the most dramatic gains in income for African Americans came between 1945 and 1973, when robust economic growth combined with nondiscrimination policies.[44] The onset of affirmative action, however, coincided with the energy crisis and the slowed economic growth of the 1970s, and also with a great surge of legal and illegal immigration that steadily increased competition between minorities for jobs and wages. Economic growth resumed in the mid-1980s, but the Reagan and Bush administrations curtailed the enforcement budget of the OFCC and limited class-action enforcement by the EEOC.[45] Macroeconomic studies of affirmative action since the 1960s nonetheless showed little or no significant impact on the average employment status or income of black men.[46] Between 1973 and 1987 the income of the middle quintile of black families as a percentage of white income increased only 1.26 percent (from 56.1 percent to 59.2 percent). Aggregating the data for all African Americans, however, conceals more than it reveals. The most striking economic trend during the era of affirmative action since the early 1970s has been the sharp internal bifurcation in black society.

Most economic indicators for the 1970s and 1980s show a widening gap between the black middle class and the black underclass in America. Economic studies of affirmative action that compared federal contract firms with noncovered firms showed that government pressure to hire and promote minorities was effective for black workers who were skilled, better educated, managerial, and female.[47] As sociologist William Julius Wilson pointed out in *The Declining Significance of Race* (1980) and *The Truly Disadvantaged* (1987), affirmative-action programs worked well for those already advantaged, swelling the ranks of the black middle class, but did little to improve the status of the least advantaged.[48] Moreover, like most government programs that benefit middle-class constituencies (home mortgage subsidies, college aid, medical benefits), affirmative-action programs developed powerful "iron triangles" of political support. The growing network of institutions committed to affirmative action by the 1980s included the House and Senate judiciary committees, civil rights oversight committees, and the Congressional Black Caucus; the civil rights enforcement agencies in the federal government, especially Title VII enforcement under the EEOC and Title VI enforcement under the OFCC; the equal employment and human rights offices created in state and local governments and in private firms; the minority studies programs created on college and university campuses; public-interest law firms for minority concerns, such as the NAACP and its Latino counterpart, the Mexican-American Legal Defense and Education Fund; and specialized lobbying organizations, such as the Minority Business Enterprise Legal Defense and Education Fund.

In the American system of interest-group pluralism, government programs backed by a support network as extensive as this become well entrenched in the political process. The rapid growth of the black middle class during the 1970s and 1980s was not dependent on these affirmative-action programs, but its prosperity was greatly accelerated by the programs' powerful incentives.[49] Between 1973 and 1987 income growth for the top 60 percent of black families increased significantly faster than for the top 60 percent of white families. Income for the top fifth of black families grew by 33.3 percent, while growing by only 24.5 percent among the top fifth of white families. Meanwhile, however, the bottom 40 percent of black families fell further behind. The income share of the bottom fifth of black families *decreased* by 17.6 percent between 1973 and 1987. A striking growth in income inequality characterized the Reagan era for whites and blacks alike, but the polarization was much sharper among African Americans. In 1987 the income of the top fifth of white families was nine times greater than the income of the bottom fifth. But among black families in 1987 the top fifth had incomes *sixteen* times greater than families in the bottom fifth.[50]

These polarizing trends can by no means be laid at the feet of affirmative-action policies. In the complexity of economic and social life, government programs are rarely that efficacious, especially in the face of such external events as massive immigration, the growth of drug addiction and crime, and the globalization of economic competition. But the growth of affirmative-action programs coincided with and reinforced the worsening of income inequality in American. Although all African Americans were entitled to government preference under affirmative action, in practice the programs accelerated the gap between the black middle class and the black poor. Far more troublesome politically, however, affirmative-action policies increasingly granted preference to prosperous blacks while the economic status of lower-income whites was declining.[51] In 1987, the average income of the bottom 40 percent of white families was $12,979. Income-earners in these families were required by law to yield preference in economic competition to the top fifth of black families, whose average income was $38,583. Small wonder, then, that the moral and legal claims of African Americans as a class for government preference were viewed with increasing skepticism during the 1970s and 1980s by nonminorities.

The Political Consequences of Affirmative Action

There is a consensus among students of American politics and government that race has been the key issue since 1968 in breaking up the

Roosevelt Democratic coalition and enabling conservative Republicans to capture the presidency and the federal courts.[52] Until the late 1960s the New Deal coalition had successfully united the majoritarian economic interests of the poor, working-class, and lower-middle-class voters in the traditional liberal alliance. Following the Democratic loss of the presidency in 1968, however, the party's leadership shifted to a different coalition base. Procedural reforms sponsored by Senator George McGovern shifted power in party councils to an upper-middle-class, college-educated, culturally liberal elite, recruited from the ranks of the civil rights, antiwar, feminist, and student movements.[53] This new leadership was linked to an array of Democratic clientele groups seeking an expansion of rights and benefits that had spun out of the Great Society—job and education rights for minorities, reproductive and workplace rights for women, constitutional protections for the criminally accused, equal opportunity for the handicapped, gays, and lesbians. Republicans emphasized the unpopular constituencies and demands of the "rights revolution"—free-speech rights for pornographers, entitlements for welfare queens, marital benefits for homosexuals, welfare rights for illegal immigrants. Richard Nixon took the lead in identifying radical constituencies with the Democratic party, and in the process of crushing McGovern in 1972 Nixon detached from the New Deal coalition both the lower-income white populists of the South and the European ethnic voters of the northern cities.

During the 1980s Presidents Reagan and Bush added to Nixon's partisan achievement the appeal of the tax revolt that surged out of California in 1978 with the passage of Proposition 13. The Reagan Republicans captured the presidency in the 1980s by developing a populist stance around the issues of race and taxes, asking blue-collar and middle-class voters to join in slashing the taxes that fed the welfare programs.[54] Reagan and Bush built a coherent conservative majority by persuading working-class and lower-middle-class voters to join an alliance with affluent business interests against high Democratic taxes and social welfare expenditures. Ironically, one of the main policy consequences of the Republicans' neopopulist strategy was a sharp redistribution of income from the bottom to the top.[55] Despite this economic slide, the "Reagan Democrats" remained loyal to the Republican presidency because unemployment and inflation remained low during the prosperous middle and late 1980s, and because the Democratic slates of Walter Mondale and Geraldine Ferraro in 1984 and Michael Dukakis and Lloyd Bentsen in 1988 to the Republicans' patented attacks. Mondale pledged to raise taxes, Dukakis supported the parole program that freed black murderer

Willie Horton to commit rape, and both Democratic nominees were required to perform an extended courtship dance to win the favor of Jesse Jackson—who *Washington Post* columnist Mark Shields called the "president of black America."

When Congress in 1990 passed a civil rights bill that reaffirmed several affirmative-action policies that the Rehnquist Court had curtailed, President Bush vetoed it as a "quota bill."[56] Then in 1991, running for reelection, Bush signed a slightly modified version of the 1990 bill. The Civil Rights Act of 1991 was so ambiguous in crucial sections of its language that only years of litigation would likely clarify its meaning. By 1992 the deepening recession had made the Bush presidency vulnerable to an economics-centered, class-based attack by Arkansas governor Bill Clinton, who carefully kept his distance from the more strident Democratic interest groups, including Jesse Jackson. Clinton's politically astute campaign won a plurality in a three-way race in which the Democrats won strong support from black and Latino voters. The policy consequences for civil rights of the Democrats' presidential victory, like the policy consequences of the Civil Rights Act of 1991, remained unclear. Both before and after the Bush presidency, however, public opinion polls showed a widening racial gap on affirmative-action issues.

The Widening Gap in Racial Attitudes

During the 1970s the proponents of affirmative action defended minority preferences as a temporary necessity, a catch-up adjustment to compensate for past discrimination. Justice Harry Blackmun, justifying his vote against Allan Bakke's admission to medical school because of his race, explained that America was going through a regrettable but necessary period of "transitional inequality."[57] Blackmun hoped that "within a decade at most" American society would "reach a stage of maturity where acting along this line is no longer necessary." In the *Bakke* case, the University of California defended the minority admissions set-aside at Davis as a temporary necessity. "Colorconscious special-admissions programs are not viewed as a permanent fixture of the admissions landscape, the university maintained. "The underlying philosophy of programs like the one at Davis is that they will eliminate the need for themselves and then disappear."[58]

When the support base for affirmative-action programs, however, continued to grow in Congress during the 1980s and spread to new venues in federal programs and state and local governments, it appeared that nei-

ther the minority preference programs *nor* controversy over their legitimacy were temporary. Indeed, both support and opposition appeared to
be intensifying along racial lines. When a *New York Times* poll asked a
national sample of respondents in May 1985 if they favored preference in
hiring or promotion for blacks in areas where there had been discrimination in the past, 42 percent said yes and 46 percent said no. Asked the
same question in December 1990, 32 percent said yes and 52 percent said
no.[59] When a 1990 survey by the Times-Mirror Corporation asked a
national sample of more than three thousand people whether they agreed
that "we should make every possible effort to improve the position of
blacks and other minorities, even if it means giving them preferential
treatment," white men disagreed by a margin of 81 to 16 percent. White
women, who comprise 40 percent of the U.S. voting population, and who
have benefited greatly from nondiscrimination policy since the 1960s and
relatively little from gender preferences under affirmative action, agreed
with the opinion of white men.[60] A study commissioned in 1990 by the
Leadership Conference on Civil Rights found that white voters typically
saw civil rights proposals and expressing the narrow concerns of particular-
ized groups instead of promoting a broad policy opposing all forms of
discrimination. Using a national poll and focus groups, the investigators
did not find intensified racism but did find strong opposition to discriminatory practices based on race, gender, age, or disability.[61]

While white opinion was hardening against minority programs, African American attitudes were growing more favorable. The racial gap had
been small during the 1970s, when black survey respondents favored
"ability" standards over "preferential treatment" almost as strongly as did
whites.[62] But during the late 1980s black support for traditional merit
standards began to fade in competition with minority preferences. In a
1989 Gallup poll, 82 percent of whites but only 56 percent of blacks
favored "ability, as determined by test scores" over "preferential treatment [to] make up for past discrimination in getting jobs and places in
colleges."[63] In 1991 Gallup posed this question: "Do you believe that
because of past discrimination against black people, qualified blacks
should receive preference over equally qualified whites in such matters as
getting into college or getting jobs?" Only 19 percent of whites but 48
percent of blacks said yes, while 72 percent of whites and 42 percent of
blacks opposed such preference.[64]

In March 1993, twenty-five years after Martin Luther King was assassi-
nated in Memphis and two months into the new Clinton administration,
the New York Times/CBS News Poll asked a national sample of respondents: "Do you believe that where there has been job discrimination in

the past, preference in hiring or promotions should be given to blacks today?" Two-thirds of blacks thought preference should be given and 58 percent of whites thought it should not.[65] When asked whether race relations in the United States were generally good or generally bad, two-thirds of blacks said they were bad and 55 percent of whites agreed with them. Polls indicated that in the racial polarization of attitudes over affirmative action, two protected-class groups—women and Asians—generally agreed with white men and disagreed with African Americans. A third protected-class group, Latinos, held traditional preferences for meritocratic values but showed signs of movement toward the preferential policies advocated by Latino political leaders.[66]

IV
Civil Rights Policy and the Irony of History

History, during the three decades since 1964, has been operating as a powerful independent variable to shape national civil rights policy, but it has been doing so in two contradictory directions. One direction of development has been traditional. For two centuries our collective historical experience under the Constitution has shaped our national political culture—our beliefs and values about fairness and justice, about the proper balance between liberty and equality, and about the legitimate role of government. For civil rights and race relations this has meant a conflict for the white majority between the American Creed of equal rights and opportunities and the historic practice of racial discrimination and inequality. Gunnar Myrdal in his monumental study of 1944 called this conflict the American Dilemma.[67] Since Myrdal wrote, the history of civil rights policy has been a painful but successful story of resolving the dilemma in favor of the American Creed. Indeed, the liberal accord of 1964–68 enacted the creed into national policy. Postwar public opinion polls show a soaring consensus on the core principles at the heart of the accord. This poses an optimistic prospect—that a citizenry united by belief in these values shares an interest in the fading of historical discrimination into a racist past. Knowledge of history is thus liberating, not confining; historical self-knowledge can free us from history's heavy burdens. As Justice Blackmun explained in his *Bakke* opinion, we work toward a society where "persons will be regarded as persons" and racial discrimination will be "an ugly feature of history that is instructive but that is behind us."

The other use of history, operating as an independent variable in shaping civil rights policy since 1964, is novel and drives policy in an opposite direction. The sins of our past, captured and entrenched in the values and procedures of our institutions, justify and require policies that will purge the accumulated toxin. Our racist past is institutionalized in the present and hence poisons the future. History used this way becomes a trigger for affirmative-action remedies, which produce group benefits around which "iron triangles" grow. This poses a pessimistic prospect—that beneficiary groups, in order to maintain and expand redistributive programs, will develop a vested interest in their victim status. Racist history will not be allowed to fade into the past; instead, it will be marshaled to the present, summoned to the front to justify future policy.[68]

The tension between these two conflicting uses of history in policymaking will be illustrated by a final example. In 1989 the Supreme Court, in *City of Richmond v. Croson,* ruled that Richmond's set-aside requirement (that at least 30 percent of the total dollar amount of all public contracts must go to minority subcontractors) violated the Fourteenth Amendment's equal protection clause. Writing for the majority in *Croson,* Justice Sandra Day O'Connor explained that unlike Congress, which enjoys broad discretion in enforcing the Fourteenth Amendment (as the Court acknowledged in *Fullilove*), state and local governments are bound by the Court's strict scrutiny test when they make racial classifications (as, for example, in school segregation statutes and antimiscegenation laws).[69] This meant that the kinds of racial categories common in affirmative-action programs could be used only to remedy identified discrimination, and then only if the measures were narrowly tailored and employed and only after race-neutral remedies had failed.[70] Richmond, controlled by a black-majority government since the 1970s, had offered "no evidence," Justice O'Connor wrote, "that qualified minority contractors have been passed over for City contracts or subcontracts, either as a group or in any individual case."[71] Proper findings documenting specific violation, not broad societal claims to historic discrimination, O'Connor declared, "are necessary both to define the scope of the injury and the extent of the remedy necessary to cure its effects." To the Court majority in *Croson,* racial preferences in government policy were permissible under the Fourteenth Amendment, but only under documented circumstances governed by traditional judicial norms of violation and remedy.

The *Croson* decision created almost overnight a lively consultant's market in "disparity studies." In order to obtain findings of discrimination in contract operations and especially in the construction industry, which for two decades had been operating under the minority hiring requirements of the Philadelphia Plan, local jurisdictions hired consultants to document discrimination in the historical record. Tax dollars were used not to defend city governments from charges of discrimination, but instead to help prove them guilty.[72] Major consulting firms moved into the disparity study field, such as KPGM Peat Marwick. Atlanta's study, which ran to 1,034 pages and cost Atlanta's taxpayers $532,000, was prepared by Andrew Brimmer, a University of Massachusetts economist and the first black member of the Federal Reserve Board, and Ray Marshall, professor of public policy at the LBJ School and former secretary of labor in the Carter administration. Between January 1991 and June 1992, state and local governments spent $13 million on disparity studies to prove the need for their set-aside programs, and the federal government's Urban Mass Transit Authority alone spent $14 million. The consultant business promised to remain brisk as post-*Croson* litigation bubbled up from the federal district courts.

The disparity studies illustrate how far the uses of history in making and justifying policy had polarized since 1964, mirroring the racial split in public attitudes toward affirmative action. On the one hand, the catechism of the liberal accord of the mid-1960s—national enforcement of individual, universal, and timeless rights under a color-blind Constitution—seemed by the 1990s to be naively idealistic and quaintly optimistic. Old-fashioned nondiscrimination seemed an archaic canon, inappropriate for a poststructuralist society that had lost its innocence in the fires of the 1960s. On the other hand, history as represented by the disparity studies, providing post-hoc rationalizations for political decisions, was history as a hired gun, cynically screening our collective memory for incriminating evidence. At its worst this was law-office history or Beltway-bandit social science. Client-centered in its epistemology, it began inquiry, like a lawyer's brief, with the answer.

Despite the polarization of American opinion over civil rights issues since the 1960s, there is evidence of an equilibrium cycle in American political life. The presidential campaign and election of William Jefferson Clinton in 1992 can be seen in part as an initiative by center-left liberals in the Democratic party to narrow a history a gap in the public eye that placed them too far from the economic and individual rights of the New Deal tradition and too close to the New Left groups of the McGovern party. In nonelective politics, the *Croson* decision itself may be seen as an initiative by center-right conservatives of Republican persuasion to narrow the judicial history gap by disclaiming purist standards of constitutional color-blindness while at the same time limiting the reach of future claims against a discriminatory past. Whatever the outcome of the struggle over civil rights policy in the 1990s, policymakers will address their arguments to the nation's historical legacy in ways that were alien to the leaders of 1964.

Vanderbilt University

Notes

1. Hugh Davis Graham, "The Stunted Career of Policy History: A Critique and an Agenda," *Public Historian* 15 (Spring 1993): 15–37.

2. See, in general, Hugh Davis Graham, *The Civil Rights Era: Origins and Development of National Policy, 1960–1972* (New York, 1990).

3. Morroe Berger, *Equality by Statute* (Garden City, N.Y., 1952); Jack Greenberg, *Race Relations and American Law* (New York, 1952); Michael I. Sovern, *Legal Restraints on Racial Discrimination in Employment* (New York, 1966).

4. Charles Whalen and Barbara Whalen, *The Longest Debate: Legislative History of the Civil Rights Act of 1964* (Cabin John, Md., 1985).

5. Steven F. Lawson, *Black Ballots: Voting Rights in the South, 1944–1969* (New York, 1976); Graham, *Civil Rights Era*, 153–76.

6. U.S. Commission on Civil Rights, *The Federal Fair Housing Enforcement Effort* (Washington, D.C., 1979); John M. Goering, ed., *Housing Desegregation and Federal Policy* (Chapel Hill, 1986); Graham, *Civil Rights Era*, 258–77.

7. On voting-rights enforcement, see Steven F. Lawson, *In Pursuit of Power: Southern Blacks and Electoral Politics, 1965–1982* (New York, 1985); Abigail M. Thernstrom, *Whose Votes Count? Affirmative Action and Minority Voting Rights* (Cambridge, Mass., 1987); Hugh Davis Graham, "Voting Rights and the American Regulatory State," in Bernard Grofman and Chandler Davidson, eds., *Controversies in Minority Voting* (Washington, D.C., 1992), 135–76.

8. Jeremy Rabkin, "Office for Civil Rights," in James Q. Wilson, ed., *The Politics of Regulation* (New York, 1980), 304–53. For an opposing view of civil rights regulation, see Hanes Walton, Jr., *When the Marching Stopped: The Politics of Civil Rights Regulatory Agencies* (Albany, N.Y., 1988).

9. Elizabeth Jacoway and David R. Colburn, eds., *Southern Businessmen and Desegregation* (Baton Rouge, La., 1982).

10. Numan Bartley and Hugh D. Graham, *Southern Politics and the Second Reconstruction* (Baltimore, 1975); Alexander P. Lamis, *The Two-Party South* (New York, 1984); Lawson, *In Pursuit of Power*.

11. *Green v. County Board of New Kent County*, 391 U.S. 430 (1968); *Swann v. Charlotte-Mecklenburg Board of Education*, 402 U.S. 1 (1971); J. Harvie Wilkinson III, *From Brown to Bakke: The Supreme Court and School Integration, 1954–1978* (New York, 1979).

12. Graham, *Civil Rights Era*, 258–77.

13. James W. Button, *Black Violence: Political Impact of the 1960s Riots* (Princeton, 1978).

14. *Report of the National Advisory Commission on Civil Disorders* (New York, 1968).

15. Allen J. Matusow, *The Unraveling of America: A History of Liberalism in the 1960s* (New York, 1984), 360–75; Button, *Black Violence*.

16. Paul H. Norgren and Samuel E. Hill, *Toward Fair Employment* (New York, 1964); Alfred W. Blumrosen, *Black Employment and the Law* (New Brunswick, N.J., 1971).

17. See Lee Rainwater and William L. Yancey, *The Moynihan Report and the Politics of Controversy* (Cambridge, Mass., 1967).

18. Lyndon B. Johnson, Memorandum on Reassignment of Civil Rights Functions, *Public Papers of the Presidents of the United States, 1965,* II (Washington, D.C., 1966), 1017–19; Executive Order 10246, 30 *Federal Register* 12327 (1965).

19. Lawrence H. Silberman, "The Road to Racial Quotas," *Wall Street Journal,* 11 August 1977.

20. *The Civil Rights Act of 1964* (Washington, D.C., 1964), 115–16.

21. In 1971 John Rawls provided a philosophical treatise to justify contractarian obligations for compensating benefits to society's least advantaged members in *A Theory of Justice* (Cambridge, Mass., 1971). On the eve of the *Bakke* decision, Ronald Dworkin published a defense of preferential treatment in *Taking Rights Seriously* (Cambridge, Mass., 1977), 223–39.

22. *Public Papers of the Presidents: Lyndon B. Johnson, 1965* (Washington, D.C., 1966), 1:636.

23. Louis L. Knowles and Kenneth Pruitt, eds., *Institutional Racism in America* (Englewood Cliffs, N.J., 1969); Joe R. Feagin and Clairece B. Feagin, *Discrimination American Style: Institutional Racism and Sexism* (Englewood Cliffs, N.J., 1978).

24. David Vogel, "The 'New' Social Regulation in Historical and Comparative Perspective," in *Regulation in Perspective,* ed. Thomas K. McCraw (Cambridge, Mass., 1981), 155–86; Michael D. Reagan, *Regulation* (Boston, 1987), 45–71, 85–111.

25. Hugh David Graham, *Civil Rights and the Presidency* (New York, 1992), 223–32.

26. Wilkinson, *From Brown to Bakke,* 108–18.

27. *Griggs v. Duke Power Company,* 401 U.S. 424 (1971); Donald L. Horowitz, *The Courts and Social Policy* (Washington, D.C., 1977); Cass R. Sunstein, *After the Rights Revolution* (Cambridge, Mass., 1990).

28. Taylor Garth, Paul B. Sheatsley, and Andrew M. Greeley, "Attitudes Toward Racial Integration," *Scientific American* 238 (June 1978): 42–51; Howard Schuman, Charlotte Steeh, and Lawrence Bobo, *Racial Attitudes in America: Trends and Interpretations* (Cambridge, Mass., 1985), 86–104; Seymour Martin Lipset and William Schneider, "The Bakke Case: How Would It Be Decided at the Bar of Public Opinion?" *Public Opinion* 2 (April 1978): 38–44.

29. Kevin P. Phillips, *The Emerging Republican Majority* (New York, 1970).

30. Drew S. Days III, "Fullilove," *Yale Law Journal* 96 (1987): 453–85.

31. George R. LaNoue, "Split Visions: Minority Business Set-Asides," *Annals of the American Academy of Political and Social Science* 523 (September 1992): 104–16.

32. Daniel Levinson, "A Study of Preferential Treatment: The Evolution of Minority Business Enterprise Assistance Programs," *George Washington Law Review* 49 (1980): 61–71.

33. Mark Eddy, *Federal Programs for Minority and Women-Owned Businesses* (Washington, D.C., 1990).

34. *Fullilove v. Klutznick,* 100 Supreme Court Reporter 2758 (1980).

35. *University of California Regents v. Bakke,* 438 U.S. 265 (1978).

36. *United Steelworkers of America v. Weber,* 99 Supreme Court Reporter 2855 (1979).

37. Robert Belton, "Reflections on Affirmative Action After *Paradise* and *Johnson,*" *Harvard Civil Rights and Civil Liberties Review* 23 (Winter 1988): 115–37.

38. Summary of the Activities of the Committee on Small Business, House of Representatives, 94th Congress (1976).

39. Steven P. Erie, *Rainbow's End* (Berkeley and Los Angeles, 1988).

40. John Hurst and Ronald B. Taylor, "Fraction of Indian Blood Worth Millions in Business," *Los Angeles Times,* 27 December 1990.

41. William Steinberg and Mathew C. Harrison, Jr., *Feeding Frenzy: The Inside Story of Wedtech* (New York, 1989); Marilyn W. Thompson, *Feeding the Beast: How Wedtech Became the Most Corrupt Little Company in America* (New York, 1990).

42. The direct cost of civil rights regulation to taxpayers and of compliance by employers are difficult to aggregate. For a recent antiregulatory attempt, see Peter Brimelow and Leslie Spencer, "When Quotas Replace Merit, Everybody Suffers," *Forbes*, 15 February 1993.

43. Thomas Sowell, *Markets and Minorities* (New York, 1981), *The Economics and Politics of Race* (New York, 1983), and *Preferential Policies: An International Perspective* (New York, 1990).

44. John P. Smith and Finis Welch, *Closing the Gap: Forty Years of Economic Progress for Blacks* (Santa Monica, Calif., 1986); Gerald David Jaynes and Robin M. Williams, Jr., eds., *A Common Destiny: Blacks and American Society* (Washington, D.C., 1989), 269–328.

45. Criticizing the Reagan record from the left is Norman C. Amaker, *Civil Rights and the Reagan Administration* (Washington, D.C., 1988); criticizing from the right is Robert Detlefson, *Civil Rights Under Reagan* (San Francisco, 1990).

46. John P. Smith and Finis Welch, "Affirmative Action and Labor Markets," *Journal of Labor Economics* 2 (April 1984): 269–301; Jonathan S. Leonard, "What Was Affirmative Action?" *American Economic Review* 76 (May 1986): 359–63.

47. Jonathan S. Leonard, *The Impact of Affirmative Action* (Berkeley, Calif., 1983), 215–21; Leonard, "Anti-discrimination and Reverse Discrimination: The Impact of Changing Demographics, Title VII, and Affirmative Action on Productivity," *Journal of Human Resources* 19 (Spring 1984): 145–74.

48. William Julius Wilson, *The Declining Significance of Race* (Chicago, 1980); Wilson, *The Truly Disadvantaged: The Inner City, the Underclass, and Public Policy* (Chicago, 1987).

49. John J. Donohue III and Joseph Heckman, "Continuous Versus Episodic Change: The Impact of Civil Rights Policy on the Economic Status of Blacks," *Journal of Economic Literature* 29 (December 1991): 1603–43; Richard B. Freeman, "Changes in the Labor Market for Black Americans, 1948–1972," in Arthur Okun and George Perry, eds., *Brookings Papers on Economic Activity* (Washington, D.C., 1973), 67–132.

50. Thomas Byrne Edsall with Mary D. Edsall, *Chain Reaction: The Impact of Race, Rights, and Taxes on American Politics* (New York, 1992), 231–34.

51. Dave M. O'Neill and June O'Neill, "Affirmative Action in the Labor Market," *Annals* 523 (September 1992): 88–103.

52. See, for example, Byron E. Shafer, *Bifurcated Politics* (Cambridge, Mass., 1988); Carl Everett Ladd, Jr., *Transformations of the American Party System* (New York, 1978); Edward G. Carmines and James A. Stimson, *Issue Evolution: Race and the Transformation of American Politics* (Princeton, 1989); E. J. Dionne, Jr., *Why Americans Hate Politics* (New York, 1991); Edsall and Edsall, *Chain Reaction*.

53. Byron E. Shafer, *Quiet Revolution: The Struggle for the Democratic Party and the Shaping of Post Reform Politics* (New York, 1983); Edsall and Edsall, *Chain Reaction*, 3–16.

54. The strategic linkage of race and taxes for Reagan Republicans is explicated by the Edsalls in *Chain Reaction*, 1–16, 116–53.

55. Between 1977 and 1989, 90 percent of the nation's real income growth went to the top 10 percent of American families and real income doubled for the top 1 percent. During those same years the bottom 60 percent of American families lost real income and the bottom 10 percent, falling back by 10 percent, experienced a downward social mobility on a scale not seen since the Great Depression.

56. The main target of congressional liberals was the Supreme Court's 1989 decision in *Wards Cove Packing Co. v. Antonio*, in which the Court's post-1988 conservative majority revised the *Griggs* standard of 1971 for proving "disparate impact" discrimination. In *Wards Cove* a 5–4 majority shifted much of the burden of proving discrimination from employers to employees and held that employer hiring practices that produced a disparate impact on minorities need only meet a standard of reasonable "business justification," not the stringent standard of "business necessity" set by *Griggs*.

57. *Regents of the University of California v. Bakke*, 438 U.S. at 403.

58. Brief of Petitioners, *University of California v. Bakke*, 42–43.

59. Peter Applebome, "Rights Movement in Struggle for an Image as Well as a Bill," *New York Times*, 3 April 1991.

60. Peter A. Brown, "Ms. Quota," *New Republic*, 15 April 1991, 18–19.

61. Thomas Byrne Edsall, "Rights Drive Said to Lose Underpinnings," *Washington Post*, 9 March 1991.

62. George H. Gallup, *The Gallup Poll: Public Opinion, 1972–1977*, (Wilmington, Del., 1978), 2:1059.

63. *Gallup Poll Monthly*, 19 December 1989, 18.

64. Seymour Martin Lipset, "Equal Chances Versus Equal Results," *The Annals* 523 (September 1992): 66–69.

65. *New York Times*, 4 April 1993. The polling sample contained 1,368 adults (1,056 white and 229 black).

66. Press release, Latino National Political Survey, Washington, D.C., 15 December 1992. For a discussion of Latino attitudes, see Peter Skerry's essay in this volume.

67. Gunnar Myrdal, *An American Dilemma: The Negro Problem and Modern Democracy* (New York, 1944).

68. By the early 1990s pessimism was growing on both the right and left about civil rights prospects and policy in America. On the right, see Peter Collier and David Horowitz, eds., *Second Thoughts About Race in America* (Lanham, Md., 1991); on the left, Derrick A. Bell, *Faces at the Bottom of the Well: The Permanence of Racism* (New York, 1992).

69. *City of Richmond v. Croson*, 488 U.S. 469 (1989).

70. George R. LaNoue, "Social Science and Minority 'Set-Asides,' " *The Public Interest* 110 (Winter 1993): 49–62; LaNoue, " 'But for' Discrimination: How Many Minority Businesses Would There Be?" *Columbia Human Rights Law Review* 24 (Winter 1992–93): 93–133.

71. *City of Richmond v. Croson*, 488 U.S. at 510.

72. Consultants were obliged to reach deeply enough into history to avoid tainting any current government officials or contracting companies, since that would raise the issue of sanctions against the discriminator and could lead to a rebuttal. See LaNoue, "Minority 'Set-Asides,' " 52–60.

JANE SHERRON DE HART

Equality Challenged: Equal Rights and Sexual Difference

"ERA Won't Go Away!" The words were chanted at rallies and unfurled on banners at countless marches as the deadline—June 30, 1982— approached for ratification of the Equal Rights Amendment. To include in the Constitution the principle of equality of rights for women, supporters insisted, was an essential of republican government in a democratic society. Congress had shared that perception in 1972, passing a series of measures aimed at strengthening and expanding federal legislation banning discrimination on the basis of sex. Included was a constitutional amendment simply stating that "Equality of rights under the law shall not be denied or abridged by the United States or any state on account of sex." Thirty-five of the thirty-eight states necessary for a three-fourths majority needed to amend the Constitution had given their approval.

The failure to secure the additional three endorsements for what had originally seemed to be a straightforward extension of civil rights to women understandably enraged supporters. Yet one of the most striking aspects of the ten-year ratification struggle is how suspect the very concept of equality had become in the wake of two decades of litigation, legislation, and executive orders on behalf of civil rights for minorities. Public opinion polls indicated that more and more Americans favored equality in principle. But by the 1980s the meaning of gender equality and its legitimacy as a goal for women were being challenged on so many fronts as to render problematic both principle and policy.

The nature of that challenge is the subject of this essay. The first section highlights key themes in the popular attack on sexual equality that emerged in the ratification struggle of the 1970s; the second, after briefly tracing the transformation of this popular discontent into administration policy during the Reagan-Bush era, focuses primarily on key Supreme Court decisions and secondarily on federal legislation involving women's rights during the 1980s and early 1990s; the third examines responses to the stalemate and defeats of the 1980s by feminist scholars. Feminist legal scholarship is particularly effective in illuminating the limitations of rights theory and the problem that female difference poses in the creation of gender-just law and policy. My primary purpose is to provide insight into how our understanding of equality has changed as appreciation has grown of the profound complexities and ambiguities involved in translating principle into policy.

I

Debate over ERA was never symmetrical in the sense that every argument for ratification was met by a counterargument addressed to that particular way of understanding the issue. Rather, arguments, whether public rhetoric or private statements, were layered with feelings, perceptions, ideology, and historical consciousness. Representing individual strands in a pattern of meaning, antiratificationist arguments were especially revealing of the cultural context in which opposition to equality emerged in the 1970s.[1]

Equality as Intrusive and Unreasonable Government

One woman's letter to her U.S. Senator urging him to vote against the ERA consisted of three short sentences. "*Forced* busing, *forced* mixing, *forced* housing. Now *forced* women! No thank you." At legislative hearings on ratification, another woman pleaded, "Please don't desexigrate us." The linkage between racial equality and sexual equality permeated debates on ERA. Although both statements may have been infused with racism and antistatism, at issue were the specific judicial decisions and executive orders that transformed the principle of equality into practice. A Supreme Court that had not only mandated racial integration but prohibited prayer in the public schools and struck down bans on birth control, abortion, and pornography, many Americans believed, could no longer be trusted to allow people to live the way they wanted to live in their own localities. When ratificationists said that the implementation of a constitutional ban on sexual discrimination would be left to the Supreme Court, conservatives were profoundly suspicious. Their train of thought was evident in the frequency with which anti-ERA lawmakers in

North Carolina, for example, mentioned the Court's enforcement of voting rights as indicative of the Court's thinking. Such suspicions were not
confined to disgruntled government officials in the South. The numerous
hostile references to busing and to the dictates of HEW (Department of
Health, Education, and Welfare) that surfaced in Massachusetts during
debate on a state ERA made clear that people throughout the nation
believed that court-enforced sexual equality, like racial equality, would
further diminish the power exercised by state and local government.[2]

Such logic also illuminates charges, mystifying to ratificationists, that
ERA would destroy the family. To understand such charges requires recognition of the meaning attached to the busing of children to achieve racial
balance in the schools, perhaps the most controversial of the various policy
initiatives designed to end racial discrimination. Although ERA proponents saw the measure as having nothing to do with private relationships,
many Americans saw busing, constitutionally required by federal courts to
achieve racial equality, as a direct attack on the family, a denial of parent's
rights to educate their children where and how they pleased. The moving of
children literally from their parents' door to faraway schools was perceived
as state intrusion into the private domain of the family, subverting the
influence of parents who preferred to rely on neighborhood institutions to
reinforce parental values. Such perceptions provided a pattern of plausibil-
ity to charges from ultraconservative spokeswomen such as Phyllis Schlafly
who invoked a post-ERA world in which mothers, no longer financially
able to remain at home, would be forced to surrender their children to
government-sponsored day-care centers. There childcare personnel would
supplant parental authority and family identity with loyalty to the state.

Schlafly's apocalyptic vision of what would happen if Big Brother or,
more appropriately, Big Sister, had her way in Washington resonated
with social conservatives who had seen what a federal agenda in feminist
hands would look like at the International Women's Year Conference in
Houston in 1977. A meeting subsidized by the U.S. government and
attended by the wives of three Presidents of the United States had endorsed not only women's rights and ERA but government-sponsored
childcare, federal funding of abortions for poor women, contraception for
minors without parental consent, and gay rights. That the threat was seen
as moral as well as political was made clear by the 1980 White House
Conference on Families with its acknowledgment of multiple family
forms. To adopt the definition of family favored by feminists and to apply
the term to a group of people unrelated by blood, marriage, or adoption,
or to unmarried heterosexual couples, or, worse still, to lesbians bringing
up a child was to provide government sanction to the deviance and

immorality that traditionalists associated with the cultural rebellion of the Sixties. Despite assurances that the ERA was concerned only with discrimination in the law, opponents felt they knew better. The way they had experienced the implementation of policies designed to achieve racial integration warranted a vote of no confidence in a government whose policies promoting women's rights would further erode local authority, traditional social arrangements, and established norms and values—all in the name of equality.[3]

Equality as Equal Opportunity—and Female Disadvantage

"I am a widow," declared an ERA opponent, "have three children, and work to make ends meet. I am still against the ERA. I am a woman—and want to be treated as a woman—not as a man." The refrain "We don't want to be men" permeated the discourse of antiratificationists, frustrating ratificationists who insisted that voiding classification by sex in the law had nothing to do with the masculinization of women. The apprehension, defensiveness, and anger that suffused such statements came from women who identified the ERA with feminism and the repudiation of traditional roles from which they, as self-styled "family-oriented women," derived meaning and identity. The issue had little to do with whether or not women worked outside the home—many anti-ERA women did. Rather, the concern was the price of integration into a male world. Women who supported the ERA, opponents believed, were women who had adopted masculine values, behavior, and jobs. They had become aggressive, demanding, and competitive—which is to say, they behaved like men. Women, observed an antiratificationist, whether at work or at home, should "ease into what was peaceful and productive" and "competing with a man" was neither. Antiratificationist women seemed to be saying: "You feminists have forced your way into a man's world, competed with men, and won. But you have become men in the process. Now with the ERA you want to impose upon us your standard of behavior, your definition of equality. You want to make us the same as men."[4]

The conclusion that feminists/ratificationists wanted to be—and wanted all women to be—men is a measure of the difficulty ERA opponents had separating sex from gender. It was also a measure of how they understood equality. Although variously defined, equality within the American context has generally meant equality of opportunity, which in turn is associated with work and competition. Liberal feminists, mostly middle-class, educated, and eager for access to "meaningful" jobs outside the home, had

reinforced that linkage in the early years of the feminist movement. But if
they found much to celebrate in Gloria Steinem's quip, "We have become
the men our mothers wanted us to marry," antiratificationist women did
not. In the work world of secretarial pool and assembly line, assumptions
about sexual difference, codified in protective legislation and symbolized by
the coffee klatch and ladies' lounge, was the only thing that protected
women. "Being a woman" was not an appeal to be placed on a pedestal.
Rather, it was a realistic assessment of what equality meant in a workplace
where most women lacked the psychological attributes and physical
strength associated with males. "If it were possible for you to stroll through
[my] plant unseen," insisted an ERA opponent, "you would find more
women working harder most of the time than did men. You would also find
that women do not have the respect of the men that they once had. It is not
because of the fact that morality is any less, but because of equality. . . . If
we become equal [to men], we will have to load 44 lb cases of cigarettes into
box cars and also receive these same cases from conveyor belts and stack
them on pallets higher than our heads. There are also many other jobs that
women will have to do in a place like ours because of straight line seniority
and equality."

So closely linked were work, competition, and masculinity in the
American context that opponents literally could not extract male values
from the presumably gender-neutral ethos associated with ERA. What
they heard in debate over ERA was not the traditional language of suffrage seeking to legitimate *women's* action in the polity, but rather feminist demands for equality *with men*, using men as the measure of female
action and value. What the language of rights and equality evoked, therefore, were images not of liberation but of loss. The idea of the autonomous
individual freed from the constraints of gender hierarchy and oppression,
which came so naturally to women who framed their claim to equality
within an emancipatory tradition of rights consciousness, was both alien
and alienating. For anti-ERA women, the image that emerged was not of
individuals free to choose social roles and careers on the basis of talent
and preference rather than stereotype, but of women *forced* to be men and
thus bereft of the values and female relationships that had defined and
sustained women historically.

Equality as Denial of Difference

Equality not only disadvantaged women, antiratificationists argued, it also
endangered them. The charge gained credibility in debate about the impli-

cations of gender-neutral law for military service. Ratificationists agreed
that women would be subject to the draft, were conscription reinstated, but
not *all* women would have to serve—most men, in fact, had never had to do
so. As for combat assignments, military commanders could make those
assignments on the basis of physical strength and individual preference—
many women in the military wanted such assignments. Antiratificationists, with their images of war shaped by televised depictions of the
Vietnam War, did not find such reassurances convincing.

"Today," a mother wrote after ERA had passed the U.S. Senate, "I am
ashamed and terrified at what the future holds for my three little girls.
Will my shy, sweet Tommy be drafted in six years? So modest I can't even
see her undress. Oh, God! I can't stand it. I just can't bear it. You must
pass a law allowing parents to have girl children sterilized. This would be
the only solution. Then women would not have to worry about or prevent
pregnancy just like men. Everyone would be truly equal. Dear God in
heaven—help us women."

Her words did not constitute a linear analysis of cause and effect, but a
cry of anguish in which images of innocence, ravage, and death commin-
gled. The fusion of the ERA and sterilization shrieked danger. To deny
sexual distinction in the law was to leave women vulnerable to the power
of men in its most violent expression. But the danger Tommy faced was
not just sexual violation in barracks or on battlefield; it was ultimate,
elemental obliteration of self—and of all the values and norms that had
shaped her in the first place. No more Tommy; no more Tommys. "Oh
God," she cried, "I just can't bear it." Moral failure and existential terror
fused in the eruption of her feelings. The anguish, also evident when
other anti-ERA women spoke of the ERA, sex, and self, suggests that
what was at issue was the basic meaning of life itself. Certitude about the
role of sex in shaping person identity, private obligation, family life, and
social responsibility was, for many women opposing ERA, essentially a
religious conviction. Tommy's mother did not say to her U.S. Senator
that ERA was unbiblical or un-Christian, but that it would destroy little
girls. Addressing God did not mean that she was especially religious,
although she may have been, but that she had assigned to her daughter's
gender an absolute quality.

Gender, in short, was sacred. It was a given; a biologically, physically,
defined thing; a clear definite division of humanity into two; a basic
reminder of the orderliness of Nature. For women living in a world in
which personal identity, social legitimacy, economic viability, and moral
order were rooted in traditional gender categories, insisting that gender
was a social construction made no sense. Calling into question those

categories—making men and women "the same" in the name of gender-neutral law—represented to anti-ERA women both ultimate folly and ultimate danger. In denying biological difference, equality thus imperiled the very group it was supposed to benefit.

Such perceptions did not defeat the ERA. But they do help to explain: (1) the ease with which opponents transformed a simple guarantee of legal equality into an absolute assurance of gender revolution; (2) the reluctance of conservative legislators to endorse a measure whose implementation they believed would mean further intrusions of federal power that could threaten business, family, locality, and their own power to govern; and (3) the division over the amendment among women themselves, which allowed conservative lawmakers to vote their apprehensions and still claim they were responsive to the needs and wishes of female constituents. Those same perceptions were part of a larger process by which equality as a principle was gradually delegitimized and resistance to policies mandating racial integration was validated. The result would be a new and very different civil rights agenda in the 1980s.

II

After the presidential campaign of 1980, in which the President-elect promised to get government "off the backs of the American people," critics of civil rights policy were confident that at last they had a friend in the White House. To what extent Ronald Reagan would succeed in reversing the trend of expanding civil rights activism on the part of the federal government remained to be seen. There was no mistaking the intent, however, as the administration moved swiftly to recast the Commission on Civil Rights with conservatives, transform the Equal Employment Opportunity Commission, make the attorney general the point man for an attack on affirmative action in the courts, and eventually to transform through new judiciary appointments the Supreme Court itself.

Affirmative-action policy was a natural target. Resentment at the way in which nondiscrimination had evolved into minority preferences and racial quotas had been building throughout the 1970s; so too had dismay at the extent to which equality of opportunity had given way to equality of results. Affirmative action, critics charged, entailed not only excessive costs and paperwork but also resulted in unqualified hires and reverse discrimination against white men. Justice Department statements from the Reagan administration reflected that discontent. According to the attorney general, quotas, numerical goals, and timetables should be rejected as means of redressing the present consequences of past discrimination. Evidence of discrimination should consist of intent to discriminate on the part of the employer rather than on statistical disparities. And remedies should be limited to specific individuals who had actually suffered discrimination.[5]

Clearly, nothing short of "an intellectual sea change" in civil rights policy was the goal.[6] To the extent that the Supreme Court was persuaded by arguments advanced by the Justice Department, women as well as racial minorities stood to lose. Efforts to achieve equality in the workplace had been a key objective of the women's movement since its reemergence in the 1960s. Affirmative action had been essential to those early gains, just as had Title IX of the Educational Amendment Act, Title VII of the Civil Rights Act, the Equal Pay Act, and the abortion rights conferred by *Roe v. Wade*.[7] To weaken any one of those tools would weaken the drive for sexual equality, advocates of women's rights insisted, for collectively they embodied a whole set of assumptions about women and their roles and choices in life. How the Court would rule on cases involving affirmative-action preferences for women, pregnancy in the workplace, comparable worth, and other sex-discrimination issues thus assumed critical importance, both as an indicator of how well the administration had succeeded in reorienting civil rights policy and as a key to judicial understanding of the meaning of sexual equality, sexual difference, and equal rights in the absence of a constitutional mandate.

A Divided Court: Affirmative Action and Pregnancy Disability

Although the first case to come before the Supreme Court in which preferences for women was the primary issue was not heard until 1987, affirmative-action advocates must have awaited the decision in *Johnson v. Transportation Agency* with apprehension. That the administration's interpretation of civil rights policy was taking hold in the lower courts was already evident in the notorious Sears case. A sex-discrimination investigation initiated by the Equal Employment Opportunity in the 1970s, the case came to trial in 1986. The issue was gender segregation in the workplace. The crux of the dispute involved the absence of women from higher-paying jobs as commission salespersons. Was the low number of women in these jobs the result of women's own choices, as Sears claimed, or of societal discrimination and employers' reluctance to make those jobs available? Although the case gained notoriety for its use of expert testimony from historians—feminist scholars testified on opposing sides—the argument constructed by Sears's lawyers proved both compelling and exculpatory. The judge, a Reagan appointee, found statistical disparities inadequate evidence of employer discrimination. There was no intent to discriminate—Sears had an affirmative-action plan in place—and there were no victims present who had actually suffered discrimination. Rather, Sears's female employees had simply made different job choices from those of males, as typically both sexes had done historically. The decision was a victory not only for Sears but for the administration in that it nicely fitted with the logic of Reagan conservatism. In the meantime, however, the focus was on the Supreme Court.[8]

Initially the Court had proven resistant to administration arguments— at least in cases involving racial minorities. It had not only rejected requirements of "intent" as well as the "victim-specific" approach, but affirmed the use of hiring "goals" (to be used sparingly) and court-ordered highly specific "catch-up" quotas (to be used in extreme cases). The Justice Department, undaunted by these rebuffs, had plowed ahead, urging the Court in 1987 to strike down an affirmative-action plan of Santa Clara County that provided preferences for female workers.[9]

The problem, as in the Sears case, was the segregation of women into low-paying jobs. Diane Joyce had been promoted to road dispatcher over Paul Johnson, a white male, in a voluntary effort by the Santa Clara Transportation Department to redress the paucity of women in the higher-paying, skilled-craft category. Johnson, who had scored two points higher than Joyce on an oral exam, claimed to be a victim of reverse discrimination. Attorney General Edwin Meese III agreed with the male plaintiff. Neither sex-based nor race-based preferences were lawful, he insisted, when used solely "to achieve some numerical proportion or balance of race and gender" in a workforce or to make up for the "mere history" of discrimination. Although Joyce has produced evidence of sex bias in her case, there was no formal finding that the Santa Clara Transportation Agency had discriminated against women in the past.[10]

In a 6–3 decision, the Court found in favor of the agency. Justice William J. Brennan, Jr., writing for the majority, insisted that it was indeed "appropriate to consider as one factor the sex of Ms. Joyce in making the decision. . . . the plan," he pointed out, "sets aside no positions for women. . . . Rather, the plan merely authorizes that consideration be given to affirmative action concerns when evaluating qualified applicants." Brennan claimed that this type of voluntary program is important to correct "a conspicuous imbalance in traditionally segregated job categories." In essence, the majority affirmed that "mere history of discrimination" did indeed matter, that discrimination need not be victim-specific, and that different treatment was legal when it furthered equality of opportunity.[11]

That same principle was reaffirmed in *California Federal Savings and Loan Association v. Guerra* a year later—a decision that further illuminated judicial thinking about equality and difference. The issue was pregnancy as a temporary disability. In 1978, feminists and their allies had succeeded in obtaining congressional passage of legislation that amended the Civil Rights Act of 1964, requiring employers to give workers physically disabled by pregnancy and childbirth the same benefits given to other disabled workers. The problem, however, was not yet resolved for the many smaller companies that typically provided no disability coverage at all. Equal (the same) treatment in such situations actually penalized women employees unable to work because of pregnancy-related illness. Recognizing that the procreative rights of female employees were burdened while the comparable rights of male employees were not, lawmakers in California had responded by stipulating that employers must provide pregnant workers unpaid leave for the period of disability even if such "coverage" was not available to other workers. Employers complained that this constituted "preferential" treatment for women and thereby discriminated against men. California Federal Savings and Loan Association won a federal court order invalidating the state law after a receptionist asked for a reinstatement from a three-month pregnancy leave. Pointing to the federal Pregnancy Discrimination Act, which mandated that pregnant workers be treated the same as other employers for all employment-related purposes, Cal Fed asserted that since it did not guarantee men their jobs back after disability leave, it could not treat women any differently.[12]

After the U.S. Ninth Circuit Court of Appeals reinstated the pregnancy disability statute, the defendant appealed to the Supreme Court. Writing for the majority, voting to uphold the California law, Justice Thurgood Marshall went to the heart of the matter, claiming that "while federal law mandates the same treatment of pregnant and non-pregnant employees, it would be a violation of the spirit of the law to read it as barring preferential treatment of pregnancy." The California law, he reasoned, "promotes equal employment opportunities because it allows women as well as men to have families without losing their jobs." Any "state laws based on 'stereotypical notions' that pregnant workers suffered from an inherent handicap, or denying opportunities to them," Marshall concluded, "would violate Federal law."[13]

The Court's reading of Title VII with respect to pregnancy was further illuminated when it addressed the controversial issue of fetal protection policies in *UAW v. Johnson Controls, Inc.* Johnson Controls, a major producer of batteries, had excluded "women with childbearing capacity" from its battery division. Motivating company policy were concerns about potential harm that exposure to lead might have on fetal development and potential tort liability for resulting injuries. Although the company's concerns were legitimate ones, union leaders had concerns of their own. Such fetal protection policies, if enforced, could close as many as 20 million industrial jobs to women. The United Automobile, Aerospace, and Agricultural Implement Workers of America (UAW), several UAW locals, and a group of individual employers brought suit, alleging that Johnson Controls' fetal protection program violated Title VII as amended by the Pregnancy Discrimination Act of 1978. The lower courts found for Johnson Controls, ruling that the company had established significant risk of harm and that, while the policy of denying employment to fertile women was sex-biased, it could be sustained under Title VII's bona fide occupational qualification (BFOQ) defense. Johnson Controls' concern for industrial safety was an essential part of the company's battery manufacturing business and the fetal protection policy was "reasonably necessary" to maintain industrial safety.[14]

The Supreme Court disagreed. For employers to exclude women from the workplace on the ostensibly benign grounds of protecting women's unconceived offspring, while ignoring evidence of the debilitating impact of lead exposure on the male reproductive system, represents the overt gender discrimination explicitly forbidden by Title VII, the Court reasoned. Further bolstering its conclusion, Justice Blackmun cited the Pregnancy Discrimination Act of 1978 and its legislative history. Congress had stipulated that discrimination on the basis of a woman's pregnancy or capacity to become pregnant is sexual discrimination. In choosing to treat all of its female employees as "potentially pregnant," unless they furnished proof that they were incapable of reproducing, Johnson Controls was engaging in sexual discrimination. Moreover, that discrimination could not be defended as a BFOQ. The Supreme Court had interpreted "bona fide occupational qualifications" to mean job-related skills and aptitudes. In attempting to expand the narrow BFOQ exception to cover safety to fetuses by making sterility an occupational qualification for women, the lower courts had erred. "Fertile women, as far as appears in the record, participate in the manufacture of batteries as efficiently as anyone else," Blackmun observed. "In other words, women as capable of doing their jobs as their male counterparts may not be forced to choose between having a child and having a job. . . . It is," he concluded, "no more appropriate for the courts than it is for individual employees to decide whether a woman's reproductive role is more important to herself and her family than her economic role. Congress has left this choice to the woman as hers to make."[15]

The Court's rulings delighted feminists and vindicated ERA ratificationists who had long argued that a commitment to substantive equality would require the Court, in essence, to separate sex from gender, taking into account "real difference" while rejecting gender-based stereotypes and restrictions that served to deny equal opportunity. But such victories were less definitive than they appeared to be. The 6–3 vote in *Johnson* did not indicate a strong consensus. As students of the Court pointed out, Justice Sandra Day O'Connor had concurred in the result but not in the reasoning; in a future case, she indicated she might vote differently. Justice Lewis Powell also did not support all affirmative-action plans and might shift as well, leaving staunch supporters in a minority.[16] Nor was pregnancy policy resolved. The Court had ruled in a little-publicized case only a few months after the *California Federal* decision that states may deny unemployment compensation to women whose employers refuse to reinstate them after leaving their jobs to give birth.[17]

As new Reagan-Bush appointees took their place on the federal bench and ultimately on the Court itself, narrower interpretations of sex-discrimination law and new restrictions on abortion rights would ultimately prevail. Heralding a shift of the Court toward conservatism, these new rulings would also signal the force of the Reagan-Bush administration's assault on equality. However, the administration's one-two punch would also generate popular and congressional resistance, highlighting the limits of Rightist efforts to redefine both principle and policy.

Narrowing the Scope of the Law:
Education Equity and Abortion Rights

One of the first equality issues to suffer involved education. In *Grove City College v. Bell*. (1984), the Court weakened significantly the impact of Title IX of the Equal Educational Opportunities Act. Since the act's passage in 1972, equal-rights advocates had relied on a broad interpretation of the anti-sex-discrimination provision that held that an entire college or university risked loss of federal aid if any program or department receiving federal funds was found guilty of discrimination. Under the Reagan administration, the Office of Civil Rights, which enforced Title IX, had revised its interpretation, making the provision program-specific. The implications were clear. So long as the particular programs receiving federal money did not discriminate, the institution need not fear federal sanction. The Court concurred in its *Grove City* ruling, stipulating that penalties must be restricted to the offending department. Equal-rights advocates immediately appealed to Congress to pass the Civil Rights Restoration Bill, which would restore the original reading. The bill finally passed in 1988, but with a stipulation that refusal to provide abortion services would not be considered discrimination against women—another indication of how precarious abortion rights were becoming in the Reagan-Bush era.[18]

That abortion is considered a right and an equality issue is a testament of the effectiveness of modern feminism. While the move to legalize abortion in the 1960s came from a coalition of groups driven by different concerns, feminists were at the forefront. Calling for decriminalization was a way of claiming women's right to sexual pleasure as well as attacking a sex-segregated labor market and cultural expectations about women's roles. "It allowed women to argue (and symbolically demonstrate) that although childbearing was important, it was not the single most important thing in a woman's life," sociologist Kristen Luker has pointed out. But first and foremost, access to abortion was critical because reproductive control was the prerequisite for other choices—labor market participation was only the most obvious. The right to a legal abortion was thus closely linked to other rights essential to sexual equality. That federal policymakers agreed seemed evident, at least to opponents. Congressional passage of the Equal Rights Amendment was followed within months by *Roe v. Wade*.[19]

Opposition to legalized abortion, which mounted swiftly in the wake of *Roe*, had as its moral basis certain religious tenets shared by social conservatives, whether Catholic, Fundamentalist Protestant, or Mormon. Its political home, however, would ultimately prove to be the Republican party of Ronald Reagan and George Bush. While anti-abortion forces in the late 1970s had managed to strip funding for abortions from Medicaid—actions the Court upheld—they did not make other significant gains until the 1980s. Eager to placate New Right elements within the party, Reagan and, subsequently, Bush closely aligned their administrations with anti-abortion forces, naming anti-choice officials to head key federal agencies and withholding funds to family-planning agencies that counseled clients about abortion or provided referrals. Far more significant, however, was the decision to make reorientation of abortion policy a key factor in the selection of new judges. With three openings on the Supreme Court and a new Chief Justice to pick, Reagan succeeded in making abortion policy a part of the judicial agenda. After sixteen years of rejecting state restrictions on abortion, the Court changed course in 1989.[20]

In a decision that left the author of the majority opinion in *Roe v. Wade*, Justice Blackmun, fearful both "for the liberty and equality of millions of women" and for the "integrity of, and public esteem for" the Court itself, a majority of the justices seemed willing to so restrict abortion as to leave in doubt whether they were still willing to consider the right to terminate a pregnancy a fundamental right. Although the Court rejected Attorney General Meese's call to overturn *Roe* entirely, its *Webster* decision validated a Missouri law banning abortions by publicly paid medical personnel in publicly funded facilities unless the woman's life was in danger. Lawyers who followed constitutional developments closely were not surprised by that portion of *Webster* upholding the ban on abortions in public hospitals. In 1977 and 1980, the Court had held that it was not an infringement on a woman's fundamental right for the government to deny funding for abortions, even therapeutic abortions. What did generate concern was the Court's clear signal in *Webster* that restrictions on abortion would be permitted—an invitation, in effect, for future test cases that would provide an opportunity to reconsider *Roe*. Given the thinking of a plurality of the justices in *Webster*, the outcome of such cases would undoubtedly be a further narrowing of abortion rights. The ultimate result, predicted Justice Blackmun in his dissent, would be "to return to the States virtually unfettered authority to control the quintessentially intimate, personal and *life-directing* decision as to whether to carry a fetus to term."[21]

When two of Court's strongest supporters of abortion rights, Justices William J. Brennan and Thurgood Marshall, retired, Blackmun's pessimism seemed well founded. New Bush appointees David H. Souter and Clarence Thomas were in place by the time the Court agreed to review *Planned Parenthood v. Casey*, and either justice could determine the fate of *Roe*. The case itself involved a Pennsylvania law requiring spousal notification for wives and parental consent for minors, a twenty-four-hour waiting period, medical counseling about alternatives before an abortion could be performed, and the requirement that physicians or clinics make statistical reports to the state. Feminists saw the law as a blatant reassertion of patriarchal authority. Abortion-rights lawyers saw it as a probable defeat in which some, if not all, of the restrictions would be upheld.

Though the decision did not overturn *Roe*, it upheld all of the Pennsylvania regulations except the one requiring spousal notification. In reaching its decision, the Court applied for the first time a standard of "undue burden" to determine whether a state abortion regulation would present a "substantial obstacle" to a woman seeking an abortion. Despite the Court's determination that most of the Pennsylvania regulations would not pose an undue burden, abortion-rights advocates were dismayed, contending that these regulations would make it more difficult and expensive for women, who would be required to make two trips to abortion clinics that might be far from their homes. Abortion-rights supporters also worried that the court decision provided doctors with reasons to refuse to offer abortion services, knowing that their statistical reports to the state would set them up for harassment by anti-choice activists. In short, by upholding the Pennsylvania regulations, the Supreme Court paved the way for new state regulations to restrict abortion.[22]

Restoring Rights: The Congressional Response

The task of reversing this assault on equality fell to a Congress in which Democrats, although a majority, lacked sufficient votes to override a presidential veto. Civil rights legislation, therefore, was slow to emerge and was embedded in compromise. The Civil Rights Restoration Act of 1988 finally garnered enough votes to overturn the *Grove City* decision by reestablishing "institution-wide" rather than "program-specific" standards for withdrawing federal funding in educational institutions discriminating on the basis of sex. The Civil Rights Act of 1991, designed to reverse many of the affirmative-action decisions made by the Court in its 1988–89 term, had been successfully blocked for three years by a threatened presidential veto of any measure leading to "quotas." Finally passed in 1991, it was subjected to so many compromises that certain portions of the final version were unclear; the act nonetheless accomplished its basic objective.[23]

The new law restored the rights of women and other groups to sue for discrimination in the workplace and to collect both compensatory and punitive damages through a jury trial in cases of intentional discrimination. With respect to unintentional discrimination, the act shifted back to employers the burden of proof in justifying hiring and promotion policies that on the surface seemed neutral, but that in practice had a disparate and adverse impact on employment opportunities for women or minorities. In dual-motive cases in which both nondiscriminatory and discriminatory factors were involved, employers were required to prove that only legitimate criteria such as job performance—not gender, race,

or disability—were factors in an employment decision. In situations in
which gender (or race or disability) was a motivating factor, employers
who could show that the "same decision" would have been made even in
the absence of impermissable motivation, were spared payment of damages. In cases in which damages were awarded to victims of discrimination, the amount was limited. However, the fact that the 1866 Civil
Rights Act set no caps for damages in racial suits meant that in practice
limits were set on awards to women for job discrimination, but not for
minorities.[24]

Civil rights advocates admitted the bill was not perfect; its intention-
ally vague and open-ended language would likely require years of clarifica-
tion on the part of the Supreme Court. Nonetheless, the bill was probably
the best that could be achieved under the Bush administration. Other
legislation was in the works, including a freedom-of-choice bill compelling states to keep abortion legal and uniformly available and a bill dealing
with escalating violence against women. In addition, a number of gender-
equity measures awaited action from a new Congress and a new Democratic president in 1993.[25]

To the extent that policy reversals in the area of civil rights could be
accomplished by presidential appointments and Executive Orders, Bill
Clinton acted quickly. With respect to abortion rights, for example, the
President issued an executive memorandum on his second day in office
reversing some of the anti-choice measures promulgated by his Republican predecessor. Among the most important were the Title X "gag rule,"
which had prohibited family planning clinics receiving federal funds from
counseling low-income women about abortion as an option, and the ban
on abortions in overseas military hospitals. In addition, the President
mandated a review of the ban on imports of RU-486, the French-
developed abortifacient, into the United States for personal use. But a
stroke of the Clinton pen could not strip the federal judiciary of its more
conservative appointees or equality of its intensely contested meaning.

The meaning of equality, in fact, was exposed as the real issue to be
addressed. If, as supporters, promised, the ERA would not go away in the
1980s and 1990s, neither would the emotional and intellectual baggage
with which opponents had encumbered the amendment in the 1970s.[25]
The equal rights model on which the ERA was based is clearly fraught
with ambiguities and complexities, which antiratificationist women had
intuited and which Reagan-Bush appointees exploited. Years of political
debate and conflict compelled feminists themselves to reconsider the
intellectual foundations of their positions.[27]

III

That equal rights as a goal for women had become so hotly contested over the course of two decades was primarily (although not exclusively) the doing of vulnerable, suspicious women, conservative (mostly male) legislators, and hostile political and judicial appointees. All embraced in varying measure philosophies and policies associated with neoconservatism or the New Right. But critics could come from the Left as well as the Right, from within feminism as well as without. At the cutting edge of feminist criticism were legal scholars, who, in probing the complexities of accommodating equality and difference in American law, would expose the limitations of rights analysis and argue for recasting approaches to gender justice, for the most part, within a "renewed" and "redeemed" liberalism.[28]

Feminist legal scholars understood the emancipatory vision associated with rights consciousness—how "deliciously empowering" equal rights feels for those who have been denied them.[29] During the early years of a resurgent women's movement, they had celebrated the efforts of liberal feminists to end sex-based discrimination and secure reproductive freedom and political representation. By the 1980s, however, there was little to celebrate. The ERA's defeat, retrenchment on abortion rights, and escalating violence against women highlighted the fragility of other gains during the Reagan-Bush years. Sobering reminders of the depth of the popular backlash against equality fueling administration policy, these developments contributed to new recognition of the persistence of sex-based disadvantage. That recognition, in turn, invited reassessment of the strategies and theoretical frameworks used to achieve gender equality in the 1970s.

Feminist legal theorists were not the first critics of rights discourse and liberal ideology. Legal theorists, influenced by Marxism and identified with the Critical Legal Studies movement, had led the way in the 1970s. The law, they pointed out, is neither neutral nor objective, but reflective of dominant ideological, political, and economic forces that it also reinforces and rationalizes.[30] Scholars from a variety of disciplines reached somewhat similar conclusions from other perspectives. Drawing on literacy and philosophical approaches identified with poststructuralism, theorists pointed out how meanings are reproduced differentially, through contrasts and oppositions, and hierarchically, through the assignment of primacy to one term and subordination to the other. Binary pairings such as objective/subjective, public/private, equality/difference, and male/female are key examples. The interconnectedness of the asymmetrical relationship is important to recognize, many concluded, "because it suggests that change is more than a matter of the adjustment of social resources for a subordinated group, more than a question of distributive justice."[31]

Absorbing and assessing this scholarship,[32] as well as that generated by other feminists in the academy,[33] feminist legal scholars immediately began to fashion their own critiques. As they did so, they came to understand the contingent, constructed character of presumably neutral, universal concepts and principles. One of the most telling examples focused on eighteenth-century liberal ideology.

The Androcentrism of Rights Theory

Liberalism, now the dominant political ideology of twentieth-century Western society, had long been assumed to be about people in general. Upon closer scrutiny, however, analysts demonstrated the extent to which it is in fact grounded in patriarchal structures and unstated gender hierarchies normative in English society at the time.[34] Women, to the extent they were considered at all, were assumed to be participants in the social contract, but in real life most were not even allowed to sign a contract. When seventeenth- and eighteenth-century rights theorists, seeking to assert the importance and autonomy of the individual against authority based on divine right, posited an abstract, autonomous, rational individual, their model, not surprisingly, was male. Subsequently incorporated into the constitutional and statutory judicial doctrines of the United States, that autonomous individual, critics pointed out, is a male construct. To those persons who can match the picture of the abstract autonomous individual, rights analysis offers "release from hierarchy and subordination," according to Harvard's Martha Minow; to those who cannot, rights analysis can be "not only un-responsive, but punitive."[35]

It was that punitive quality that antiratificationist women had intuitively grasped when they complained that equality would require them to "compete" as "men." That the result of competition, celebrated under the aegis of equality in a capitalist economy, has been and continues to be socioeconomic inequality they recognized. As political conservatives, they did not challenge that reality, believing it to be the result of natural differences having little to do with disparities associated with class, race, or ethnicity. As women, however, antiratificationists understood that inequalities are compounded by male advantage. No matter what individuals might accomplish, women as a group lacked the resources that would enable them to compete with the advantaged group on its own terms. Their concerns thus illustrated precisely what critics of rights discourse meant when they charged that equal rights, by masking the inequality inherent in the status quo, can indeed be marginalizing rather than emancipating.[36]

The androcentrism and individualism of rights theory, which feminist scholars had been so quick to identify, also had other implications that troubled antifeminists.[37] One ERA opponent spoke of rights advocates who seemed to be on "an ego trip." That association had seemed inappropriate until the phrase was identified with antiratificationist revulsion at the self-dramatization of the 1960s. Rights and ego were linked in a reference to public demonstrations and to men who thought that "rights" were more important than relationships. The association of rights and individual autonomy with (male) ego and masculine attributes on the part of "family-oriented women," if only a visceral response to rights rhetoric, nonetheless suggests a valid concern. If women had to be men, how could they continue to be women? The question pointed to a deficiency in rights discourse to which political theorists such as Jean Bethke Elshtain have also pointed: the absence in concept and in law of affiliative virtues associated with the private sphere of home and family, where connectedness to and concern for others are central. At the core of these scholarly critiques of "predatory individualism" was a plea for difference. But difference, specifically female difference, is at the very heart of the problem.[38]

Rights Theory and Group Difference: The Difference Dilemma

Rights theory "preserves rather than alters the dilemma of difference."[39] Although the term "difference dilemma" is a new one, the problem is not.[40] Difference can come in many forms: race, sex, and religion are but a few of the traits to which law and society have attached entitlements and status. The dilemma occurs not in the guaranteeing of rights to which all persons of equal moral worth and citizenship status are now entitled, but rather in the defining of equality in relation to difference.

Equality is presumed to mean sameness, not only because it rests on an image of fundamental human sameness, but because in America it carried with it the principle of interchangeability, as historian J. H. Pole has pointed out.[41] Individuals were assumed to be interchangeable if disassociated from religion, class, and race and given the requisite training and experience. Only as Victorian sexual polarities were gradually eroded by the forces of modernity, Pole notes, were women seen as includable into the classes of people to whom equality might apply. Inasmuch as the principle of interchangeability, like the concept of equality, has hidden within presumably neutral language an implicit male norm, difference with respect to sex has thus always meant women's difference. The courts ensured that meaning through an approach embodied in the Constitution's "similarly situated" requirement: similarly situated individuals should be treated alike.[42] As claimants of equal rights, the problem for women—and especially for women of color—has been how to handle difference without reviving the disadvantage associated with it.[43]

Feminist policy strategists of the 1970s and 1980s found the problem no less tractable than had their predecessors. The question whether to emphasize sameness or difference had divided feminists historically, leading them to oscillate between androgyny and female uniqueness in their quest for liberation. Suffragists, for example, had emphasized sexual difference as well as sameness in their demand for the ballot, insisting that women should have to vote both as a right of citizenship and as an acknowledgment of the state's need for their distinctive female attributes. But if women's rights advocates in the first women's movement were prepared to rest their claim for equality on both sameness and difference, their successors seemed more inclined to choose. Liberal and radical feminists for the most part emphasized basic commonalities between the sexes, while cultural feminists valorized female difference.[44]

Liberal feminists, for example, were aware of how sexual difference had served as the basis for different and unequal treatment historically. Familiar with the history of protective legislation, they had come to understand how classification by sex, sanctioned by the Court in *Muller v. Oregon* (1908), had resulted in overclassification in law that stereotyped women. They had just discovered through EEOC findings how legislation designed to protect women workers had actually been used by employers to discriminate.[45] The key to equality seemed therefore to lie in rejecting biological essentialism and transcending gender difference through an appeal to equal individual rights. As the branch of the modern feminist movement most interested in public policy, equal-rights advocates carried the day. The ERA was seen as the quintessential expression of an equality strategy that presumed the sexes are reasonably fungible. As the definitive legal analysis of the amendment pointed out, it would require treating all individuals under the law the same, except in cases such as childbirth, which constituted a "real" sex difference.[46]

Yet the choice was never so clear-cut or internally consistent as it appeared to be. The same policy strategists who placed an equal rights amendment on their agenda in 1967 engineered the inclusion of sex in Executive Order 11246 that same year.[47] By including sex discrimination in affirmative-action policy, advocates of women's rights once again placed women in a special category by virtue of the way difference disadvantaged women in the marketplace. Policy options were thus pursued that sought to end sex-based discrimination in law by downplaying difference (ERA) and in employment by categorizing employees on the basis of difference (affirmative action). With both approaches, however, strategists promptly found themselves impaled on the horns of the difference dilemma. Affirmative action would symbolically reinforce difference, both for the women who benefited and the men who did not, as principals in the Johnson case would demonstrate. And the ERA, opponents charged, by ignoring difference, would also reinforce it by further disadvantaging those women who did not conform to male norms.

The Difference Dilemma and the Courts

The complexity of the problem became even more apparent to feminist scholars when examining other legal cases of the mid 1980s in which sexual difference was central. Consider, for example, the *Sears* case. Leaving aside such matters as whether statistical evidence of discrimination alone, without corroborating anecdotal evidence, was sufficient to justify liability, the crux of Sears's defense rested on its insistence that the under representation of women employees holding higher-paying jobs in commission sales was not the result of discrimination but rather of women's choices. Female employees, by virtue of socialization, family responsibilities, and other factors, had different job preferences and expectations, the defense argued, and therefore made different job choices than their male counterparts, preferring lower-level, less competitive positions. By viewing the status quo as neutral and the issue as one of *either* discrimination *or* women's difference, the Court ruled out more complex explanations that were less totalizing and categorical. By making the argument one of sameness versus difference, differences among women were obscured and gender stereotypes reinforced. More important, the court obsured the way in which the very notion of difference can be manipulated to mask inequities so that difference becomes essentialized and social inequity naturalized.[48]

But if the very notion of difference can preclude equality by masking inequities, so can the denial of difference. Nowhere was this more apparent than in developments surrounding the *California Federal* case. Recognizing the extent to which inequality has been explained and justified by biological sexual difference, feminist legal scholars who helped draft the Pregnancy Discrimination Act provided legislation dealing with pregnancy and childbirth that mandated equal treatment in the workplace. Employers were required to treat pregnancy and childbirth in the same manner as any other physical condition that can temporarily disable workers. The aim was not the stigmatizing of pregnancy as a disability, but the "demythologizing [of] pregnancy by linking it in the work context with conditions that have a comparable effect on ability to work." To single out pregnant workers for special treatment was to label those workers as "different" and, from the standpoint of employers, "a burden."[49]

Yet in those companies that did not provide disability coverage to their workers, denial of difference penalized female employees who were "disabled" by childbirth and lacked job-protected unpaid leaves. Identical treatment in this instance did not produce equality because "there is no comparable male disability that systematically keeps men as a class out of the workforce and causes them to lose seniority and job tenure benefits in the way pregnancy does for women."[50] The Court upheld in *California Federal* the California statute that sought to redress this inequality by mandating reasonable leaves of absence for temporarily disabled pregnant workers. A few months later, however, it upheld an apparently sex-neutral state policy in Missouri that denied unemployment benefits to women whose employers would not reinstate them after taking "voluntary" pregnancy leave. Since pregnancy was not singled out as a basis for denying benefits, there was no discrimination, the Court reasoned. The federal antidiscrimination statute did not *require* "preferential treatment" for pregnancy.[51]

What such cases highlight, feminist legal scholars point out, is the inherent difficulty of realizing equality within conventional approaches associated with rights analysis for those who fail the test of sameness. In the area of sexual assault, abortion, and reproductive control the problems are compounded.[52] The dichotomies that are set up between sameness and difference, equal treatment and special treatment, public and private, are false dichotomies. They leave women the option either of being assimilated into a preexisting, predominantly male world that reflects white male middle-class interests and values or of being treated as a human being who cannot live up to a male standard. With these as the available options, sex-based inequalities are reinforced as often as they are challenged. In sum, rights theory and practice, while providing a qualified guarantee of equal treatment, serve as a problematic basis for the kind of far-reaching change required to ensure sexual equality. If this is indeed the case, what are the alternatives?

Alternative Approaches

Some feminists legal scholars, like their counterparts in Critical Legal Studies, have largely given up on rights, convinced that liberalism is fundamentally flawed. The liberal state, argued Catherine MacKinnon in her widely acclaimed *Toward a Feminist Theory of the State,* is one in which male "dominance reified becomes difference," in which "the rule of law—neutral, abstract, elevated, pervasive—both institutionalizes the power of men over women and institutionalizes power in its male form."[53] Robin West, who also posits a feminist jurisprudence, but one based on female connectedness rather than on male dominance, is similarly dismissive of liberal theory and law.[54] Many feminist legal critics, however, have rejected such categorical critiques.[55] They can admire the skill with which critics have converted theoretical insights about sexual subordination into a legal actionable wrong: MacKinnon's transformation of sexual harassment in the workplace into a legal prohibition, for example. They can appreciate new (and contingent) epistemological perspectives, the importance of human interdependency, and the need to shift the emphasis from rights to responsibilities in various areas of law.[56] But they are also mindful of the coercive power of the state and hence unwilling to relinquish liberal concepts such as autonomy.[57] First and foremost, however, they recognize the enormous progress achieved under the rubric of rights by subordinate groups who have found rights to be a source of self-definition and empowerment.[58] Obliged to use rights-based strategies, feminist scholars and activists focus not surprisingly on the structural inequalities and ideological underpinnings that underlie specific issues, challenging and subverting rights discourse and practice from within.

The central problem with rights-based frameworks, as Deborah Rhode argues, "is not that they are inherently limiting but that they have operated with a limited institutional and imaginative universe." The objective of feminist legal criticism must be "not to delegitimate such frameworks but rather to recast their content and recognize their constraints."[59] Or as Patricia Williams would put it, to appropriate and redirect the law's magic of right; or as other legal theorists would argue, to expand older notions of individual rights so that rights embrace connection, a communal dimension that can expand opportunities for women as a class.[60] With respect to difference, the commitment must be neither to embrace nor to suppress it, but to "challenge the dualism and make the world safe for differences." Strategies for doing so may vary, but the emphasis, Rhode insists, must be on historically situated contextual analysis.[61]

One example may suffice. Consider again the difference dilemma and the vexing problem of pregnant workers. Attempting to prevent discrimination against pregnant workers in the form of job dismissals, the Pregnancy Discrimination Act, as we have seen, required identical treatment of workers. Pregnancy-related disability had to be treated in the same manner as any other medical disability. But in companies providing no disability coverage for workers, pregnancy-related illness and childbirth, as we have also seen, often resulted in loss of jobs—and, in some cases, unemployment benefits as well. By adhering to equal treatment in this instance, the male norm is left in place, the workplace remains a place for men (and nonpregnant women), and pregnant women either bear the costs themselves or have their difference reinforced with "special treatment."

Suppose the framework in which gender issues are debated is shifted,[62] as it was in the making of the *California Federal* decision. The crucial issue becomes not difference, but the *difference that difference makes.* Then the issue is not whether legal recognition of difference constitutes "special treatment," but whether that legal recognition is likely to reduce or reinforce gender disparities. Does it empower women and enable them to participate as full members of society?[63] In the *California Federal* case, a majority of the Supreme Court shifted the focus to pregnant women, and away from the male norm, without substituting a new female norm for claiming equality. The public/private dichotomy was also eliminated: both male and female workers were understood to have workplace and family duties. By replacing the old unstated norm of the male worker *without* family duties with a new norm of male and female workers *with* family duties, the issue then, and only then, became equality and sameness. Because California's pregnancy-disability-leave statute "allows women, as well as men, to have families without losing their jobs," no conflict was found between the Pregnancy Discrimination Act and the challenged California statute.[64]

The challenge for the Court, as indeed for all policymakers, is to think seriously, consistently, and with clarity about difference. The place to begin is to recognize that difference itself is *relational:* "I am no more different from you than you are from me," Minow reminds us.[65] Understanding that the distinctions that help us think by categorizing also carry within them hidden assumptions of value and hierarchy, we can examine how those labeled "different" in social and legal discourse can be—and often are—marginalized and penalized. By focusing on *each specific context,* we begin to challenge our conventional understandings, in Minow's words, by "challenging and transforming the unstated norm used for comparisons, taking the perspective of the traditionally excluded or marginal group, disentangling equality from its attachment to a norm that has the effect of unthinking exclusion, and treating everyone as though he or she were different." Otherwise, she concludes, a commitment to equality—"to treating likes alike"—will inevitably remain caught in contradiction.[65]

Passage of the ERA, insisted supporters in 1973, would be "simple justice." But justice and equality are seldom simple. If, during the last three decades, more and more Americans have come to affirm equality in principle, they have also come to agree less and less on the policies required to realize equality in practice. The paradigmatic liberal prescription, equal opportunity, which inspired egalitarian policies of the past, has proven to be as necessary to achieve equality for women as it has for minority groups—and as insufficient. Those who benefited most from equal-access policies—Title VII of the Civil Rights Act and Title IX of the Educational Amendments Act—have been for the most part young, educated, and middle class. Even the modest goal of assimilating women into mainstream institutions has proven more complicated than anticipated. Institutional structures and cultures have proven to be as deeply gendered as feminists had claimed them to be, requiring additional policies to deal with such knotty issues as pregnancy disability, sexual harassment, child care, and combat participation.

Policies themselves have often proven, at best, incremental in effect and, at worst, divisive in impact, pitting the Paul Johnsons against the Diane Joyces, both hardworking, deserving individuals, and leaving the road department of Santa Clara Transportation Agency little changed— "predominantly white, predominantly male."[67] If the remedies associated with affirmative action divided men and women, the ERA and abortion rights debates revealed profound differences among women that are moral and ideological at least as much as they are political. Divisions over policy, while less polarized than those between liberal feminists and conservative antifeminists, have emerged among feminists as well. Women's rights organizations, while agreeing on the desirability of job-secure leaves for any temporary disability, filed *amicus* briefs on both sides of the litigation in the *California Federal* case. Such actions revealed recurrent disagreements about strategy—special treatment (gender-specific childbirth policies) versus equal treatment (gender-neutral policies). They also revealed recurrent tensions within feminism between maximizers (those who emphasize sexual differences, whether biological or cultural) and minimizers (those who downplay differences). Even more fundamentally, they underscore the dilemma of difference.

The complexity—and especially the conflict—surrounding egalitarian policies has, in turn, slowed progress in the political sphere. Popular discontent with the legislative and administrative equal-rights and affirmative-action remedies of the 1960s and 1970s was both reflected in and exploited by the Reagan-Bush administrations during the 1980s. The result, if not the total "roll back" for women and minorities that archconservatives had hoped for and liberals feared, left defenders of those policies too preoccupied with damage control to press for new gains. The positive legal legacy of Court decisions affecting women also became problematic during the 1980s as the Court handed down decisions on a wide variety of issues, ranging from abortion to pregnancy in the workplace. Whether, from the vantage point of the twenty-first century, the mid-seventies and eighties may appear as a brief stall in a long upward trend line remains to be seen.

What is clear is that the stall generated unprecedented attention from feminist scholars. The timing of so rigorous a critique of rights theory has left liberals feeling that equality is under siege from the Left as well as the Right. Such reactions, however, while understandable, miss the import of much of this work. By demystifying the relationship between law and gender and theory and policy, feminist legal theorists have exposed the limits as well as the potential of legal reform to bring about fundamental social change. By showing how the articulation of rights allowed new contradictions to unfold, they have helped to clarify what sexual equality *really* requires. Finally, by revealing that rights can be what we make of them, they identify themselves first and foremost as reforgers—talented artisans eager to shape and sharpen the tools needed to resume dismantling the tenacious, interlocking, and sometimes invisible hierarchies that permeate our society.

University of California, Santa Barbara

Notes

I am grateful to Valery Garrett and Daniel Gomes for research assistance and to Hugh Graham and Laura Kalman for helpful suggestions. I owe a special debt to Joan Williams and Martha Chamallas who attempted to save me from mistakes in the legal sections. For any remaining inaccuracies, I am, of course, responsible.

1. For a fuller discussion of opposition to the ERA, see my "Gender on the Right: Meanings Behind the Existential Scream," *Gender and History* 3 (Autumn 1991); also Donald G. Mathews and Jane Sherron De Hart, *Sex, Gender, and the Politics of ERA: A State and the Nation* (New York, 1990), chaps. 2, 6–8.

Unless otherwise noted, Part I of this essay is based on interviews with opponents of ERA, broadsides and information sheets disseminated by STOP ERA and other anti-ERA groups in North Carolina (in author's files, some of which have been turned over to the University of North Carolina at Greensboro, or in the papers of all persons mentioned in this note), extensive correspondence to the chief opponent of ERA in the U.S. Senate, Samuel J. Ervin in the Southern Historical Collection (hereafter SHA), University of North Carolina at Chapel Hill, as well as the extensive collection of letters and published document in the ERA Collection, North Carolina Department of Archives and History (hereafter NCDAH). Included in the NCDAH collection are the papers of the following North Carolina legislators: Representatives J. Allen Adams, A. Heartwell Campbell, David H. Diamont, Peter W. Hairston, Edward S. Holmes, Robert B. Jones, Margaret Keesee, Larry E. Leonard, Ernest B. Messer, Robie Nash, Ned R. Smith, and Margaret Tennille. To allow for a degree of anonymity agreed upon at the time of the interviews, quotations from interviews are not cited. For a full list of interviews, see Mathews and De Hart, *Sex, Gender, and the Politics of ERA*, app. 4.

2. For the initial quotation, see Violet S. Devieux to Senator Sam J. Ervin, Jr., 23 March 1972, Samuel J. Ervin Papers, #3847 SHA. The plea not to "desexigrate" was made at hearings held on 11 March 1975 by the North Carolina General Assembly, at which the author was a participant observer. For arguments against a state ERA in Massachusetts, see the following sample from Massachusetts newspapers, Frances Scoledge, "Vote No," *Amesbury News*, 15 September 1976; "Our Readers Write," *Melrose Evening News*, 2 August 1976; *Amherst Record*, 15 September 1976; *Lawrence Eagle-Tribune*, 14 September 1976; Boston *Pilot*, 9 July 1976; Lynn *Sunday Post*, 17 October 1976.

3. Schlafly's arguments are elaborated in Phyllis Schlafly, *The Power of the Positive Woman* (New York, 1977). The symbolic significance of both conferences for opponents was evident to participant observers at the Houston meeting and at the pro-family conference in Washington, which was called to counter the White House Conference on Families. See copies of notes of Roxie Nicholson and Donald Mathews, in possession of the author. See also Rebecca Klatch, *Women of the Right* (Philadelphia, 1987), 122–27.

4. Lois J. Watkins to Representative Margaret Kessee, 24 February 1973, copy, author's files (now at the university of North Carolina at Greensboro).

On the occupational status as well as the ideological and political orientation of anti-ERA activists, see, for example, Theodore S. Arrington and Patricia A. Kyle, "Equal Rights Activists in North Carolina," *Signs* 3 (1978): 660–80; Kent L. Tedin, "Religious Preferences and Pro/Anti Activism on the Equal Rights Amendment Issue," *Pacific Sociological Review* 21 (1978: 55–67; Carol Mueller and Thomas Dimieri, "The Structure of Belief Systems Among Contending ERA Activists," *Social Forces* 60 (1982): 657–73; Jerome L. Himmelstein, "The Social Basis of Antifeminism: Religious Networks and Culture," *Journal of the Scientific Study of Religion* 25 (1986): 1–15. For anti-ERA sentiment among the general public, see Val Burris, "Who Opposed the ERA? An Analysis of the Social Basis of Antifeminism," *Social Science Quarterly* 64 (1983): 305–17; Joan Huber, Cynthia Rexroat, and Glenna Spitze, "A Crucible of Opinion on Women's Status: ERA in Illinois," *Social Forces* 57 (1978): 549–65. According to poll data from the Institute for Research in the Social Sciences at the University of North Carolina at Chapel Hill, "Survey of North Carolina Women" (1978), women in the workforce most likely to oppose ERA were those holding either blue- or pink-collar jobs.

5. Tom Wicker, "One Voice, In Retreat," *New York Times*, 22 April 1983, sec. I, p. 31.

6. The characterization of the policy reversal as a "sea change" was made by Morris B. Abram, vice-chairman of the Civil Rights Commission. See Robert Pear, "Civil Rights Agency Splits in Debate on Narrowing Definition of Equality," *New York Times*, 14 October 1985, sec. I, p. 17.

7. Title IX, by banning sex-based discrimination in educational institutions, allowed women to secure the necessary credentials for employment; Title VII banned sex-based

discrimination in employment; the Equal Pay Act mandated equal pay for the same work.

8. *Equal Employment Opportunities Commission v. Sears, Roebuck & Co.*, 628 F. Suppl. 1264, U.S. District Court for the Northern District of Illinois, 1986. The judge was John A. Nordberg. While the initial accounts of journalists and scholars focused on the expert witnesses and their testimony, subsequent accounts, whether by historians, political scientists, or legal scholars, emphasize the relationship of difference and inequality. See, for example, Joan W. Scott, "Deconstructing Equality-Versus-Difference: Or, the Use of Post-structuralist Theory for Feminism," *Feminist Studies* 14 (1988): 33–48; Zillah R. Eisenstein, *The Female Body and the Law* (Berkeley and Los Angeles, 1988), 110–16; Christine A. Littleton, "Equality and Feminist Legal Theory," *University of Pittsburgh Law Review* 48 (1987): 1043–59; and Martha Minow, *Making All the Difference: Inclusion, Exclusion, and American Law* (Ithaca, N.Y., 1990), 70–75.

9. Stuart Taylor, Jr., "Supreme Court, 6–3, Extends Preferences in Employment for Women and Minorities," *New York Times*, 26 March 1987, sec. 1, p. 1.

10. Al Kamen, "Supreme Court Upholds Affirmative Action Hiring," *Washington Post*, 26 March 1987, sec. 1, p. 1; David G. Savage, "Landmark Ruling Upholds Job Preferences for Women," *Los Angeles Times*, 26 March 1987, sec. I, p. 10; Taylor, "Supreme Court, 6–3, Extends Preferences in Employment for Women and Minorities." For a much fuller treatment of the case, see Melvin I. Urofsky, *A Conflict of Rights: The Supreme Court and Affirmative Action* (New York, 1991).

11. *Johnson v. Transportation Agency*, 107 S. Ct. 1442, 1475 (1987).

12. Al Kamen, "Court Upholds Pregnancy Leave Laws," *Washington Post*, 14 January 1987, sec. A, p. 1; David G. Savage, "Justices Uphold Pregnancy Leave," *Los Angeles Times*, 14 January 1987, sec. I, p. 11; Stuart Taylor, Jr., "Job Rights Backed in Pregnancy Leave," *New York Times*, 14 January 1987, sec. A, p. 1.

13. *California Federal Savings & Loan Association v. Guerra*, 107 S. Ct. 683.

14. *International Union, United Automobile, Aerospace, and Agricultural Implements Workers of America v. Johnson Controls, Inc.* 886 F. 2d 898, U.S. Court of Appeals for the Seventh Circuit (1989).

15. *International Union, United Automobile, Aerospace, and Agricultural Implement Workers of America v. Johnson Controls, Inc.* 111 S. Ct. 1196 (1991). Although all nine justices agreed that Johnson Controls' policy violated the Civil Rights Act of 1964, the Court divided over the BFOQ; a majority agreed with Blackmun's narrow interpretation of the BFOQ, while the more conservative minority argued for a broader interpretation that would allow employers greater leniency.

16. For an account of the positions of various members of the Court, see Urofsky, *A Conflict or Rights*, 154–74.

17. *Wimberly v. Labor & Industrial Relations Commission* 107 S. Ct. 821 (1987).

18. Veronica M. Gillespie and Gregory L. McClinton, "The Civil Rights Restoration Act of 1987: A Defeat for Judicial Conservatism," *National Black Law Journal* 12 (Spring 1990): 65–66.

19. Kristin Luker, *Abortion and the Politics of Motherhood* (Berkeley and Los Angeles, 1984), 120. An excellent outline of the varying goals of the groups that coalesced around legalization of abortion is provided in Lee Epstein and Joseph F. Kobylka, *The Supreme Court and Legal Change: Abortion and the Death Penalty* (Chapel Hill, 1992), 145. See *Roe et al. v. Wade*, 93 S. Ct. 705 (1973).

20. For an account of the road from *Roe* to *Webster*, including discussion of the Hyde Amendment banning Medicaid funding of abortions for poor women, which was upheld by the Supreme Court in *Harris v. McRae* (1980), see Epstein and Kobylka, *The Supreme Court and Legal Change*, 203–98.

21. *Webster v. Reproductive Health Services*, 109 S. Ct. 3040 (1989) 3067. (Emphasis added.)

22. *Casey v. Planned Parenthood of Southeastern Pennsylvania*, U.S. (1992). Linda Green-house, "High Court, 5–4, Affirms Right to Abortion but Allows Most of Pennsylvania's Limits," *New York Times*, 30 June 1992; Ruth Marcus, "Supreme Court Declines to Over-rule Roe," *Washington Post*, 30 June 1992.

23. Milton Zall, "What to Expect from the Civil Rights Act," *Personnel Journal* (March 1992): 50; Julia C. Ross, "New Civil Rights Act," *ABA Journal* 78 (January 1992): 85; Susan M. Benton-Powers, "Sexual Harassment: Civil Rights Act Increases Liability," *HR Focus* 69 (February 1992): 10; Bob Smith, "The Burden of Proof Grows Heavier," *HR Focus* 69 (February 1992): 1–2.

24. Other provisions of the act included a federal "glass ceiling" commission to study factors inhibiting women and minorities from achieving high corporate positions. I am grateful to Martha Chamallas for pointing out the impact of the Civil Rights Act of 1866.

25. The Family and Medical Leave Act, which provides job protection for employees needing time off for family and medical emergences, was signed by Clinton during his first month in office. Other measures include the Women's Health Equity Act and the Eco-nomic Equity Act, both omnibus measures, portions of which have already been enacted.

26. The difficulty of getting a new amendment through Congress unencumbered by restrictions proved impossible in the 1980s. See Mary Frances Berry, *Why ERA Failed: Politics, Women's Rights, and the Amending Process of the Constitution* (Bloomington, 1986), 101–9. The possibility of "clean" Freedom of Choice Act is likely to prove as difficult.

27. Most feminists, whatever their reservations about the amendment, ultimately rallied behind ERA inasmuch as it became symbolic of feminism for both feminists and antifeminists during the ratification struggle. Radical feminists, however, had never equated rights-based equality with the kind of transformation in male-female relations they believed necessary; therefore, they found little rethinking of positions necessary. For a scholarly critique not just of ERA but of "legal liberalism" in general and the gendered inequalities that the juridical equality of women masks, see Joan Hoff, *Law, Gender, and Injustice: A Legal History of U.S. Women* (New York, 1991).

28. Anne C. Dailey, "Feminism's Return to Liberalism," *Yale Law Journal* 102 (1993): 1266. In arguing, as does Dailey, that feminist legal scholars would by the 1990s "return to liberalism," it is not my intent to ignore the very different approaches that reside within contemporary feminist jurisprudence or to imply that all fit comfortably within a "re-deemed" liberalism. How to characterize those various approaches is itself a matter of disagreement. "Liberal," "cultural," "dominance," and "postmodernist" are labels often employed. Although I subsequently cite authors associated with each approach, an exten-sive discussion of each is beyond the scope of this essay.

29. Patricia J. Williams, *The Alchemy of Race and Rights: Diary of a Law Professor* (Cambridge, Mass., 1991), 164–65. Williams's comment, which was made with respect to African-Americans, is applicable to white women, as my study of ERA supporters demon-strates. See Mathews and De Hart, *Sex, Gender, and the Politics of ERA*, chaps. 3–5.

30. For an introduction to the critical legal studies movement, see Robert Gordon, "New Developments in Legal Theory," in David Kairys, ed., *The Politics of Law: A Progres-sive Critique* (New York, 1982); also Allan Hutchinson, ed., *Critical Legal Studies* (Totowa, N.J., 1987).

31. For a discussion of the use of deconstructive methodology in legal scholarship in general, see Christopher Norris, "Law, Deconstruction, and Resistance to Theory," *Journal of Law and Society* 15 (1988). Use of deconstructive methodology by feminist legal scholars is evident in the work of Martha Minow and Marie Ashe, for example. See Minow, *Making All the Difference: Inclusion, Exclusion, and American Law* (Ithaca, N.Y., 1990); also Marie Ashe, "Law-Language of Maternity: Discourse Holding Nature in Contempt," *New En-gland Law Review* 22 (1988): 521–59. The quote is that of Joan Scott, "Women's History," in Peter Burke, ed., *New Perspectives on Historical Writing* (University Park, Pa., 1991), 57–58. Scott is perhaps the best example of a historian who employs poststructuralism as a

more radical epistemology than Marxism from which to analyze structures, institutions, and, indeed, theory itself. See her application of poststructural analysis to equality doctrine and the *Sears* case in "Deconstructing Equality vs. Difference."

32. A few feminists were part of the early critical legal studies movement (CLS) and contributed to Kairys's classic collection of essays. See, for example, Nadine Taub and Elizabeth Schneider, "Perspectives on Women's Subordination and the Role of Law," and Diane Polan, "Toward a Theory of Law and Patriarchy," both in David Kairys, ed., *The Politics of Law,* 117–38. While some feminist legal scholars have remained within the movement, others, such as Patricia Williams and Elizabeth Schneider, have expressed reservations over the extent of the CLS attack on rights. Williams took issue with the CLS preference for "needs" over "rights," arguing that the former may be appropriate for whites but not for blacks. African Americans have found in rights a political mechanism, Williams argues, that can confront the historical denial of need. Schneider takes a similar tact, acknowledging the limitations of rights discourse to achieve fundamental social change. Yet rights, she insists, have played an important symbolic and political role in the women's rights movement and must remain an essential part of any legal and political strategy. See Patricia J. Williams, "Alchemical Notes: Reconstructing Ideals from Deconstructed Rights," *Harvard Civil Rights—Civil Liberties Law Review* 22 (1987): 418; and Elizabeth M. Schneider, "The Dialectic of Rights and Politics: Perspectives from the Women's Movement," *New York University Law Review* 61 (1986): 589–652.

33. Particularly influential for some feminist legal critics is Carol Gilligan's work on moral theory. Gilligan's description of a female ethic of care and a male ethic of justice made *In a Different Voice* (Cambridge, Mass., 1982) a seminal work that has generated an extensive literature, some of it highly critical. See, for example, Linda K. Kerber et al., "On *In a Different Voice:* An Interdisciplinary Forum," *Signs* 11 (1986): 303–33; and also Gertrude Nummer-Winkler, "Two Moralities? A Critical Discussion of an Ethic of Care and Responsibility Versus an Ethic of Right and Justice," in William W. Kurtines and Jacob L. Gewirtz, eds., *Morality, Moral Behavior, and Moral Development* (New York, 1984): 348–61. Legal scholars such as Robin West, Lucinda Finley, and Katharine T. Bartlett, borrowing from Gilligan, seek to integrate a female ethic of care into the law in a variety of areas. See Robin West, "Jurisprudence and Gender in Feminist Legal Theory," *University of Chicago Law Review* 55 (1988): 1–72; Lucinda Finley, "Transcending Equality Theory: A Way Out of the Maternity and Workplace Debate," 86 *Columbia Law Review* (1986): 1118–80; Katharine T. Bartlett, "Re-Expressing Parenthood," *Yale Law Journal* 98 (1988): 293–340. Other legal scholars, such as Joan Williams, are critical of Gilligan, arguing that she is attempting to attribute to women two influential critiques of contemporary Western culture: one a critique of traditional Western epistemology and the other a critique of possessive individualism. See Williams, "Deconstructing Gender," *Michigan Law Review* 87 (1989): 798–845.

34. The feminist critique of liberal theory is extensive and focuses on both the absence or subordination of women in political theory and the gendered structure of the societies in which the theorists lived. A partial list of early critics includes: Susan Miller Okin, *Women in Western Political Thought* (Princeton, 1979); Jean Bethke Elshtain, *Public Man, Private Woman: Women in Social and Political Thought* (Princeton, 1981); and Lorenne M. G. Clark, "Women and John Locke: Who Owns the Apples in the Garden of Eden?" in *The Sexism of Social and Political Theory: Women and Reproduction from Plato to Nietzsche,* ed. Lorrene M. G. Clark and Lynda Lange (Toronto, 1979). See also Carole Pateman, *The Sexual Contract* (Stanford, Calif., 1988), and Carole Pateman and Elizabeth Gross, eds., *Feminists Challenges: Social and Political Theory* (Boston, 1987).

35. Minow, *Making All the Difference,* 147. For an introduction to the British version of this debate, see Elizabeth Kingdom, *What's Wrong with Rights? Problems for Feminist Politics of Law* (Edinburgh, 1991).

36. See, for example, Elizabeth H. Wolgast, *Equality and the Rights of Women* (Ithaca, N.Y., 1980). chap. 1; also idem, *The Grammar of Justice* (Ithaca, N.Y., 1987), 39.

37. See note 29 for a partial listing. Feminists were not the only political theorists critical of the individualism of liberal theory. See Crawford B. MacPherson, *The Political Theory of Possessive Individualism: Hobbes to Locke* (Oxford, 1962).

38. For an example of the early criticism of liberalism emphasizing affiliative values, see Jean Bethke Elshtain, "Antigone's Daughters," *Democracy* 2 (1982): 46–59. For more recent critiques, see Elshtain, *Power Trips and Other Journeys: Essays in Feminism as Civic Discourse* (Madison, 1990); Elizabeth Fox-Genovese, *Feminism Without Illusions: A Critique of Individualism* (Chapel Hill, 1991); also Wolgast, *Grammar of Justice*, 25–27. Both Elshtain and Fox-Genovese, who consider themselves feminists, equate contemporary feminism with individualism and the striving of elite women for male-defined success in patriarchical institutions. Their emphasis on traditional institutions (family for Elshtain, community for Fox-Genovese) is shared by many antifeminists.

On the "female" ethic of care and responsibility versus the "male" ethic of right, see the discussion of Gilligan and her influence on feminist legal scholars in note 31.

39. See Minow, *Making All the Difference*, 147. The same point is made by others, especially Deborah L. Rhode, *Justice and Gender: Sex Discrimination and the Law* (Cambridge, Mass., 1989); also Christine A. Littleton, "Equality and Feminist Legal Theory."

40. Martha Minow, "The Supreme Court 1986 Term Forward: Justice Engendered," *Harvard Law Review* 101 (1987): 12–15.

41. J. R. Pole, *The Pursuit of Equality in American History* (Berkeley and Los Angeles, 1978), 293–94.

42. See, for example, Royster Guano, 253 U.S., 415 ("[T]he classification must be reasonable, not arbitrary, and must rest upon some ground of difference having a fair and substantial relation to the object of the legislation, so that all persons similarly circumstanced shall be treated alike.") While significant gains have flowed from this concept, the limitations of equality analysis soon became apparent to feminist legal scholars, as I shall demonstrate. In Canada, the "similarly situated" test has been rejected as deficient for producing equality, the Supreme Court noting that it would have justified the formalist separate-but-equal doctrine of *Plessy v. Ferguson*. See Catharine A. MacKinnon, "Reflections on Sex Equality Under Law," *The Yale Law Journal* 100 (1991): 1281–1328, esp. n. 67.

43. Black feminist scholars have long been sensitive to the problem of gaining recognition of and relief from oppression occasioned by multiple forms of difference. See, for example, Kimberle Crenshaw, "Demarginalizing the Intersection of Race and Sex: A Black Feminist Critique of Antidiscrimination Doctrine, Feminist Theory, and Antiracist Politics," in Katharine T. Bartlett and Rosanne Kennedy, eds., *Feminist Legal Theory: Readings in Law and Gender* (Boulder, Colo., 1991), 57–80.

44. Although there are many varieties of feminism, participants in the contemporary feminist movement in the United States are usually grouped into three categories: liberal, radical, and cultural or relational. In the early stages of the movement, the division was predominantly between radical and liberal feminists, often referred to as women's liberationists and women's rights advocates, respectively. Liberal feminists believed that equality could be achieved by bringing women into the public sphere and providing them with equal rights. Radical feminists insisted that women's inequality in the public domain had its roots in their subordination in the family and that equality required not merely the sexual integration on mainstream institutions, but a radical transformation of cultural values. Both, however, emphasized that gender was socially constructed. Cultural/relational feminists, who had superseded radical feminists by 1975, chose instead to emphasize male/female difference, whether biologically or socially constructed, and to valorize the female. By focusing on personal rather than social transformation, they functioned more as a counterculture than as agents of political change. For an overview of the contemporary feminist movement, see my essay "The New Feminism and the Dynamics of Social

Change," in Linda K. Kerber and Jane Sherron De Hart, eds., *Women's America: Refocusing the Past* (New York, 1991), 493–521. On the shift from radical feminism to cultural feminism, see Alice Echols, *Daring to Be Bad: Radical Feminism in America, 1967–1975* (Minneapolis, 1989).

45. For the emerging views of key women's advocates on these issues in the 1960s, see Cynthia Harrison, *On Account of Sex: The Politics of Women's Issues, 1945 to the 1960s* (Berkeley and Los Angeles, 1988). For an important early statement on legal classification of sex as overclassification, see Mary O. Eastwood and Pauli Murray, "Jane Crow and the Law: Sex Discrimination and Title VII," *George Washington Law Review* 34 (1965): 232–65.

46. Barbara A. Brown, Thomas I. Emerson, Gail Falk, and Ann E. Freedman, "The Equal Rights Amendment: A Constitutional Basis for Equal Rights for Women," *Yale Law Journal* 80 (1971): 871–985. For the extent to which both pro- and anti-ERA supporters regarded the Emerson article as definitive, see Mathews and De Hart, *Sex, Gender, and the Politics of ERA*, 44–50. The legal expression of this approach, which was modeled on antidiscrimination doctrine developed in conjunction with race, is evident in sex-discrimination cases argued in the 1970s by Justice Ruth Bader Ginsburg.

47. Harrison, *On Account of Sex*, 198–207.

48. See Scott, "Deconstructing Equality." Joan Williams argues that the defense's use of difference allowed Sears's lawyers, with Judge Nordberg's help, to enshrine gender stereotypes at the core of Title VII in ways that constitute a "dramatic reversal of existing Title VII law." See Williams, "Deconstructing Gender," 819. For a related argument that attempts to move judges beyond explanations of either women's choice or employers' coercion, see Vicki Schultz, "Telling Stories About Women and Work: Judicial Interpretations of Sex Segregation in the Workplace in Title VII Cases Raising the Lack of Interest Argument," *Harvard Law Review* 103 (1990): 84–131.

49. Nadine Taub and Wendy W. Williams, "Will Equality Require More than Assimilation, Accommodation, or Separation from the Existing Social Structure? *Rutgers University Law Review* 37 (1985): 833–35; also Wendy W. Williams, "Equality's Riddle: Pregnancy and the Equal Treat–Special Treatment Debate," *New York University Review of Law and Social Change* 13 (1985): 325–80.

50. Martha Minow, "The Supreme Court 1986 Term—Leading Cases," *Harvard Law Review* 101 (1987): 326–27.

51. For an incisive comparison of the two cases, see Minow, "Supreme Court 1986 Term Forward: Justice Engendered," 41–43.

52. MacKinnon is especially eloquent on this point in her "Reflections on Sex Equality Under Law," in which she develops the argument for reproductive control and abortion as sex equality issues.

53. Catharine A. MacKinnon, *Toward a Feminist Theory of the State* (Cambridge, Mass., 1989), 238. See also her earlier article, "Feminism, Marxism, Method, and the State: An Agenda for Theory," *Signs* 7 and 8 (1982–83): 515–44, 635–58.

54. West rejects both liberal legalism and critical legalism as "masculine" and, following the lead of Gilligan, attempts to construct a feminist jurisprudence based on female connectedness and lived experience. See Robin West, "Jurisprudence and Gender," *University of Chicago Law Review* 55 (1987): 81–145.

55. The theories of feminist jurisprudence associated with MacKinnon and West, though recognized as powerful and incisive, are vulnerable to criticism on a variety of grounds. Some scholars reject the gender essentialism embodied in the thought of both. They point out that MacKinnon, in emphasizing the pain and suffering of female subordination exemplified in rape, and West, in stressing the joy of female connectedness to others through such biologically based activities as pregnancy, breastfeeding, and heterosexual intercourse, rest their analysis on an assumption of fundamental sexual difference. Critics such as Drucilla Cornell point to the totalizing and reductive consequences of such assump-

tions and, in the case of MacKinnon, the extent to which the logic leads to a reversal rather than a displacement of gender hierarchy. African-American legal scholars such as Angela Harris are understandably critical of how notions of women's "true nature," combined with the failure to examine how hierarchies of difference interact, serve to marginalize women of color. See Angela P. Harris, "Race and Essentialism in Feminist Legal Theory," *Stanford Law Review* 42 (1990): 581–616; also Drucilla Cornell, *Beyond Accommodation: Ethical Feminism, Deconstruction, and the Law* (New York, 1991), 4–78 passim. (Cornell is more sympathetic to West, disagreeing with her approach but not with her conclusions.)

56. The issues raised by West and relational feminism are widely reflected in feminist legal scholarship. Note, for example, Marie Ashe's emphasis on the nature of the female bodily experience in pregnancy with respect to surrogacy in "Law of Maternity"; Finley's argument for supplementing rights analysis by incorporating responsibility into legal discourse concerning pregnant women in "Transcending Equality Theory"; and Leslie Bender's argument for recognition of relational as well as financial loss in tort law in "Feminist (Re)Torts: Thoughts on the Liability Crisis, Mass Torts, Power, and Responsibilities," *Duke Law Journal* (1990): 848–912.

57. For a critique of West and other relational feminists for tossing out the proverbial baby with the bath water, in this instance liberal conceptions of autonomy and rights, see Linda C. McClain, " 'Automistic Man' Revisited: Liberalism, Connection, and Feminist Jurisprudence," *Southern California Law Review* 65 (1992): 49–109. I am grateful to Joan Williams for calling the McClain article to my attention.

58. See, for example, Schneider, "Dialectic of Rights and Politics"; Patricia Williams, "Alchemical Notes"; Kimberle Williams Crenshaw, "Race, Reform, and Retrenchment," *Harvard Law Review* 101 (1988): 1366–69.

59. Deborah Rhode, "Feminist Critical Theories," *Stanford Law Review* 42 (1990): 617–38. Subsequent quotations in this paragraph, unless otherwise noted, are also from this article.

60. Williams, *The Alchemy of Race and Rights*, 164–65; Martha Minow, "Rights for the Next Generation: A Feminist Approach to Children's Rights," *Harvard Women's Law Journal* 9 (1986): 1, 24; Schneider, "Dialectic of Rights and Politics," 648–52.

61. In concurring with Rhodes's overall assessment, I recognize that this reading is not the only one that can be made of feminist legal theory. For an alternative reading far more sympathetic to the cultural feminism of West, see Hoff, *Law, Gender, and Injustice*, 350–75.

62. It is this shifting anti-essentialist perspective associated with postmodernism that many feminist scholars find to be the most promising approach.

63. The question is essentially MacKinnon's. I have adapted the paraphrased version posed by Sylvia Law in another context. See Sylvia A. Law, "Rethinking Sex and the Constitution," *University of Pennsylvania Law Review* 132 (1984): 955–1040, esp. 968. In commenting on the debate over abortion and "working" mothers, Joan Williams makes the same point. See her "Gender Wars: Selfless Women in the Republic of Choice," *New York University Law Review* 66 (1991): 1163–64. See also Minow, *Making All the Difference*.

64. See note 13.

65. Minow, "The Supreme Court 1986 Term Forward: Justice Engendered," 13.

66. Minow, *Making All the Difference*, 16, 374.

67. The assessment, that of California union officials involved in the Johnson case, is quoted in Urofsky, *A Conflict of Rights*, 188.

PETER SKERRY

The Ambivalent Minority: Mexican Americans and the Voting Rights Act

In the countless conversations about U.S. immigration policy that I have had with Mexican Americans of varied backgrounds and political orientations, seldom have my interlocutors failed to remind me that "We were here first," or that "This was our land and you stole it from us."[1] Even a moderate Mexican American politician like former San Antonio Mayor Henry Cisneros sounds the same theme in a national news magazine:

> It is no accident that these regions have the names they do—Los Angeles, San Francisco, Colorado, Montana. . . . It is a rich history that Americans have been led to believe is an immigrant story when, in fact, the people who built this area in the first place were Hispanics.[2]

Echoing the strident claims of Chicano activists during the 1960s, such assertions today confirm the fears of many Americans that bilingual education programs are not, as Mexican American leaders often claim, intended to move Spanish-speaking children into the American mainstream, but rather to maintain a distinct culture and language. Many Americans similarly regard bilingual ballots not as a matter of voting rights, but as a device concocted by Mexican American leaders to maintain control of their people in isolated barrio enclaves.

Morris Janowitz, the distinguished University of Chicago sociologist, has been one of the few academic observers to give voice to such anxieties:

> Mexicans, together with other Spanish-speaking populations, are creating a bifurcation in the social-political structure of the United

States that approximates nationality division. . . . Thus, the presence of Mexico at the border of the United States, plus the strength of Mexican cultural patterns, means that the "natural history" of Mexican immigrants has been and will be at variance with that of other immigrant groups. For sections of the Southwest, it is not premature to speak of a cultural and social irredenta—sectors of the United States which have in effect become Mexicanized and therefore, under political dispute.[3]

Or, as the question is often put to me, "Don't we have in the Southwest today the makings of our own Quebec?"

My short answer to this query is no. Despite their separatist rhetoric, Chicano activists in the heady 1960s typically argued not for secession from the United States, but for a vaguely defined self-determination (influenced by then fashionable notions of community control) within the existing political framework. Reincorporation of the American Southwest into Mexico was certainly not advocated.[4] More generally, the widespread suspicion that the growing Mexican American community either cannot, or will not, become part of mainstream America is simply not sustained by the evidence.

I argue instead that as a nation we are presented with a much more complicated and troublesome question: Will Mexican Americans define themselves as traditional ethnic immigrants or as victims of racial discrimination? By the phrase "immigrant ethnic group" I refer to those—Irish, Germans, Jews, Italians, Greeks, Poles—who were not conquered, enslaved, or otherwise subjugated by the United States, but who chose to come here voluntarily.[5] Such groups have no special claims on the American conscience; nor are they inclined to make any. This does not mean that immigrant ethnic groups, particularly as new arrivals, have never experienced prejudice or discrimination. But such discrimination—unlike that endured by "racial minority groups" such as black and Native Americans—has not been systematic or sustained over generations. In part, this is because the cultural characteristics that demarcate immigrant ethnic groups (language, religion, dress) are mutable, whereas racial characteristics are not.

This analytic distinction is seldom clear-cut, however, either in scholarly or in popular usage. Black Americans, for example, are frequently referred to as an ethnic group as well as a racial group because, along with certain racial traits, they share many distinctive cultural traits. Indeed, recent moves by such leaders as Jesse Jackson to change the designation "black" to "African American" reflect a disposition to reorient the group's self-image away from that of a victimized racial minority toward a positive identification with its ethnic and cultural heritage.[6]

Historically, the distinction between immigrant ethnic and racial minority group has translated into very different political strategies. For the last great wave of immigrants to arrive here earlier this century, political power was gained through strong local party organizations that, through face-to-face contact and material incentives, helped politically unsophisticated newcomers and their offspring make tangible connections between their own self-interest and the political system. For racial minorities, especially blacks, this avenue of locally based machine politics was either unavailable (in the South) or inadequate in overcoming racial animosities and barriers (in Chicago or New York City, for example). That is why the civil rights movement of the 1950s and 1960s pursued a strategy that sought redress principally from the national government in Washington. Through protest, media attention, and litigation in the federal courts, black Americans finally broke down the barriers excluding them from the political process, and then went on, amid controversy, to fashion affirmative-action remedies enforced by the federal government.

Are Mexican Americans an Ethnic Group or a Racial Minority?

The question is: Where do Mexican Americans fit into this schema? Which historical model is appropriate for them, and which political strategy are they most likely to pursue? The answer is not simple or straightforward, because the Mexican American experience contains *both* a history of territorial conquest and racial subjugation (particularly in the Southwest) *and* a pattern of massive, ongoing immigration and subsequent upward mobility. Perhaps more than any other group, Mexican Americans feel a profound ambivalence: on the one hand, bitter memories and deep-seated resentments about how, at certain times and places, they have been treated by other Americans; on the other hand, hopes and dreams in the classic immigrant mold. As Mexican Americans frequently say, "Some of us have been here for three hundred years, some for three days."

Because of this ambivalence, there is nothing automatic or preordained about the political strategy that Mexican Americans are likely to pursue. Taken as a demographic whole, Mexican Americans conform more to the immigrant ethnic pattern than to the racial minority one. Indeed, most Mexican Americans are recent arrivals. At the close of hostilities between Mexico and the United States in 1848, Mexicans comprised barely 4 percent of the population of the Southwest—or about 80,000 people.[7] Since this was only about 1 percent of Mexico's population at the time, very few Mexican Americans today can trace their lineage back to that conquest. The vast majority are either immigrants themselves or the descendants of immigrants who arrived here in one of the various waves that have swept across the border since the turn of the century. As demographers Frank Bean and Marta Tienda conclude:

> The idea, then, that Mexican Americans must be viewed as different from other national origin groups who have immigrated to the United States because they are a conquered people instead of voluntary immigrants seems hard to justify in light of these statistics.[8]

Socioeconomic data further bear out the immigrant ethnic facet of the Mexican American experience. Intermarrriage data reveal that they marry outside their group at rates comparable to those exhibited by European immigrants earlier this century.[9] Similarly, residential mobility studies reveal that Mexican Americans differ markedly from black Americans in gradually moving up and out of initially settled urban enclaves.[10] And subjectively, Mexican Americans by no means agree that they constitute a racial minority. When asked to classify themselves racially in the 1990 census, 50.6 percent said they were "white."[11]

Such evidence makes it all the more striking that the dominant institutions of contemporary American society unhesitatingly define Mexican Americans as a racial minority. One of the earliest manifestations of this perspective emerged during the 1967 congressional hearings on bilingual education. At that time Senator Ralph Yarborough of Texas, principal sponsor of the Bilingual Education Act, argued that bilingual programs were appropriate for Mexican Americans because, unlike other non-English-speaking groups in the United States, they had not come here voluntarily but had been conquered and "had our culture imposed on them."[12] Nongovernmental institutions are equally disposed toward designating Mexican Americans a racial minority. A good example is *Daedalus*, the prestigious journal of the American Academy of Arts and Sciences. In a special issue entitled "American Indians, Blacks, Chicanos, and Puerto Ricans," editor Stephen Graubard asserts:

> It is obvious that these four peoples—the "victims" of conquest—men and women who did not choose America, who have long suf-

fered exclusion and discrimination because of their origins, live over-
whelmingly in conditions substantially different from those common
to other groups in the United States.[13]

Similarly, the editors of the *Harvard Educational Review* describe a special
issue of their journal, entitled *Facing Racism in Education,* as having articles from contributors who "represent those groups who have historically
been the targets of racism in the United States: Asian Americans, Blacks,
Latinos, and Native Americans."[14] Not coincidentally, these are the
groups covered by the Voting Rights Act, as well as by affirmative-action
requirements in general.

One reason mainstream elites have so readily designated Mexican
Americans a racial minority is that Mexican American elites are so intent
on this perspective. This is certainly true of Mexican American academ-
ics, who typically view themselves as part of a colonized people.[15] As for
political leaders, Rodolfo de la Garza's research concludes: "Chicano
elites consider racism to be a defining characteristic of the Chicano experience that continues to plague them today."[16] An important reason why
Mexican American leaders claim racial minority status is that our post–
civil rights regime offers significant incentives to do so.

In other words, neither history nor contemporary socioeconomic trends
alone can resolve the question whether Mexican Americans are an immigrant ethnic group or a racial minority group. Indeed, the choice facing
Mexican Americans—indeed, all Americans—is fundamentally a political one. The resolution of Mexican American ambivalence must come, if
at all, through the workings of the contemporary American political
system, where enormous changes have been wrought during the past
twenty-five years. And the full impact of those changes is suggested by a
case study of Mexican American political leadership in the voting-rights
politics of Los Angeles.

In metropolitan Los Angeles, the Mexican American population has
grown from 9 percent of the population in 1960 to 38 percent in 1990.
Unlike the more settled Mexican American communities of South
Texas, those in Los Angeles have had to seek political power in an
environment characterized by intensifying immigrant isolation, weak
community organization, and political leadership committed to the racial minority model of litigation politics as pioneered by the Legal
Defense Fund of the NAACP. A key institutional actor in Los Angeles
has been the Mexican American Legal Defense and Education Fund
(MALDEF), the strongest institutional expression of the racial minority
view of Mexican Americans.

MALDEF'S Racial Minority Strategy

Since the 1960s the Voting Rights Act has been the most significant elite initiative toward Mexican Americans in the national arena. Today, the VRA is the single strongest incentive for Mexican Americans and their leaders to define themselves as racial minority claimants. But it was not always thus. Not until 1975 was the original 1965 Act amended to designate Asians and "persons of Spanish heritage" as "language minorities" subject to the same extraordinary protections that had, until then, been exclusively afforded to black Americans. Indeed, as Abigail Thernstrom reveals in her meticulous study of the VRA, Mexican Americans were brought under its umbrella despite spotty evidence that they had been subjected to the kind of systematic racial discrimination experienced by blacks.[17] At the time black leaders knew better, and objected strenuously. But Anglo elites in Washington remained ignorant of the subtleties of group relations in the distant Southwest. From their viewpoint, the Mexican American situation was analogous to that of blacks, and that was that.[18]

The resentment among black leaders over the Hispanic drive for inclusion under the VRA was perhaps understandable but ironic, since the leading Hispanic rights organization in this effort, MALDEF, was consciously modeled on the NAACP Legal Defense Fund by its sponsoring and funding organization, the Ford Foundation. Announcing the foundation's $2.2 million start-up grant in May 1968, Ford president McGeorge Bundy explained: "In terms of legal enforcement of civil rights, American citizens of Mexican descent are now where the Negro community was a quarter-century ago."[19] NAACP Legal Defense Fund executive director Jack Greenberg was appointed to MALDEF's first board of directors. Moreover, NAACP staff attorney Vilma Martinez helped prepare the initial grant application to Ford, and then served as liaison between the two public-interest law firms. Martinez subsequently served as MALDEF's executive director.

Though scarcely the oldest Mexican American organization in the nation, MALDEF has for almost a quarter century been the most visible Mexican American presence in the national arena. The 1973 *San Antonio v. Rodriguez* litigation, which challenged Texas's school finance program, was MALDEF's first major foray—and most notable defeat, since the Supreme Court rejected its argument that the program violated a fundamental, constitutionally protected right to education. MALDEF had to wait a decade for a major victory, which came in 1982 when the Supreme Court upheld its argument (in *Plyer v. Doe*) that Texas public schools

were constitutionally required to educate the foreign-born children of
illegal immigrants. Significantly, the *Plyer* case reflected Vilma Martinez's
decision to follow a legal strategy modeled on that of the NAACP a
generation earlier: laying the groundwork for illegal immigrants' rights
litigation by focusing on the educational disadvantages of children.[20]

Yet there is a striking difference between MALDEF and the NAACP
Legal Defense Fund. Unlike the latter, MALDEF has never been tied to a
mass membership organization.[21] To be sure, MALDEF has ties to the
Mexican American professionals and businessmen who contribute to it
financially and sit on its board. But it has no membership base among the
larger Mexican American population. Throughout its history, MALDEF
has been financially dependent on the Ford Foundation, with additional
help from a handful of other major foundations, corporate sponsors, and
even the federal government. During the 1980s, MALDEF received from
one-third to almost half of its total annual revenues from Ford alone.[22]
MALDEF has been far and away the single largest recipient of all foundation grants to Hispanic organizations.[23]

This base of support raises questions about MALDEF's strengths and
liabilities as a champion of Mexican American interests. In the first place,
there is no single, dominant Mexican American interest that can be
plausibly represented by one organization. Experiencing more mobility
and less discrimination than blacks, Mexican Americans embody interests
too diverse to be channeled into any one organization working in the
highly focused way that the NAACP worked to end legal segregation.
Indeed, the NAACP itself has recently lost membership and become
divided as to its mission.[24] If it no longer makes sense for blacks to
conceive of themselves as defined by a single, overriding interest, then it
arguably makes even less sense for Mexican Americans to do so.

Yet the most important question about MALDEF is not *who* it represents, but *how* it represents them. As the work of various observers suggest, MALDEF is typical of public-interest organizations, which generally
lack a membership base and rely on corporate and foundation support.[25]
Such third-party support allows political entrepreneurs to represent interests or groups that might otherwise be left out of the political process.
This "vicarious representation," as James Q. Wilson calls it,[26] reveals a
troubling differentiation of our political institutions from the social structure. When such entrepreneurs are environmenalists or campaign finance
reformers, questions about whose interests actually get represented are
appropriate. When those being vicariously represented include illegal
immigrants and noncitizens, such questions are imperative.

One characteristic of public-interest law firms like MALDEF is their

tendency to litigiousness. When twelve students from East LA's Garfield
High School were accused by the Educational Testing Service of cheating
on their Advanced Placement math exams, MALDEF's immediate response was to file suit against the Princeton-based testing conglomerate.
The students' teacher, the now-famous Jaime Escalante, demurred and
sought other means of redress, which eventually vindicated him and his
students.[27] Such lawyerly behavior highlights the structure of incentives
within which MALDEF functions. In one sense the organization behaves
like any group of ambitious, well-trained lawyers. But without any members
or clients to which it is answerable, MALDEF can take a much broader,
longer view than any conventional law firm. This was of course what the
Ford Foundation had in mind when it established MALDEF. By contrast,
membership organizations are constrained by the needs of actual members.
Such constraints, though frustrating to agenda-setting foundation execu-
tives and public-interest litigators, are nevertheless one basis of the account-
ability we typically expect of group spokesmen in a democratic society.

Even more striking is the contrast between public-interest organizations
like MALDEF and the strong, neighborhood-based party organizations that
facilitated the political assimilation of earlier generations of immigrants.
One facet of this contrast is the difference between functional and territorial representation. Sociologist Morris Janowitz argues that neighborhood-
based, territorial organizations encourage a weighing and balancing of the
diverse interests within a territorial jurisdiction, thereby prefiguring, however imperfectly, some notion of the public interest:

> In the local community, the person and his household have the
> opportunity—by no means generally realized—to both internalize
> and aggregate the cost and benefits of alternative public policies. At
> least the aspiration of the public interest is not lost as a goal. Each
> citizen is forced to consider his definition of the "good community"
> and to confront the costs he will have to endure for such a social
> order.[28]

For Janowitz, the critical outcome is that territorial representation fosters
more informal, prepolitical resolution of tensions and conflicts where they
arise—a process he refers to as "social control."[29] In essence, geographi-
cally based political organizations are proto-governing institutions. Some
even explicitly seek to govern. By contrast, functionally defined interest
groups are, in Janowitz's pithy formulation, "prepared to bargain but without aspiring to rule."[30] Unrestrained by the responsibilities of actually
governing, interest groups pursue their narrow objectives unmindful of

broader public concerns. Increasing in number and influence without
benefit of the moderating influence of political parties, these groups ever
more energetically press their demands on the state, and the result is
political overload and governmental paralysis.[31] Such tendencies are only
exacerbated when an interest group like MALDEF does not even have a
membership to whom it must answer.

Still, such objections would carry less weight if elite initiatives like
MALDEF genuinely advanced the political standing of Mexican Americans. Yet the evidence is that the legal strategies pursued by MALDEF are
actually counterproductive. The point has been made forcefully by
Charles V. Hamilton about black politics:

> Instead of concentrating time and resources on being politically astute
> (mobilizing, bargaining, compromising), black leaders had to concen-
> trate on being legally precise and Constitutionally alert. As useful as
> this training is in a political democracy, it is hardly the sort that
> prepares a constituency for viable *political* participation. In an impor-
> tant sense, then, an effective black elite developed keen legal skills
> (and in turn both influenced and encouraged the enforcement of
> American Constitutional law). But it was unable to develop those
> skills required for mobilizng masses and maneuvering in the political
> marketplace. Blacks, in other words, developed plaintiffs rather than
> precinct captains. And except for a few places in Northern cities like
> New York and Chicago, they developed legal warriors, not political
> ward leaders.[32]

Hamilton's point applies *a fortiori* to Mexican Americans. For the disaffec-
tion with politics that they bring with them from their homeland is
reinforced by their illegal and noncitizen status in this country. In the
present context, of course, such political inertness only increases pressure
for the remedies of public-interest entrepreneurs. Yet the vicarious representation provided does nothing about the primary causes of that inertness, arguably exacerbating it by conveying to the presumed beneficiaries
the message that the fruits of politics may be had without resort to its
messy processes.

The Politics of Voting Rights in Los Angeles

It is in Los Angeles that the full impact of the VRA on Mexican Americans can best be assessed. In 1986 the Justice Department launched a suit

challenging the 1981 redistricting of the Los Angeles City Council on the grounds of inadequate Hispanic representation. Widely regarded as a Reagan administration move to embarrass Democratic Mayor Tom Bradley, then running for governor, this suit led to the creation of a new Hispanic-majority district, from which Assemblywoman Gloria Molina was elected to the council in 1987.

In 1988 the Republicans in Washington made another election-year effort to ingratiate themselves with Hispanics. That year, the Reagan Justice Department initiated proceedings for a similar suit, this time charging the Los Angeles County Board of Supervisors with discriminating against Hispanics in its 1981 redistricting plan. In what was reportedly the largest VRA suit ever brought, costing the litigants in excess of $12 million, *Garza v. County of Los Angeles* resulted in the creation of a Hispanic majority district from which Molina was elected in 1991 as the first Mexican American to sit on that powerful five-person body since 1875.

In this particular episode, the role of the media is especially worthy of note.[33] The *Los Angeles Times*'s endorsement of Molina helped her overcome the superior financial resources of her principal rival, State Senator Art Torres. But of much greater relevance was the rhetoric the *Times* brought to bear on behalf of Molina. Praising the reasoning of the federal district judge who upheld the plaintiffs' arguments against the board's 1981 redistricting, the *Times* intoned:

> That kind of racial or ethnic gerrymandering is illegal under federal law and is as offensive as poll taxes, literacy tests and the other racist tactics that all-white governments used to discourage African-Americans from voting during the worst days of segregation in the Deep South.[34]

From such rhetoric one would never guess that the historical evidence brought to light in this litigation[35] revealed nothing like the treatment experienced by blacks in the South. Moreover, although the federal district judge who ruled against the supervisors found "discrimination" within the definition of the Voting Rights Act, he found (as a federal appellate judge subsequently pointed out) no racial animus against Hispanics per se in the supervisors'1981 redistricting effort.[36] Instead, the district judge found intense ideological competition among two liberal Democrats and three conservative Republicans, each anxious to hold onto his own seat:

> During the 1981 redistricting process, the Supervisors' primary objective was to protect their incumbencies and that of their allies. . . .

> The Court believes that had the Board found it possible to protect
> their incumbencies while increasing Hispanic voting strength, they
> would have acted to satisfy both objectives.[37]

However self-interested or ignoble, the supervisors sacrificed the interests
of Hispanics not out of ill will or racism, but in order to hold onto their
seats.

Revealingly, one day after the federal district judge determined that "an
Hispanic candidate is unable to be elected to the Board under the current
configuration of supervisorial districts,"[38] a Mexican American woman
won the primary in the First Supervisorial District with 35 percent of the
total vote, including 68 percent of the Hispanic and 31 percent of the
non-Hispanic vote. Moreover, with the second-place finisher, an Anglo
male, winning only 20 pecent of the total vote, Sarah Flores was favored
to win the seat.[39] Nevertheless, that same judge subsequently nullified
these results, consistent with his initial finding that the supervisorial
districts were improperly drawn.

In addition to exaggerated rhetoric, the *Times* also displayed an ahistori-
cal impatience. Typical was the observation of reporter Richard Simon:
"Latinos make up one-third of the county's population, but no Spanish-
surnamed person has served on the board since 1875."[40] Simon's facts are
correct, but he seriously misleads his readers by implying that for generations a substantial segment of the county's population had been denied
representation. For throughout most of this century the Mexican-origin
population of Los Angeles was significantly smaller than it is today.

This same perspective was much in evidence the night Molina won her
county supervisor's seat. In a celebratory article entitled "In 30 Years,
History Comes Full Circle from Roybal to Molina," a *Times* columnist
quoted Molina: "This victory should have been celebrated 30 years ago.
That is why I want to dedicate this victory to Congressman Ed Roybal.
They stole the election from him 30 years ago."[41] As the article explains,
Molina was referring to a 1958 supervisorial contest that then-city coun-
cillor Roybal initially won by 393 votes, but that after four recounts and
some apparent chicanery, he subsequently lost. What the article does not
explain—thereby reinforcing Molina's claim that her victory compen-
sated for injustices against her people—is that Roybal ran in a district in
which only 23 percent of the population (not voters) was Hispanic, at a
time when Hispanics constituted only 9 percent of the county's population.[42] Indeed, about two-thirds of all Hispanics now living in the county
have arrived within the last twenty years.[43] And most of these have been
illegal immigrants. It is in fact probable that a majority of Hispanics in Los

Angeles at the time of the 1980 redistricting were not citizens.[44] Yet when it is argued that Mexican Americans have been excluded from the political process, these simple facts are usually ignored. Sympathetic media commentators constantly cater to the rhetorical claim made by Mexican American leaders that "we were here first," and imply that the entire group's present meager economic and political resources are the result of long-standing racial oppression. And as for the plaintiffs' briefs and even the judges' opinions in the *Garza* case, they are full of references to vague "demographic factors" to which the supervisors were supposed to respond. But in these documents one is hard-pressed to find the words "immigrant" or "immigration." Nor is there any acknowledgment that the supervisors' response was conditioned by the fact that only 32 percent of Hispanics in the county in 1980 were even eligible to vote.[45]

This concatenation of vague misconceptions was in full view when the *Los Angeles Times* endorsed Molina. As the editors explained, "The supervisors opted in 1981 to protect their own incumbencies by diluting the potential voting strength of the county's 3 million Latino residents."[46] Quite aside from the fact that in 1981 there were only 2 million Latinos in Los Angeles County, this 3 million figure (the county's Latino population in 1990) ignores the huge proportion of Latinos who cannot vote due to their age or legal status. Under these circumstances it is downright misleading to talk of "the potential voting strength" of 3 million Latinos. Committed to the view that the supervisors engaged in "racial gerrymandering," the *Times* simply refused to address the primary sources of the dilution of the Latino vote in Los Angeles.

Similarly ignored in the *Garza* controversy has been the residential mobility of Mexican Americans. Because compactness is one of the criteria to be considered in drawing districts, a widely dispersed group greatly complicates the process. This has certainly been the case with Hispanics in Los Angeles County. To design a Hispanic-majority district there, demographers focused on what they called "the Hispanic Core," an area composed of 229 contiguous census tracts, all but three of which had a majority of Hispanics. The Core contained 81 percent of all census tracts in the county with Hispanic population majorities in 1980, and 72 percent of its total population was Hispanic. Barely 27 percent of these Core Hispanics were voting-age citizens. But more to the point at hand, Hispanics in Los Angeles are dispersed such that the Core contained only 40 percent of the total Hispanic population in the county and just 36 percent of all citizen voting-age Hispanics.[47]

Thus, drawing Hispanic-majority districts in Los Angeles is no easy task. Indeed, in 1981, when Mexican Americans constituted 28 percent of the county population, it was simply not possible to draw a supervisorial district with a Hispanic voting majority.[48] Significantly, none of the experts for the plaintiffs or defendants in the *Garza* case ever argued otherwise. Even the Chicano activists who in 1981 singlehandedly challenged the supervisors' redistricting plan never asked for such a district. Instead, they sought two "influence districts" in which Hispanics would hold less than a voting majority, but would nevertheless have the potential either to elect one of their own to the board or to exert significant clout over whoever did get elected.[49] Moreover, throughout the 1980s creating a Hispanic voting-majority district remained problematic, with demographers and political scientists disagreeing as to exactly when in the decade it was feasible.[50] When the new district was finally created by order of the courts in 1990, Hispanics constituted 71 percent of its population and 59 percent of its voting-age citizens, but just 51 percent of its registered voters.[51]

For all these reasons, it is no wonder that MALDEF hesitated for almost a decade before bringing suit against the supervisors. The organization declined to join forces with Chicano activists in 1981 when they challenged the county redistricting plan.[52] Even after the 1982 amendments to the VRA made such suits easier (because claims to underrepresentation no longer required a demonstration of intentional discrimination), MALDEF was still reluctant to risk the enormous resources required. In the end, the catalyst was the Reagan Justice Department. Having been preempted by Justice in the 1986 Los Angeles City Council redistricting case, MALDEF could not afford to sit out a second round. So, when Justice began threatening the Board of Supervisors in 1988, MALDEF launched its suit in the midst of ongoing negotiations between the county and the feds. Shortly thereafter, Justice joined the suit.[53]

Rotten Boroughs and the Numbers Game

On the surface, *Garza* was an enormous victory for MALDEF. Yet the gain may be far less substantial than touted. Highly revealing in this regard is the disappointingly low turnout for the historic election that resulted in Molina's victory. Only 23 percent of those registered voted in the run-off between her and Art Torres.[54] Although Molina ran a more grassroots campaign than her opponent, it is not easy to overcome the enormous disincentives to neighborhood-based politics in Los Angeles.[55]

A more salient datum from this election is that out of approximately 1.8 million residents in the newly created First Supervisorial District, only

86,998 votes were cast—less than 5 percent of the total.[56] The simple fact is that this new Hispanic district does not have many residents eligible to vote. For example, when it was created, the First District had 707,651 voting-age citizens, while the predominantly Anglo Third District had 1,098,663.[57] Thus, a vote in the First weighs much more than in the Third. This imbalance arises because the federal courts have interpreted the one-person–one-vote principle as mandating districts roughly equal in total population, not in eligible voters. When laid down by the Supreme Court in *Reynolds v. Sims,* this principle was based on the assumption that equipopulous districts contain correspondingly equal numbers of electors. Yet today, under conditions of mass immigration, this assumption is often wrong.[58]

Thus, the creation of such districts, packed with large and growing numbers of individuals unable to vote, increases the number of Hispanic elected officials. But these gains do not translate into commensurate political power. These officeholders are certainly not viewed by their Anglo colleagues and allies as capable of delivering large blocks of voters—quite the contrary. The unfortunate fact is that such legalistic efforts to advance Mexican American political interests are subject to inherent constraints that cannot be overridden by impatient elites—a homely truth that has been obscured in the struggle to jump-start Mexican American politics.

Here, too, such efforts may actually hinder Mexican American political advancement. By concentrating noncitizens in highly visible districts, the problem of low Hispanic political participation is highlighted and the stereotype of Hispanics as politically passive and indifferent is reinforced. At the same time, by fostering the impression that significant political power is being acquired, pressure for more substantive political gains is reduced. And while advocates argue that an increase in the number of Mexican American officeholders raises the level of rank-and-file political involvement, the evidence from Los Angeles suggests otherwise. For with large and growing numbers of constituents ineligible to vote, Hispanics elected from these districts experience relatively little home-grown opposition. The resulting political vacuum makes it all the more likely that these elected officials respond more to the politicians or advocacy groups responsible for the creation of their districts than to those whom they formally represent. Indeed, such Mexican American officeholders not only fail to encourage voter participation, they actually discourage it. Like any officeholders, they are not eager to expand the numbers of those who might put demands on them. Moreover, they have every reason to avoid getting caught between their often conservative Mexican American base and their typically liberal Democratic allies.

In essence, these Hispanic districts represent a new type of "rotten borough." The term could not be more appropriate, since it harkens back to an era when standards of voter participation and officeholder account- ability were far less rigorous than today. The irony, of course, is that these rotten boroughs follow from today's more demanding standards. The re- sult is that we have increased Mexican American representation, but only in the most formal and delimited sense.

Even more disturbing is how the VRA seduces Mexican American leaders into playing a numbers game with ever-increasing populations of politically passive constituents. These rotten boroughs may not provide Mexican American officeholders with powerful positions, but they do provide them with secure political bases. The trouble is that, having struck this bargain, the officeholders succumb to its logic. On the one hand, they get used to the passivity of their many nonvoting constituents. On the other, in a dynamic social and political system, they cannot rest content with their relatively weak positions. Craving more clout, they know all too well the difficulties facing them if they try to expand their voting base. So they opt for the easier and safer route of relying on the increasing overall number of Hispanics. The continuing influx of newcom- ers from Mexico—illegal and legal—answers this need quite neatly.

Yet the evidence accumulates that such high levels of immigration are not necessarily in the interests of Mexican Americans generally. Economi- cally, there is evidence that immigrants undercut Mexican Americans, especially those at the lower end of the wage scale.[59] And politically, immigrants present an array of problems. For immigrants generally are not easy to organize for political goals, and immigration at the levels we have been seeing creates so much instability and transience that the task be- comes far more difficult. Large numbers of illegal immigrants only further complicate matters.

For all these reasons, Mexican American leaders used to be wary of immigration from Mexico. Rodolfo de la Garza reports that during the 1950s and 1960s, "Mexican American leaders were among the most vocif- erous of the opponents to continued Mexican immigration."[60] Given the complicated and continuing ties between Mexicans on both sides of the border, this position was often arrived at reluctantly. But for two decades after World War II, organizations such as the League of United Latin American Citizens (LULAC) and the American G.I. Forum nonetheless argued for restricted immigration from Mexico, on the grounds that large

numbers of newcomers would undermine the social and economic position of Mexican Americans struggling into the American mainstream. As
educator and political activist George I. Sanchez argued in 1966: "Time
and time again, just as we have been on the verge of cutting our bi-
cultural problems to manageable proportions, uncontrolled mass migrations from Mexico have erased the gains and accentuated the cultural
indigestion."[61]

It was not long afterward that a momentous shift occurred in leadership
views toward immigration. Today's Mexican American leadership is over-
whelmingly in favor of adopting a de facto open-borders stance, while
Mexican Americans generally seem as sharply divided as ever.[62] For example, the Latino National Political Survey found that in 1990 three-fourths
or more of all Mexican Americans (citizens and noncitizens alike) agreed
that "there are too many immigrants coming to this country."[63] Yet
among today's leadership, there is certainly no voice comparable to Sanchez's objecting to the present influx.

The critical factor accounting for this widely ignored sea change in
leadership attitudes toward mass immigration, from disapproval to induce-
ment, is the VRA and similar efforts that now reward Mexican American
leaders not for their group's political clout at the polls, but for its population totals at census time. The affirmative-action logic that now pervades
our political culture means that steadily increasing numbers of Mexican
immigrants readily translate into demands for steadily increasing quotas
for Hispanic employees and Hispanic-majority electoral districts. Thus,
Mexican American leaders have not only acclimated to immigration from
Mexico at high levels, but they have in fact become dependent on it as
the source of their visibility and influence.[64]

The VRA offers concrete benefits to various political elites, most obvi-
ously advancing the careers of Mexican American leaders whose electoral
opportunities have been significantly expanded by it. It also fosters the
affirmative-action logic whereby such leaders generally can press their
special claims as the spokesmen and representatives of an aggrieved racial
minority whose numbers happen to be growing. Yet this dynamic makes
these leaders dependent on continuing high levels of immigration that in
fact weaken the group politically—and perhaps economically. As a result,
the political fortunes of Mexican American leaders are substantially at
odds with the organizational and political strength of Mexican Americans
as a group.

But Mexican American leaders are hardly the sole beneficiaries of this
regime. VRA-mandated districts also reassure concerned Anglo elites
that the interests of Hispanics are getting represented. More specifically,

these rotten boroughs speak to the specific needs of Democratic party leaders in California and elsewhere. Quite aside from the objective difficulties of organizing Mexican Americans under the conditions I have been describing, Democrats are not eager to mobilize large numbers of new voters who might further complicate the problems of putting together winning coalitions.[65] Rotten boroughs allow party leaders to avoid this risk while at the same time responding to Mexican American demands for representation. At the same time, electoral redistricting to create Hispanic-majority districts benefits Republicans. For as Reagan and Bush administration officials well understood, concentrating Hispanics (or blacks) in such districts simultaneously permits the creation of safer Anglo—that is, Republican—seats.[66]

Again, Hamilton's work on black politics is extremely pertinent. In a seminal article written at the end of the 1970s, Hamilton sought to explain the decline in black political participation and power in New York City.[67] He did so by identifying a curious political dynamic he called "patron-recipient politics," which he traced back to the War on Poverty and then contrasted with the "patron-client politics" of the urban ethnic machines. Of direct relevance to my analysis of Mexican American politics is the distinction Hamilton draws between the impersonal, one-directional nature of patron-recipient ties and the multifaceted, face-to-face relationships that characterized the ethnic machines. Hamilton observes:

> The party official provided favors, divisible benefits, jobs for the constituents. In return, grateful constituents gave their votes on election day. . . . At all times, both patron and client clearly understood the basis of the relationship: *quid pro quo*. . . . The recipient receives from the patron and is asked to do nothing *but* receive the benefits. . . . The client becomes a political actor; the recipient remains a political nonactor.[68]

As Hamilton emphasizes, the patron-recipient tie, because it is fleeting and transient, lacks the organizational dimension that characterizes the patron-client relationship:

> The patron expects to service a revolving recipient group, which becomes one measure of the patron's viability: the numbers of *different* recipients served. This is so, because the basis of the relationship is the recipient's needs, not necessarily the patron's resources. Presumably, that need can be met. Therefore, it is not expected that a permanent or even long-term relationship be developed between the patron and

the recipient. Again, unlike the patron-client association, it is hoped that the particular patron-recipient relationship will be ephemeral and transitory. It is difficult, therefore, to perceive a viable, sustained political foundation being built upon such an orientation.[69]

Lacking strong organizational bases, practitioners of patron-recipient politics resort, when necessary, to protest tactics. Once again, no lasting relationships between leaders and rank-and-file are forged. Finally, Hamilton argues that patron-recipient politics, contrary to the intentions of those who often support it, depoliticizes its intended beneficiaries. Although he does not put it in such terms, Hamilton's work suggests that patron-recipient politics fosters the political equivalent of welfare dependency.

Hamilton's analysis is, if anything, more relevant to an understanding of Mexican American than black politics—because, due to various cultural and structural factors, Mexican Americans are more prone to political passivity than blacks. Certainly it puts into perspective the implicit strategy of Mexican American political elites who, contrary to what their critics typically charge, are not concerned to organize or control an insulated barrio constituency, but rather to represent—vicariously—a continually expanding and assimilating body of constituents to whom they have only the most tenuous ties.

The Mexican American Experience and Contemporary Institutions

The historical experience of Mexicans in the United States is a complicated one that points to no single or obvious set of policies vis-à-vis Mexican Americans today. To be sure, Mexican American leaders are focused on the injustices visited on their people, but whether these justify extraordinary rights-oriented remedies such as the Voting Rights Act is highly problematic. In large part, coverage of Mexican Americans under the VRA reflects the understandable impatience of leaders to advance their group in a political system that is hardly of their own making.

But these are leaders, it is also important to note, who are by and large unmindful or simply unaware of the historical experiences of other groups that have had to struggle to become part of American society. Mexican Americans, even the most sophisticated and educated, typically react with disbelief when told of the discrimination and prejudice encountered by Irish, Polish, Jewish, and Italian immigrants to this nation. They are similarly brought up short when reminded, for example, that the Irish, who began arriving here in substantial numbers during the 1820s and 1830s, did not capture the mayor's office in New York until 1880; in Boston until 1884; or in Chicago until 1893.[70] Do such historical examples mean that Mexican Americans should expect to wait for half a century before one of their own becomes mayor of Los Angeles? No, but they do counsel a degree of patience and proportionality lacking among Mexican American leaders.

What these leaders lack perhaps even more fundamentally are alternatives to the prevailing racial minority perspective, as they attempt to make sense of the inevitable hurts, injustices, and discontents that arise with entry into the mainstream of American life. But, once again, this is hardly a situation entirely of their own making. For the dominant society's elites have adopted this same racial minority perspective and have moreover institutionalized it, for example, with MALDEF.

In this regard, as we have seen in the Los Angeles case, the media have played a critical role. Like generals, they are fighting the last war: which in this case is the struggle for black civil rights during the 1960s.[71] Sustained by the moral capital accumulated during that period, and fortified by Watergate and other Washington scandals, journalists, particularly those in the national media, are keen to play this role again. This predisposition, in addition to the time constraints under which they work, means that journalists tend to accept uncritically the racial minority interpretation of the Mexican American experience offered by advocates and activists.

Eager for change, and steeped in the history of the Southwest, Mexican American leaders are understandably impatient. Much more surprising is the impatience displayed by non-Mexican-American, Anglo elites. Their response may in part reflect a sense of urgency about the need to incorporate a large and growing number of immigrants, quite regardless of their legal status, into our political system. But more fundamentally, these elites are acting on lessons absorbed in the 1960s, long before the present influx. It was during that period they learned, from the civil rights movement, that if tolerance is a virtue, so is impatience. At least, having once been roundly—and justifiably—criticized for counseling patience to the victims of racial discrimination, these elites are now determined not to make the same mistake again.

Yet impatience may be a mistake when dealing with the problems of recent immigrants. In this article I have posed the question whether Mexican Americans are in fact a racial minority group entitled to the same special benefits afforded black Americans. My reading of the evidence inclines me to say no. But beyond this specific response lies my broader concern that we have as a society not adequately considered our de facto response to this question. In our impatience with the wrongs suffered by racial minorities, we forget what a long and arduous process it is for immigrants to become full participants in American life. We forget our own history—not just that of Mexicans in the Southwest, but that of immigrant groups back East. And we indulge our impatience, insisting that newcomers be fully represented and participate in all our institutions before they have had the time to build up any real political strength. In sum, by trying to jump-start the process, we end up short-circuiting it.

Center for American Politics and Public Policy, UCLA

Notes

This essay is excerpted from *Mexican Americans: The Ambivalent Minority* (The Free Press, 1993).

1. The same sentiment was found in the 1960s by Leo Grebler et al., *The Mexican-American People: The Nation's Second Largest Minority* (New York, 1970), 545.
2. Richard Mackenzie, "U.S. Culture with a Spanish Accent," *Insight,* 16 December 1985, 14.
3. Morris Janowitz, *The Reconstruction of Patriotism: Education for Civic Consciousness* (Chicago, 1983), 129, 137.
4. Carlos Munoz, Jr., and Mario Barrera, "La Raza Unida Party and the Chicano Student Movement in California," *Social Science Journal* 19 (1982): 111; Walker Connor, "Who Are the Mexican-Americans? A Note on Comparability," in Walker Connor, ed., *Mexican-Americans in Comparative Perspective* (Washington, D.C., 1985), 16–18.
5. The distinction I draw here parallels that made by John U. Ogbu, "Minority Status and Literacy in Comparative Perspective," *Daedalus* 119(1980): 145–46, 150. I am indebted to Paul Peterson for bringing this article to my attention.
6. See Ben L. Martin, "From Negro to Black to African American," *Political Science Quarterly* 6 (1991): 83–107.
7. Frank D. Bean and Marta Tienda, *The Hispanic Population of The United States* (New York, 1987), 107.
8. Bean and Tienda, *The Hispanic Population,* 107–9.
9. Edward Murguia, *Chicano Intermarriage: A Theoretical and Empirical Study* (San Antonio, Tex., 1982), 40–41, 48–49.
10. See Douglas S. Massey and Nancy A. Denton, "Trends in the Residential Segregation of Blacks, Hispanics, and Asians: 1970–1980," *American Sociological Review* 52 (1987): 802–25. Also Joan Moore and Harry Pachon, *Hispanics in the United States* (Englewood Cliffs, N.J., 1985), 60.
11. Of the remainder, 1.2 percent of Mexican Americans said they were "black" and 46.7 percent "other race." Confirming these data are the findings of the Latino National Political Survey. Conducted around the same time as the 1990 census, the Survey reports that 51 percent of Mexican Americans identify themselves as racially "white." See Rodolfo O. de la Garza et al., "Will the Real American Press Stand Up: A Comparison of Political

Values Among Mexicans, Cubans, Puerto Ricans, and Anglos in the United States," paper presented at the annual meeting of the American Political Science Association (1991), 16.

12. Quoted in Diane Ravitch, *The Troubled Crusade: American Education, 1945–1980* (New York, 1983), 271.

13. Stephen R. Graubard, "Preface," *Daedalus* 110 (1981): vii.

14. I quote here from an advertising circular. For the actual publication, see *Harvard Educational Review* 58 (1988): 265–432.

15. See, for example, Mario Barrera, *Race and Class in the Southwest: A Theory of Racial Inequality* (Notre Dame, Ind., 1979); or David Montejano, *Anglos and Mexicans in the Making of Texas, 1836–1986* (Austin, Tex., 1987), passim and especially 261.

16. Rodolfo O. de la Garza, *Public Policy Priorities of Chicano Political Elites*, working Paper, U.S.-Mexico Project Series, No. 7 (Washington, D.C.: Overseas Development Council, July 1982), 22.

17. Abigail M. Thernstrom, *Whose Votes Count? Affirmative Action and Minority Voting Rights* (Cambridge, Mass., 1987), 43–62.

18. On the Voting Rights Act and its extension to Mexican Americans, see Thernstrom, *Whose Votes Count?*, 43–62. For evidence that the discrimination experience by Mexicans even in as extreme a context as Texas was less intense than what blacks endured, see Greber et al., *The Mexican American People*, 389–90. See also Montejano, *Anglos and Mexicans in the Making of Texas*, though my inferences from Montejano's data differ from his own.

19. Karen O'Connor and Lee Epstein, "A Legal Voice for the Chicano Community: The Activities of the Mexican American Legal Defense and Educational Frund, 1968–1982," *Social Science Quarterly* 65 (1984): 248.

20. Ibid., 253.

21. For an analysis of the structure and incentives of the NAACP and its spinoff, the NAACP Legal Defense and Educational Fund, see James Q. Wilson, *Political Organizations* (New York, 1973), 171–81, 321. See also Joel F. Handler et al., "Public Interest Law and Employment Discrimination," in Burton A. Weisbrod et al., *Public Interest Law: An Economic and Institutional Analysis* (Berkeley and Los Angeles, 1978), 272–73. On MALDEF specifically, see ibid., 273–74.

22. Data compiled from MALDEF and Ford Foundation annual reports.

23. Blanca Facundo, *Responsiveness of U.S. Foundations to Hispanic Needs and Concerns: Results of a Survey on Institutional Policies and Procedures Relevant to Hispanics and an Analysis of Grant Information in the 1977 and 1978 "Foundation Grants Index"* (Reston, Va., Latino Research Institute Division, 1980), 22–24. See also *A Study of Foundation Awards to Hispanic-Oriented Organizations in the U.S.: 1981–1982*, preliminary report (Stanford, Calif.: Stanford Center for Chicano Research, Stanford University, March 1984), 16–17.

24. See, for example, Paul Delaney, "A Purge at the Top, Confusion In the Ranks: N.A.A.C.P. Crisis," *New York Times*, 29 March 1992, sec. 4, 2.

25. See Jeffrey M. Berry, *The Interest Group Society*, 2d ed. (Glenview, Ill., 1989), 62–63; and James Q. Wilson, *American Government: Institutions and Policies* (Lexington, Mass., 1980), 215–18.

26. James Q. Wilson, ed., *The Politics of Regulation* (New York, 1980), 370–72. Wilson's discussion of vicarious representation is of course part of his broader analysis of "entrepreneurial politics," which he differentiates from "majoritarian," "client," and "interest group" politics. It is an intriguing—and not readily answered—question as to whether the political dynamics I ascribe to MALDEF are best categorized as entrepreneurial or client politics. See ibid., 367–70.

27. Jay Mathews, *Escalante: The Best Teacher in America* (New York, 1988), 172–73.

28. Morris Janowitz, *The Last Half-Century: Societal Change and Politics in America* (Chicago, 1978), 303.

29. Ibid., 27–52, 302.

30. Ibid., 302.

31. Ibid., 301–12.

32. Charles V. Hamilton, "Blacks and the Crisis of Political Participation," *Public Interest* 34 (1974): 191. Stuart Scheingold makes a similar critique of public-interest law strategies, but from a much more markedly leftist perspective. See Stuart A. Scheingold, *The Politics of Rights: Lawyers, Public Policy, and Political Change* (New Haven, 1974).

33. For a similar argument on how the media greatly oversimplied the complex issues involved in the 1981–82 debates over renewal of the Voting Rights Act, see Thernstrom, *Whose Votes Count?*, 117–20.

34. "Ending the Political Shame of L.A.," *Los Angeles Times*, 6 June 1990, B6.

35. *Garza v. County of Los Angeles*, 756 F.Supp. 1298, 1339–42 (C.D. Cal. 1990).

36. *Garza v. County of Los Angeles*, 918 F.2d 763, 778 (9th Cir. 1990) (Kozinski, C.J., concurring and dissenting in part).

37. 756 F.Supp. 1298, at 1304.

38. Ibid.

39. For the election results, see *County of Los Angeles, et al. v. Yoland Garza, et al.*, "Petition for a Writ of Certiorari to the United States Court of Appeals for the Ninth Circuit," Supreme Court of the United States, October Term, 1990; 30 November 1990, 4. For an assessment of Sarah Flores's prospects in what would have been the runoff for the supervisorial seat, see Bill Boyarsky, "The Rocky Race of Sarah Flores," *Los Angeles Times*, Nuestro Tiempo section, 11 October 1990, 1, 7.

40. Richard Simon, "Light Voter Turnout in 1st District Race," *Los Angeles Times*, 23 January 1991, A20.

41. Bill Boyarsky, "In 30 Years, History Comes Full Circle from Roybal to Molina," *Los Angeles Times*, 23 February 1991, B2.

42. J. Morgan Kousser, *How to Determine Intent: Lessons from L.A.*, Social Science Working Paper 741 (Pasadena: Division of Humanities and Social Sciences, California Institute of Technology, June 1990), 12.

43. *Garza v. County of Los Angeles*, "Appellants' Opening Brief on Appeal," U.S. Court of Appeals for the Ninth Circuit, 8–9.

44. I deduce this from the fact that 53 percent of Los Angeles Hispanics told the 1980 census they were citizens. Because we know that these self-reported census data on citizenship are artificially high, it is then entirely possible that less than this 53 percent figure— less than a majority of Los Angeles Hispanics—were citizens in 1980. See *Garza v. County of Los Angeles*, "Appellants' Opening Brief on Appeal," U.S. Court of Appeals for the Ninth Circuit, 9.

45. Derived from the data presented in *United States of America v. County of Los Angeles*, "Declaration of Dr. William P. O'Hare," U.S. District Court for the Central District of California, 26 October 1989, 10.

46. "An Election to Make History," *Los Angeles Times*, 19 February 1991, B6.

47. Figures derived from data presented in *United States of America v. County of Los Angeles*, "Declaration of Dr. William P. O'Hare," 8, 12, 14.

48. 756 F.Supp. 1298 at 1318–19.

49. For the Chicano activists' strategy in 1981, see Nancy D. Kates, *New Kingdoms for the Five Kings: Discriminatory Redistricting and the Los Angeles County Board of Supervisors*, Case Program, Kennedy School of Government, Harvard University, 1991 (draft), 7–8. See also Kousser, *How to Determine Intent*, 32–41; and 756 F.Supp 1298 at 1315.

50. 918 F.2d 763 at 769; and *Garza v. County of Los Angeles*, "Appellants' Opening Brief on Appeal," 14.

51. Richard Simon and Hector Tobar, "Deadline for 1st District Race Passes with No Surprises," *Los Angeles Times*, 1 December 1990, B3.

52. On the strategic choices facing MALDEF in 1981, see Kates, *New Kingdoms for the Five Kings*, 11. For an account, from the activists' perspective, of the events leading up to the MALDEF suit, see Steve Uranga and Marshall Diaz, "For Latinos, a Representative Case," *Los Angeles Times*, 28 July 1988, II-7.

53. This sequence of events is borne out in newspaper accounts of the negotiations culminating in the suit. See Victor Merina and Ron Ostrow, "U.S. Accuses County of Reapportionment Bias," *Los Angeles Times*, 26 May 1988, 1, 34; Victor Merina, "U.S. Vows Suit If Supervisors Don't Revamp to Aid Latinos," *Los Angeles Times*, 20 July 1988, 1, 4; Victor Merina, "Latinos Sue, Charge Bias in Districting by Supervisors," *Los Angeles Times*, 24 August 1988, II-1, II-8; and Victor Merina and Ronald J. Ostrow, "U.S. Sues to Get New Supervisor Districts Drawn," *Los Angeles Times*, 9 September 1988, 1, 28. In the latter article, a senior Justice Department official complained that voting-rights-division attorneys were caught by surprise "when MALDEF rushed in and filed suit. They picked up all the work we had done and then threw a hand grenade."

54. Lou Cannon, "Hispanic Elected in L.A. County," *Washington Post*, 21 February 1991, A5.

55. For more on this point, see Peter Skerry, *Mexican Americans: The Ambivalent Minority* (New York, 1993), 74–80, 86–90, 175–249.

56. This turnout figure is from the Los Angeles County Office of Public Information. Similarly low turnout figures for a variety of Latino (and black) constituencies in Los Angeles are presented in one of the more thoughtful articles on the 1992 Los Angeles riots. See Tim Rutten, "A New Kind of Riot," *New York Review of Books*, 11 June 1992, 54.

57. 918 F.2d 763 at 779–80 (Kozinski, C. J., concurring and dissenting in part).

58. Ibid., 781–85.

59. See especially, Kevin F. McCarthy and R. Burciaga Valdez, *Current and Future Effects of Mexican Immigration in California* (Los Angeles, 1986), 37–45, 74–75, but also Thomas Muller et al., *The Fourth Wave: California's Newest Immigrants* (Washington, D.C., 1985), 114–17.

60. Rodolfo O. de la Garza, "Mexican Americans, Mexican Immigrants, and Immigration Reform," in Nathan Glazer, ed., *Clamor at the Gates: The New American Immigration* (San Francisco, 1985), 98.

61. Quoted in Vernon M. Briggs et al., *The Chicano Worker* (Austin, Tex., 1977), 93. For more on Sanchez's views on immigration and related issues, see Mario T. Garcia, *Mexican Americans: Leadership, Ideology, and Identity, 1930–1960* (New Haven, 1989), 252–72.

62. On the divisions among Mexican Americans with regard to immigration during the 1960s, see Grebler et al., *The Mexican-American People*, 383.

63. Rodolfo de la Garza et al., *Latino Voices: Mexican, Puerto Rican, and Cuban Perspectives on American Politics* (Boulder, Colo., 1992), 101, 178, 215.

64. For a contrasting, but not very persuasive, view, see de la Garza, "Mexican Americans, Mexican Immigrants, and Immigration Reform," in Glazer, ed., *Clamor at the Gates*, 102.

65. For an elaboration of this point, see Thomas Byrne Edsall, *The New Politics of Inequality* (New York, 1984).

66. For a critique of this strategy, see Linda Chavez, "Party Lines: The Republicans' Racial Quotas," *The New Republic*, 24 June 1991, 14–16. See also Abigail M. Thernstrom, "A Republican–Civil Rights Conspiracy," *Washington Post*, 23 September 1991, A23.

67. On the decline of black turnout in northern cities generally in the pre-Reagan era, see Steven P. Erie, *Rainbow's End: Irish-Americans and the Dilemmas of Urban Machine Politics, 1840–1985* (Berkeley and Los Angeles, 1988), 265–66.

68. Charles V. Hamilton, "The Patron-Recipient Relationship and Minority Politics in New York City," *Political Science Quarterly* 94 (1979): 214–15.

69. Ibid., 215–16.

70. Edward T. Kantowicz, "Voting and Parties," in Michael Walzer et al., *Politics of Ethnicity* (Cambridge, Mass., 1982), 46.

71. On television's self-conscious role in the civil rights struggle, see Michael J. Robinson, "Television and American Politics: 1956–1976," *The Public Interest* 48 (1977): 28–29.

EDWARD D. BERKOWITZ

A Historical Preface to the Americans with Disabilities Act

On 26 July 1990, President George Bush signed an ambitious new civil rights law at an emotional ceremony held on the South Lawn of the White House. Passage of the Americans with Disabilities Act (ADA, PL 101–336) brought civil rights protections for people with disabilities to a level of parity with civil rights protections already enjoyed by racial minorities and by women. What accounted for a Republican administration enthusiastically endorsing a sweeping civil rights law that might benefit as many as 43 million people? Briefly put, historical traditions within disability policy that in turn reflected broader trends within social welfare policy between 1950 and 1990 allowed the ADA to be portrayed in conservative terms that were congenial to a Republican administration.[1]

Policy Conflicts in the 1950s

In the 1950s, civil rights figured only obliquely as a theme of disability policy. Instead, policymakers located in the newly created Department of Health, Education, and Welfare (HEW) concentrated on two core projects. Managed by different sets of people, the projects often conflicted with one another. The first project concerned the expansion of the social security program, which had emerged as the nation's largest and most expensive social welfare program in 1951, to cover the risk of disability. The second project involved the expansion of federal grants to the states to assist people with disabilities in finding jobs.

Policymakers within the Social Security Administration took the lead in attempting to expand the social security program to cover the risk of disability.[2] Translated into the policy terms of social security, the project meant that retirement pensions, previously awarded only to elderly individuals and their dependents, would be broadened to include younger people who, because of a physical or mental impairment of indefinite duration, wanted to drop out of the labor force. The emphasis on retirement reflected the social security program's depression-era concern with the orderly withdrawal of people from the labor force.[3]

Policymakers within the Office of Vocational Rehabilitation, such as Mary Switzer, pressed the case for the expansion of rehabilitation services as a response to the problems of disability.[4] Switzer and her colleagues obtained a sympathetic hearing from Oveta Culp Hobby, Eisenhower's first Secretary of Health, Education, and Welfare, and from Nelson Rockefeller, the first Undersecretary of Health, Education, and Welfare. These Republican administration politicians wanted to define a distinctively Republican social welfare program. In rehabilitation, they found an approach that assumed the existence of continuing prosperity, rather than the constant threat of depression, and that highlighted the capabilities of people with disabilities, rather than their inability to compete in the labor force.

The rehabilitation approach, in fact, meshed with a more general transformation of social welfare policy in the 1950s away from the depression emphasis on income maintenance and retirement and toward a new reliance on the services of professional caseworkers to facilitate labor force participation. If social security was an entitlement or basic right, rehabilitation was a discretionary service in which professionally trained social welfare workers acted as gatekeepers and case managers. Although a successful course of rehabilitation facilitated such goals as the integration of people with disabilities into the labor force and their independence from other government benefits, it had little or nothing to do with civil rights. Nonetheless, the benefits of rehabilitation, like those from civil rights, could be expressed in the optimistic rhetoric that was common to policy discourse in the 1950s. Using the sexist language of the era, Secretary Hobby told the President, for example, that no accountant could estimate the "physical rewards, the sense of independence, pride, and usefulness, and the relief from family strains, which accrue to one of the disabled when he returns to his old job or to a newly learned job suited to his limitations, and once more take his place as a man among men."[5]

The notion of rehabilitation as a good investment in an expanding economy united vocational rehabilitation and the case made in the 1950s for civil rights laws on behalf of Negroes and other minorities. In the late-1950s discussions of social welfare policy held in elite circles as part of efforts to improve national morale and define the national purpose, participants appealed simultaneously for the expansion of rehabilitation services and the passage of civil rights laws. A 1958 report sponsored by the Rockefeller Brothers Fund on the prospect for America contained the argument that racial discrimination prevented the free flow of human capital and constituted "perhaps the most dramatic example of waste of manpower in our economy."[6] The same report recommended the expansion of rehabilitation services to the handicapped. Both goals were defined as good investments that would pay substantial dividends.[7]

The logic of social security expansion collided with the emerging faith in vocational rehabilitation and created overt political conflict in the 1950s. On a personal and far from superficial level, much animosity existed between Arthur Altmeyer, the commissioner of Social Security until 1953, and Mary Switzer, the head of the Office of Vocational Rehabilitation. Wilbur Cohen, a longtime assistant and disciple of Altmeyer, told an interviewer that Altmeyer was "always critical of Switzer."[8] Switzer, for her part, feared that the social security program, much larger than the vocational rehabilitation program, would somehow subsume her program. Her fears became acute at the end of the Eisenhower administration because, as she put it, the Democrats would concentrate "on a few issues of major mass appeal" to the detriment of her program.[9]

On an ideological level, the social security and rehabilitation leaders disagree on priorities within disability policy. Switzer feared that putting income maintenance above rehabilitation had the tendency of creating dependency when the proper focus should be on eliminating dependency. Rod Perkins, a Nelson Rockefeller adviser and Assistant Secretary of HEW for Eisenhower, noted that he opposed federal income benefits to the permanently and totally disabled because such benefits led a person "not to seek to rehabilitate himself and overcome his disability." Instead of expanding social security, Perkins recommended "large sums devoted to rehabilitation."[10]

When the leaders of social security pressed for passage of disability insurance in 1956, they found their way blocked by Mary Switzer and the supporters of rehabilitation. As Wilbur Cohen put it, Mary Switzer and E. B. Whitten of the National Rehabilitation Association were "very effective in raising questions in the minds of the Republicans" about the desirability of disability insurance.[11] When the Social security Administration succeeded in gaining passage of disability insurance in 1956, Altmeyer wrote to Cohen that "we have licked the opponents and their dupes and accomplices (the Rusks and the Switzers) on the basic proposition. Now, let's press our advantage."[12]

As a result of the passage of disability insurance in 1956 and of a major expansion of vocational rehabilitation in 1954, the decade ended with a strong government commitment to the notion that people with disabilities had the right to drop out of the labor force and a simultaneous commitment that people with disabilities should be encouraged to enter the labor force. Many people found that they were not disabled enough to qualify for disability insurance but were too disabled or demoralized to benefit from rehabilitation.

One such case concerned a United States citizen who was born in Romania before the turn of the century and who was educated in American public schools through the fifth grade. The man made his living as a paper hanger and painter. He also did various laboring jobs, such as driving a truck. Over the years he accumulated the aches and pains that accompany hard work. When he thought back over his life in 1957, at the age of fifty-nine, he remembered that he had strained the right side of his body when pushing a refrigerator over twenty years ago. Now, whenever he lifted heavy objects or exerted effort, he suffered a pain in his right side. He also had a more personal problem. He no longer had full control over his bladder due to a problem with his prostate gland. His lack of bladder control made him reluctant to take a full-time job. Even if he could get a job, he would be best qualified to perform heavy labor. His nagging backache made it difficult to do this sort of work. Other, more sedentary jobs, such as that of a watchman, were considerably more difficult to find. Perplexed, the man came to the Social Security Administration and asked for a pension. The Social Security Administration turned him down because the disability examiners felt that he had the capability to do heavy labor and that his bladder condition could be corrected through surgery. The local rehabilitation agency, which had the authority to pay for the surgery, refused to serve the man because they regarded him as a bad risk, unlikely to pay off, through public taxes and private purchases, the public funds invested in him. The man dangled between the cracks of the disability system as it was constructed in the 1950s.[13]

In general, the response to cases such as that of the Romanian laborer, was to press for the expansion of disability benefits. No one linked the man's situation with discrimination against people with disabilities. Few people saw the relevance of civil rights to disability policy.

The Coming of the Great Society

When the Kennedy administration arrived in 1961, the core projects in social welfare policy shifted from the rather vague efforts in rehabilitation and local initiatives of the Eisenhower years to the items on an agenda developed by Senate liberals in the late 1950s.[14] The central idea behind the new projects was for the federal government to close the gaps that separated the nation's performance from its potential. In particular, the Kennedy administration pushed the cause of federal aid to education and of the expansion of social security to cover the costs of medical care for the aged. In marked contrast to the items on the New Deal agenda, the new items took the form of investments in human capital rather than protections against economic catastrophe.

Although recently scholars such as Irving Bernstein have argued that Kennedy delivered on many of his promises in domestic policy, he and his administration never came close to passing either a general aid to education law or Medicare.[15] The programs of the Kennedy era tended to be more limited. They benefited well-defined professional groups or geographic regions, took a permissive form that allowed states and localities the option of participating, and relied for their implementation on bureaucratic agencies with strong congressional support, such as the Children's Bureau or the National Institutes of Health.

The Kennedy administration's greatest legislative successes in disability policy came in the area of mental retardation. The President's leadership produced a new national institute of health, devoted to the study of pediatric problems, and a plethora of new federal grants-in-aid: project grants to the states for comprehensive planning on mental retardation, grants for the construction of mental retardation research and treatment centers, centers, and grants for improving the education of "exceptional" children.[16]

The mental retardation legislation represented just the sort of small-scale, well-targeted legislation of which congressmen like Wilbur Mills (D-Ark.) approved. Medicare and aid to education remained highly contested items. Until 1965 Mills refused to support Medicare and did as much as anyone to block its passage. More limited aid to medicine, in the form of planning and facility construction grants, and more limited aid to education, in the form of grants specifically limited to the training of teachers in special education, met with much less resistance. Mills decided not even to hold hearings on his end of the legislation. Instead, he simply solicited written comments, and these comments proved sufficiently encouraging, as one observer put it, "to permit the Committee to move expeditiously."[17]

Like other policy initiatives of the era, the President's mental retardation program drew on rhetoric associated with the civil rights movement. In particular, program supporters emphasized concepts such as cultural deprivation, in which a bad environment was cited as the reason for poor educational performance and even mental retardation. The legislation relied on the perceived professional wisdom of the day, including the notion that mentally retarded people should receive community rather than institutional or custodial care.[18]

For all that the initiative was couched in contemporary rhetoric about integration, the mental retardation program consisted, at base, of federal aid to the professional caretakers of the mentally retarded. Even though what would later be called "consumers," those who actually used the programs, provided a base of support for the legislation, the legislation was not based on the concept of civil rights.

The Big Bang

In 1965, after the death of Kennedy, Johnson's election landslide, and the passage of the Civil Rights Act, the pieces fell in place for a major expansion of the American administrative state. In one of the nation's "big bangs" of legislative activity, Congress cleared aid to elementary and secondary education (ESEA) and Medicare from the agenda.[19] Behind these high-visibility items, Congress also expanded existing programs, such as vocational rehabilitation, and tied incidental concerns, such as "special education" or the education of the handicapped, to the new major legislative vehicles. In the fall of the same year as Congress passed ESEA, for example, it also passed another law (PL 89-313) that authorized aid to state agencies operating or supporting schools to handicapped children. The same Congress later added a new title to the law that established a grant-in-aid program to assist in the education of children with handicaps.

By the end of the Johnson presidency, disability policy tended to be concentrated in four major programs or centers of activity. The first and most important was Society Security Disability Insurance (SSDI), run by the Social Security Administration. The second center of activity was the traditional vocational rehabilitation program, which continued to function as it had since 1920. The Vocational Rehabilitation Act, periodically reauthorized, became a focal point for the statutory expression of the federal government's disability concerns. The third center of activity was located in HEW's Office of Education, which administered the various titles of the ESEA. The fourth and final center of activity lay in a welter of agencies with the responsibility of implementing President Kennedy's mental retardation program. These included the Mental Retardation Division of the Bureau of Public Health Services in the Public Health Service and the Children's Bureau. In 1967, these agencies gained more bureaucratic unity when, like the vocational rehabilitation program, they became parts of a new organization within the Department of Health, Education, and Welfare called the Social and Rehabilitation Service.

People in each of these centers of activity, in cooperation with the other members of their particular policy networks, worked for the expansion of their core programs. They enjoyed particular success in the Johnson years and during the first Nixon administration.[20] Social Security Administration officials pushed to make recipients of disability insurance eligible for Medicare, a goal reached in 1972. Rehabilitation advocates worked to expand federal grants for vocational rehabilitation. Mental retardation amendments in 1967 and again in 1970 (PL 91-517) broadened the definition of mental retardation to the larger concept of "developmental disabilities" and made more funds available for such activities as initiating services in community mental retardation facilities. Amendments to the Elementary and Secondary Education Act in 1970 (PL91-230) consolidated a number of previously separate federal grant authorities relating to handicapped children. This recodification became known as the "Education of the Handicapped Act." What historian W. Andrew Achenbaum has described as "incremental policymaking by analogy" predominated in each of these areas of activity.[21]

In each of the centers of activity as well, policymaking tended to be a closely held enterprise, with only the people immediately affected by the laws, often representatives of state and local governments, able to influence legislative activity. The politics of disability policy was not driven by grassroots activity so much as by the professional concerns of such groups as special educators, vocational rehabilitation counselors, or mental retardation researchers. In the same years as these centers of activity formed, other parts of the government became involved in the implementation of the three major civil rights laws passed in the Johnson years. In the early 1970s, however, disability policy and civil rights policy were still not joined.

The Arrival of Civil Rights

Then, in the mid-1970s, with little warning, theee of the four centers of disability policy acquired a new emphasis on civil rights. In 1973, Congress added a new section to the Vocational Rehabilitation Act that, among other things, adopted the provisions of Title Six of the Civil

Rights Act of 1964 to "otherwise qualified" handicapped individuals (PL 93-112).[22] The provision implied that organizations, programs, or other entities funded by the federal government could not discriminate against handicapped individuals. The same law also mandated that agencies of the federal government take affirmative action to "hire and advance in employment" persons with disabilities.[23] In 1975, Congress passed the Education of All Handicapped Children Act (PL 94-142) and the Developmental Disabilities Assistance and Bill of Rights Act (PL 94-103).

The first of these 1975 laws specified guidelines for spending federal education funds for the handicapped, such as requiring local educational agencies to develop an "individualized education plan" for each handicapped child and requiring that handicapped children be educated in the "least restrictive environment." Each time the school made a decision that would affect a child's education, it was obligated to provide the child's parents with a written notice. Parents, in turn, had the right to a "due process hearing," should they disagree with the school's decision about the placement or treatment of their child.[24]

The Developmental Disabilities Assistance and Bill of Rights Act began with a ringing declaration that persons with developmental disabilities "have a right to appropriate treatment, services, and habilitation [that] maximize the developmental potential of the person . . . and are provided in the setting that is least restrictive of the person's personal liberty."[25]

Until the 1970s, little in the histories of vocational rehabilitation, federal aid to education, or aid to the mentally retarded linked them to the notion of civil rights. From where did these assertions of individual rights come? One source, clearly, was the courts. In the early 1970s, the federal courts decided many influential cases that applied rights-based criteria to activities in which the federal government provided financial assistance. Advocates for people with developmental disabilities or people in the special education system pressed Congress to mandate that all states and all education systems comply with the court rulings. In the *Mills* case, for example, a federal district court ruled that the equal-protection clause required the provision of a free, appropriate, public education for all handicapped children, just as such an education was provided to nonhandicapped children. Lack of funds could not be used as an excuse. Instead, the District of Columbia school system, the defendant in the case, must spend its available funds so that "no child is entirely excluded from a publicly supported education consistent with his needs and ability."[26] In the 1971 *Wyatt* case, public-interest lawyers, working with an organization known as the Mental Health Law Project, successfully challenged the

state of Alabama's commitment procedures and conditions of confine-
ment for people in mental institutions.[27] This case led to more direct
efforts to achieve the removal of people from mental retardation facilities,
such as Willowbrook on Staten Island, through legal-consent decrees.[28]
In passing the disability-related civil rights laws of the 1970s, Congress
built upon a strong and growing legal foundation.

The timing of the laws coincided with a period of rising congressional
power and deteriorating economic conditions. In 1965, President Johnson had both a well-defined legislative agenda and the necessary congressional majorities to get it enacted. The policy action in many areas of
social welfare shifted briefly from the Congress and the courts to the
President. In the 1970s, during a period described by historian Kim
McQuaid as the "anxious years," the courts and the legislatures reasserted
their traditional control over social welfare policy.[29] The congressional
committees, however, lacked the cohesion that they had had in the
1960s. The profusion of subcommittees increased the power of entrepreneurial congressmen who wanted to assert control over a particular area of
policy and made Congress more receptive to penetration by new policy
networks. Older, more traditional committees could engage in program
maintenance, even as the new subcommittees expanded the old programs
to include civil rights guarantees.

In the fields of education and mental retardation, the congressional
proprietors were not unreceptive to the policy goals of the public-interest
lawyers. Mental retardation legislation and "special" education had, from
their beginnings, contained a strong bias toward such goals as desinstitu-
tionalization and mainstreaming. In the 1960s, Congress had been able to
accompany inducements to change local policies with generous grants-in-
aid. In 1974 and 1975, when GNP declined and unemployment surged to
8.5 percent, the federal government lacked the financial means to engage
in similar largesse.[30] The solution was simply to mandate responsibilities
on state and local governments. That kept the policy focus on Congress,
satisfied a growing constituency of "consumers" and public-interest lawyers of congressional sympathy with their objectives, and did not affect
either the size or even the content of existing grants-in-aid.[31]

In a sense, the new civil rights laws of the 1970s reflected the political
power of the parents of handicapped children and the elite social theorists,
now joined by the public-interest lawyers, who had succeeded in influencing President Kennedy's mental retardation legislation. To a certain extent, the laws also related to the inability of the President, in the post-
Watergate era, to discipline Congress. The new laws did not challenge the
professional autonomy of lawyers or social workers interested in main-

streaming children so much as they pressured local bureaucracies to devote more time, attention, and money to children defined as handicapped. Unlike the civil rights laws of the 1960s aimed at African Americans, the disability rights laws of the 1970s did not involve a fundamental threat to the social system of a particular region of the country. The politics of their enactment was also divorced from considerations related to party. It was therefore hard to mobilize opposition to them. Inevitably, the opponents of the laws stood to lose less than the proponents stood to gain.

Of the disability-related civil rights laws of the 1970s, the rehabilitation amendments of 1973 represented the biggest conceptual shift in disability policy. Vocational rehabilitation was a self-contained field with strong political defenders in every state and territory of the nation. These defenders protected both the basic grant-in-aid program and the professional autonomy of the rehabilitation counselors. At base, the process of psychological adjustment practiced by rehabilitation counselors was antithetical to the very concept of civil rights.[32] Because organizations representing state rehabilitation programs so tightly controlled legislative activity and because people with disabilities remained so isolated from one another, the conflict remained latent until well into the 1970s. Even so, the Vocational Rehabilitation Act became the major legislative vehicle for the civil rights of people with disabilities in the period between 1973 and 1990.

The reason that the civil rights provision (Section Five) got inserted in the vocational rehabilitation bill concerned the legislative priorities of vocational rehabilitation's defenders. Like Woodward and Bernstein, they followed the money. In 1972, influential congressmen such as Representative John Brademas (D-Ind.) and senators Jennings Randolph (D-W.V.) and Alan Cranston (D-Calif.) negotiated over legislative details related to major changes in the program's objectives and its location in the federal bureaucracy. The situation became even more complicated when President Richard Nixon vetoed two different versions of the bill for reasons having to do with budgetary politics in an election year. By the time a third version of the bill finally received President Nixon's signature, few people paid much attention to the civil rights provisions in Section Five.

This section had almost nothing to do with the vocational rehabilitation program itself, and hence it did not attract any notice from either the President, the major congressional players, or the powerful groups. From what researchers can ascertain, Representative Charles Vanik (D-Ohio) and Senator Hubert Humphrey (D-Minn.) had wanted to amend the Civil Rights Act of 1964 to include handicapping conditions. Those who defended black interests resisted broadening the civil rights legislative to encompass a large new group. How large this group was remained something of a mystery, since no one had even bothered to consider how many people considered themselves handicapped. Data existed on work limitations and on the prevalence of various health conditions, but since 1890 nothing approaching a census of the disabled had been attempted. Frustrated, the sponsors of civil rights for people with disabilities sought a new venue for their law and found it in the Vocational Rehabilitation Act. In August 1972, a congressional staff member suggested adding a civil rights provision to the vocational rehabilitation bill that was then under discussion. Another staffer hurried out of the room and came back with the wording of Title VI of the Civil Rights Act of 1964. In so doing, he created Section 504.[33]

When the regulations for Title Five came to be written, they became the responsibility of government agencies that enforced other civil rights laws rather than of the vocational rehabilitation agency. In this manner, without any grass-roots demands for the passage of a civil rights law, the lawyers in HEW's Office of Civil Rights and the Department of Labor's Office of Federal Contract Compliance began to consider how to translate civil rights concepts into terms that made sense for people with disabilities. Accustomed to negotiating with civil rights groups, these lawyers consulted leaders of disability-rights organizations. In so doing, they conveyed a sense of legitimacy to such organizations as the American Coalition of Citizens with Disabilities. In a sense, the federal government, acting through the regulatory rather than the legislative process, created the disability-rights movement.

The Ford administration gradually realized that Title Five contained political dynamite. Depending on how the regulations were framed, they might require that, for example, every college dormitory, including those constructed in the nineteenth century, be made accessible to a wheelchair. Peter Holmes, the director of HEW's Office of Civil Rights, told HEW secretary Caspar Weinberger that many schools "in physical plants built before the concept of barrier-free design was understood . . . are in precarious financial circumstances."[34] As a result of first Weinberger's and then, beginning in the summer of 1975, Secretary David Matthews's reticence to issue regulations that were potentially costly, the process of regulation writing lasted from 1973 to 1977. The Section 504 regulations became something of a political issue. In the 1976 campaign, Jimmy Carter announced that he would sign the regulations related to Section 504, and Joseph Califano, his secretary of HEW, eventually did so in April 1977.[35]

During the long period between enactment and implementation of

Section 504, the HEW lawyers developed a new vocabulary to describe civil rights for people with disabilities. They invented a lexicon of legal terms rather than a set of empirical tests that economists might have devised had they been in charge of writing the regulations.[36] It was not as though economists were without influence in social welfare policy during those years. Indeed, policy related to disability insurance, welfare reform, and health insurance was dominated by references to concepts such as marginal tax rates (as in the negative income tax), replacement rates (as in explanations for the growth of the disability insurance rolls), and marginal costs (as an explanation for rising health care expenditures). Both Gerald Ford and Carter relied on cadres of economists in such locations as the office of the assistant secretary for planning and evaluation to develop policy. Henry Aaron, the brilliant Brookings economist who worked for Joseph Califano, was particularly influential. Yet Califano, himself a lawyer, also relied heavily on the advice of lawyers, such as Stan Ross, the tax lawyer who, like Califano, had worked in the Johnson White House and who became Carter's Commissioner of Social Security.[37] The 504 regulations fell into the bailiwick of the lawyers, who proceeded to develop concepts such as "reasonable accommodation" for people with disabilities, unless such an accommodation caused "undue hardship."

In this manner, the lawyers, working in isolation from the economists who were working right down the hall but concentrating on other problems, created a civil rights policy for people with disabilities. Congress paid only cursory attention. With an institutional flexibility caused in part by the enormous number of subcommittees, Congress could change its identity instantly from a legislator of civil rights to an overseer of the excesses of regulation. Congressional guidance, Martha Derthick has written in a different context, "is unstable, changing often as Congress reacts to the consequences of previous actions." The process nicely illustrated the development of the new social regulation at a time of fiscal austerity and increasingly conservative electoral politics.[38]

The Arrival of the Americans with Disabilities Act

When the Republicans reestablished control of the White House in 1981, Ronald Reagan put Vice President George Bush in charge of a Task Force for Regulatory Relief. It was an entity that was supposed to shed the many mandates imposed by the new social regulation on the private sector and on the states and localities. It was an organization that would dismantle such administrative monstrosities as affirmative action, as defined in Section 501 of the Rehabilitation Act. It would cast social policy into a form that responded to Reagan's reading of the 1980 election: the people wanted to get government off their backs and the task force would be the contribution of George Bush, ever the cooperative team player, to the effort.

Things did not work out quite as planned. Instead of Vice President Bush presiding over the dismantling of Section 504 of the Rehabilitation Act, President Bush enthusiastically expanded civil rights protections for people with disabilities. To understand why, it helps to think of the Reagan-Bush era as similar to the Eisenhower era, a time of divided government and of a presidential desire to define a Republican approach to social welfare that would nonetheless be acceptable enough to the Democrats to clear Congress. Further, the decades bore at least a superficial resemblance to each other in terms of the widely articulated faith in the ability of the private market to solve social problems and in a reliance on job placement as the preferred solution to social welfare policy dilemmas. Hence, welfare reform in both the 1950s and 1980s concentrated on preparing people for jobs, rather than on giving people on welfare tax breaks to create work incentives. Just as Eisenhower discovered vocational rehabilitation as an alternative to disability benefits, so the Reagan and Bush administration came upon the notion of disability rights.

As early as 1983, C. Boyden Gray, the counsel to Bush's Task Force on Regulatory Relief, said that the Reagan administration and people with disabilities wanted the same thing, "to turn as many of the disabled as possible into taxpaying citizens." W. Bradford Reynolds, the Reagan administration's chief civil rights lawyer, said that the "point they're making is the difference between giving a man a fish and teaching him to catch his own. No good Republican can fault that."[39]

Although Gray and Reynolds did not know it, they could have substantiated their point with references to the public statements of prominent Republican conservatives from the era of Herbert Hoover through the era of Barry Goldwater. Even though both conservatives and liberals have supported the ideal of rehabilitating people with disabilities, the conservatives have pursued the cause with the most devotion. For liberals, rehabilitation is one of many things that people with disabilities need. For conservatives, rehabilitation is the essential thing that people with disabilities require. Hence, it is perhaps not too surprising that Representative Dan Reed, a conservative Republican from upstate New York, told his colleagues in 1939 that "I do not know of anybody who will hew closer to the line when it comes to saving money than I will, but there are certain types of expenditure which are an investment." Reed said that at a time when eleven million unemployed people were walking the street, it was heartening to find a program that allowed 120,000 "hopeless, helpless cripples" to earn their own way.[40]

Although in theory arguments in favor of civil rights proposals could be cast in conservative terms, first the Reagan administration and later the Bush administration needed to overcome the considerable stigma associated with civil rights laws in the 1980s. It was a commonplace of conservative rhetoric to complain about "quotas" and the other artifacts of the new social regulation of the 1970s. If the Republicans were to endorse a civil rights law for people with disabilities, it would have to center on employment, but not on affirmative action, and on opportunities, but not on entitlements.

A law for people with disabilities had a substantial advantage over laws for members of racial minorities because of the fact that people with disabilities belonged to both parties. The political strategy of playing upon racial resentments did not have to affect civil rights for people with disabilities who, in many people's minds, personified the deserving poor, lived in the suburbs and not just the cities, and were the antithesis of the stereotypical, menacing members of the underclass. At the same time, the number of people who belonged to the group could, by combining the young and old, working and nonworking, mentally and physically disabled, mildly impaired and severely disabled, be inflated to be as high as 50 million. That made people with disabilities, the minority with the greatest propensity to vote Republican, also the largest minority in the country.[41]

Indeed, Reagan and Bush could draw on a group of Republican disability rights activists to write a civil rights law. One center of support was the National Council on the Handicapped, a fifteen-member board appointed by the President. It was chaired by Sandra Parrino, a Westchester County civic activist and the mother of a disabled son. She fit the classic mold of a privileged person whose family experience made her conscious of the problems faced by and the capabilities of people with disabilities. Outside the National Council on the Handicapped but in close proximity to its work, Senator Lowell Weicker and journalist George Will were two other prominent Republicans who fell into the "parent" category; Reagan appointed Will's wife as the assistant secretary of education in charge, among other things, of special education and vocational rehabilitation. Each of these individuals would become an important proponent of the Americans with Disabilities Act (ADA).

Justine W. Dart Jr. also belonged to the National Council on disability

110 THE AMERICANS WITH DISABILITIES ACT

and also became a key Republican supporter of the ADA. Dart, the son of a close Reagan family friend and heir to the drugstore fortune, traveled often from his home in Texas to Washington, D.C. In Washington, as in Austin, Dart lobbied the government on behalf of people with disabilities. He invariably wore a cowboy hat and treated people with an exquisite sense of courtesy that he had learned in Japan as the founder of Japan Tupperware. Dart, who began using a wheelchair in 1948, became, upon his return to this country in the mid-1960s, a leading proponent of civil rights for people with disabilities. Within the disability rights movement, Dart became known for his conciliatory skills. He helped to draft a National Policy for Persons with Disabilities that appeared in 1983 and put a Republican stamp on the general objectives of the disability-rights movement. The statement took as the goals of disability policy the achievement of "maximum life potential, self-reliance, independence, productivity, and equitable mainstream social participation in the most productive and least restrictive environment."[42]

Two members of the National Council on the Handicapped staff also played an important role in helping to create and nurture the ADA. Robert L. Burgdorff Jr., a lawyer, worked as a research specialist for the National Council on the Handicapped staff. Lex Frieden served as the council's executive director. Friedan had been a student in electoral engineering at Oklahoma State University until he was involved in an automobile accident that left his legs paralyzed. After undergoing medical rehabilitation, Frieden, now visibly handicapped as a result of his use of a wheelchair, transferred to the University of Tulsa, changed his major to psychology, and used his considerable talents to administer an independent living center.[43]

In a 1986 report to Congress that Frieden and Burgdorff helped to write, the National Council on the Handicapped included a recommendation that "Congress should enact a comprehensive law requiring equal opportunity for individuals with disabilities." The council suggested that "such a statute should be packaged as a single comprehensive bill, perhaps under such a title as 'The Americans with Disabilities Act of 1986.' "[44]

In 1988 the first version of the ADA appeared, written largely by Burgdorff, and the House Committee on Education and Labor held two days of hearings on it. The National Council on the Handicapped explained that the bill prohibited discrimination "on the basis of handicap in areas such as employment, housing, public accommodations, travel, communications, and activities of State and local governments." The bill drew on the regulations for Section 504 in defining such terms as "physical or mental impairment."[45] In effect, it built upon the work already done to implement Section 504 and extended civil rights protections for people with disabilities from the public to the private sectors.

Although the ADA attracted many co-sponsors, including twenty-three senators, it proved too difficult a piece of legislation for Congress to handle in an election year. Both Michael Dukakis and Bush supported the legislation.[46] When Bush won the election, the ADA was an important piece of his campaign baggage.

In 1989 congressional Democrats and White House Republicans negotiated the contents of a new draft of the Americans with Disabilities Act. The new legislation was ready by 9 May, when Senator Edward Kennedy conducted a hearing on the ADA before the Senate Committee on Labor and Human Resources. Kennedy, the father of a son with a disability, described the legislation as the "most critical legislation affecting individuals with disabilities ever considered by the Congress."[47] With the legislation unveiled, it proceeded on what one analyst described as a "tortuous" legislative course through four different committees in the House. The legislation cleared the Senate on 7 September 1989, and after innumerable hearings, the legislation passed the House on 22 May, 1990. That prepared the way for the signing ceremony on the South Lawn on 26 July (for a brief summary of the contents of the law, see Appendix One).[48]

The Americans with Disabilities Act passed for two primary reasons. One was that the legislators were convinced that people with disabilities suffered discrimination in the workplace and in their daily lives that required some sort of policy response. The icon of the ADA hearings was Judy Heumann, whose biography was reprinted in nearly all of the congressional reports bearing on the ADA. Heumann had contacted polio in infancy. Throughout her life, she reenacted dramas that the civil rights movement for blacks had charged with symbolism. She told the congressmen of how she had been stopped at the schoolhouse steps at the age of five because she was in a wheelchair and the principal of her Brooklyn public elementary school deemed her a fire hazard (shades of Little Rock). She related how the housemother would not allow her to live in a college dormitory at Long Island University (James Meredith). She explained how she was not permitted to become a public school teacher in New York City because she failed the physical examination. She told a story about how she was once not allowed to travel on an airplane because she was traveling without an attendant (Rosa Parks).[49] Heumann, in the congressional idiom, made good testimony, and it appeared logical to ban discrimination against people like her: people who were intelligent, articulate (not in any way speech-impaired), and solidly middle class.

The emergence of Judy Heumann as an icon of the disability rights movement showed the differences between the agitation for civil rights law and early efforts to pass laws in aid of people with disabilities. In the 1930s, an appearance by blind people, led by seeing-eye dogs, had motivated Congress to create special grants or pensions for the blind.[50] The blind were among the most traditional members of the deserving poor, and they approached Congress with a request for money, the most traditional form of aid. In the 1990s, an appearance by people in wheelchairs, many of whom had sustained spinal-cord injuries of the sort that certainly would have led to a quick death in the 1930s, inspired Congress to enact a broad civil rights statute. People with spinal-cord injuries were not members of the traditional poor, because, considered as a group, they did not even exist in significant numbers until the 1940s. Members of this group sought the opportunity to participate in the labor force, not financial recompense for being handicapped.[51]

The other reason that the Americans with Disabilities Act passed was that it could be portrayed as a cost-saving measure at a time of fiscal stringency. In defending the Americans with Disabilities Act, Republican politicians of the Bush era unconsciously echoed the statements and sentiments of the Republican politicians of the Eisenhower era. Rehabilitation, Mary Switzer had once said, was "not a welfare program." Instead of making people dependent, it restored them to employment and produced "tangible dollar returns."[52] It was "contrary to sound principles of fiscal responsibility," said Sandra Parrino of the National Council on the Handicapped in defending the ADA, "to spend billions of federal tax dollars to relegate people with disabilities to positions of dependency on public support." "Excluding the millions of disabled who want to work from the employment ranks costs society literally billions of dollars annually in support payments and lost income tax revenues," affirmed President Bush. "Certainly the elimination of employment discrimination and the mainstreaming of persons with disabilities will result in more persons with disabilities working, in increasing earnings, in less dependence on the Social Security System for financial support, in increased spending on consumer goods, and increased tax revenues," explained Attorney General Richard Thornburgh. ADA, according to Justin Dart, was "affordable" business, and it was "good" business.[53]

Guided by this sort of rhetoric, the Republicans rediscovered the virtues of rehabilitation and led the way, with the acquiescence of the congressional Democrats who could hardly afford to oppose the basic goal of civil rights for the handicapped, in the passage of the Americans with Disabilities Act. In effect, the participants engaged in a willing suspension of disbelief. They took the cost-saving nature of the ADA largely on faith, without really knowing whether it would reduce social welfare costs. Indeed, the managers of the legislative hearings decided not to introduce expert testimony on the cost-saving nature of the ADA, preferring to make this point implicitly.[54]

As the effective date for the implementation of ADA approached, the nation discovered that its disability rolls, far from decreasing as the ADA proponents had promised, were expanding rapidly. Indeed, expenditures on disability benefits rose far more rapidly than expected in 1990 and 1991, with the result that the SSDI trust fund could be depleted by 1997.[55] On 26 January 1992 the first phase of the law went into effect, requiring businesses with twenty-five or more employees to make good-faith efforts to remove barriers to the disabled. Arguments about the cost of compliance were swiftly made. "It's not going to break Holiday Inn or Hilton Hotels to do these kinds of things. But with a mom and pop hotel it might make a real difference," one conservative policy analyst said.[56]

No one knows what will happen as the various provisions go into effect (see Appendix 2). Congress could easily shift its identity from a champion of disability rights to become a dispenser of regulatory relief. The fact remains, however, that ADA, put in place by the Republicans, is in many respects the most sweeping of the country's civil rights laws. The act itself contains the congressional finding that "43,000,000 Americans have one or more physical or mental disabilities, and this number is increasing as the population as a whole is growing older."[57]

The logic behind ADA followed from the debate in disability policy that had begun in the 1950s between proponents of the income maintenance and rehabilitation approaches. One side touted the advantages of secure entitlements to retirement pensions; the other side lamented the debilitating effects of dependence on government benefits. ADA was a restatement of the rehabilitation ideal, as tempered by nearly two decades of experience with civil rights statutes in the areas of vocational rehabilitation, mental retardation, and special education. By the 1990s, civil rights, hardly mentioned in the debates of the 1950s, had become a permanent part of the nation's disability policy.

The question of whether older programs, such as SSDI, would be recast to reflect the logic of participation of people with disabilities in the labor force and in the mainstream of American life stood at the cutting edge of the discourse among experts in disability policy in the early years of the Clinton era. Others, less versed in disability policy, pondered the costs of new and old disability entitlements in the context of growing concern about budget deficits, the ability to fund health care reform, and the tendency of the federal government to shift costs to private companies and state and local governments.

Whatever the outcome of current debates, the passage of the ADA provides another convincing demonstration of history's utility as a form of policy analysis. Disability policy has its own distinctive history that places important constraints on the ability of policymakers to respond to current problems and on the ability of grass-roots reformers to bend policy to suit their desires. Bureaucratic politics in the social security, education, mental retardation, and vocational rehabilitation programs have mattered far more to policy outcomes than have the goals of the disability-rights movement, the desires of economists to rationalize policy, or the insights of sociologists about people with disabilities as members of a minority group.

Yet, at the same time, the story of the ADA illustrates that outcomes are not static, that policy responses change over time. The disability rights constituency, itself the product of particular events in the development of the administrative state in the 1970s that enabled the iron triangle that governed vocational rehabilitation to be breached, had a particular ability to influence policy in a Republican era. Supporters of ADA effectively manipulated resonant symbols within disability policy. They put symbols developed for traditional purposes, such as the incremental expansion of vocational rehabilitation, to new uses. The ultimate result was the passage of the ADA, which must now find its place among the other historical artifacts that compose our disability policy. The policy process conserves what has come before, even as it changes constantly for reasons that historians, with their tolerance for serendipitous events and their eye for detail, are best able to explain.

George Washington University

Appendix 1: The Americans with Disabilities Act of 1990: A Brief Summary

The term disability is defined as a physical or mental impairment that substantially limits one or more of the major life activities of an individual or as having a record of such an impairment or being regarded as having such an impairment.

Title I provides that no covered entity shall discriminate against a qualified individual with a disability because of the disability in regard to job application procedures, the hiring, advancement, or discharge of employees, employee compensation, job taining, and other terms, conditions, and privileges of employed.

Qualified individual is one who, with or without reasonable accommodation, can perform the essential functions of the employment position that such person holds or desired. Business has to provide reasonable accommodation unless such accommodation would pose an undue hardship on the operation of the business. No compensatory and punitive damages.

Title II provides that no qualified individual with a disability shall be excluded from participation in or be denied the benefits of the services, programs, or activities of a public entity, or subjected to discrimination by any such entity. This title also provides specific requirements for public transportation by intercity and commuter rail and for public transportation other than by aircraft or certain rail operations. All new vehicles purchased or leased by a public entity that operates a fixed route system are to be accessible, and good-faith efforts must be demonstrated with regard to the purchase or lease of accessible used vehicles.

Title III provides that no individual shall be discriminated against on the basis of disability in the full and equal enjoyment of the goods, services, facilities, privileges, advantages, or accommodations of any place of public accommodation by any person who owns, leases, or operates a place of public accommodation. Entities to be covered by the term public accommodation are listed and include, among others, hotels, restaurants, theaters, auditoriums, laundromats, museums, parks, zoos, private schools, day-care centers, professional offices of health care providers, and gymnasiums. A failure to remove architectural barriers is not a violation unless such a removal is readily achievable. Readily achievable is defined as meaning "easily accomplishable and able to be carried out without much difficulty or expense."

Relief is injunctive relief, not damages. In addition, state and local governments can apply to the Attorney General to certify that state or local building codes meet or exceed the minimum accessibility requirements of the ADA. The Attorney General may bring pattern or practice suits with a maximum civil penalty of $50,000 for the first violation and $100,000 for a violation in a subsequent case.

Title IV adds a section to the Communications Act of 1934 providing that the FCC will ensure that interstate and intrastate telecommunications relay services are available to the extent possible and in the most efficient manner to hearing impaired and speech impaired individuals.

Appendix 2: Effective Dates for the ADA, 1992–1996

A. Public Accommodations

January 26, 1992—Existing buildings and businesses with more than 25 employees must make good-faith efforts to remove barriers to the disabled.

July 26, 1992—Businesses with 25 or fewer employees and annual revenue of 1 million must comply.

January 26, 1993—new buildings constructed for occupancy after this date must be accessible.

B. Employment

July 26, 1992—Companies with 25 or more employees
July 26, 1994—Companies with 15 to 24 employees

C. Public Transportation

January 26, 1992—New vehicles for public bus and rail systems must be accessible
July 26, 1993—Commuter rail stations must be made accessible
July 26, 1995—One car per train must be accessible
July 26, 1996—Privately owned transportation companies must buy accessible vehicles. Small operators have until July 26, 1997. New buses, trains, and subway cars have to be accessible to those in wheelchairs.

D. Telephones

July 26, 1993—Companies should have telecommunications services available 24 hours a day.

Sources: *New York Times*, 27 January 1992, A12.

Notes

1. My interpretation follows from my previous work: *Disabled Policy: America's Programs for the Handicapped* (New York, 1987); *America's Welfare State: From Roosevelt and Reagan* (Baltimore, 1991); *Creating the Welfare State: The Political Economy of Twentieth-Century Reform*, paperback edition (Lawrence, Kans., 1992) [with Kim McQuaid]; and "Disabled Policy: A Personal Postscript," *Journal of Disability Policy Studies* 3 (1992): 1–16.

2. On the bureaucratic identity of the Social Security Administration, see Martha Derthick, *Policymaking for Social Security* (Washington, D.C., 1979).

3. William Graebner, *A History of Retirement: The Meaning and Function of an American Institution, 1885–1978* (New Haven, 1980).

4. See Martha Lentz Walker, *Beyond Bureaucracy: Mary Elizabeth Switzer and Rehabilitation* (Lanham, Md., 1985).

5. Hobby to Eisenhower, 15 October 1953, in vol. 43, Nelson Rockefeller Papers, Rockefeller Archives, Pocantico, N.Y.

6. "The Challenge to America: Its Economic and Social Aspects," first published 21 April 1958, in *Prospect for America: The Rockefeller Panel Reports* (Garden City, N.Y., 1961), 316.

7. Wilbur Cohen, "Social Policies and Social Services in an Expanding Economy," October 1957, unpublished manuscript in Papers of the Rockefeller Brothers Fund, Special Studies Project, Box 30, Rockefeller Archives.

8. Blanche Coll, Oral Interview with Wilbur Cohen, 19 October 1985, transcript in oral interview file, Wilbur Cohen Personal Papers, Lyndon B. Johnson Library, Austin, Texas.

9. Hugh Calkins to Elliot Richardson, 21 April 1960, Papers of the President's Commission on National Goals, Box 9, Eisenhower Library, Abilene, Kansas.

10. No author, Memorandum for the Welfare File, 14 March 1960, Box 9, President's Commission on National Goals.

11. Wilbur Cohen, "The Situation in Social Security," 15 February 1970, Box 70, Wilbur J. Cohen Papers, Wisconsin State Historical Society, Madison. The National Rehabilitation Association was the chief lobbying group for the state vocational rehabilitation programs.

12. Altmeyer to Cohen, 8 October 1956, Cohen Papers, Wisconsin State Historical Society. Howard Rusk was a prominent rehabilitation doctor.

13. No author, Memorandum to William Greenberg, 18 August 1958, Record Group 47, Records of the Social Security Administration, Accession 67A-270, Box 1, Washington National Records Center, Suitland, Maryland.

14. James L. Sundquist, *Politics and Policy: The Eisenhower, Kennedy, and Johnson Years* (Washington, D.C., 1968).

15. Bernstein, *Promises Kept: John F. Kennedy's New Frontier* (New York, 1991).

16. Cohen to Myer Feldman, 11 January 1963, "Mental Retardation Program for 1963," Myer Feldman Papers, General File, Mental Retardation, 1/63–5/63, John F. Kennedy Library, Boston; Berkowitz, "The Politics of Mental Retardation in the Kennedy Administration," *Social Science Quarterly* (June 1980): 128–42.

17. Cohen to Mrs. Shriver, Mental Retardation Progress Report 11, 1 May 1963, Box 14, Feldman Papers.

18. Berkowitz, "The Politics of Mental Retardation."

19. Christopher Leman, "Patterns of Policy-Development: Social Security in Canada and the United States," *Public Policy* 25 (1977): 264; Hugh Davis Graham, *The Uncertain Triumph: Federal Education Policy in the Kennedy and Johnson Years* (Chapel Hill, N.C., 1984); Sherri I. David, *With Dignity: The Search for Medicare and Medicaid* (Westport, Conn., 1985).

20. By now, coached by James Patterson and others, most historians understand that the peak of social welfare spending came in the Nixon administration, not the Johnson administration. See James Patterson, *America's Struggle Against Poverty, 1900–1980* (Cambridge, Mass., 1981), 157–70.

21. W. Andrew Achenbaum, *Social Security: Vision and Revisions* (New York, 1986), 166.

22. Berkowitz, *Disabled Policy*, 212.

23. *Disability Rights Mandates: Federal and State Compliance with Employment Protections*

and Architectural Barrier Removal (Washington, D.C.: Adivsory Council on Intergovernmental Relations, April 1989), Report A-111, 28. A useful overview of the various civil rights laws and other disability-related legislation is *Summary of Existing Legislation Affecting Persons with Disabilities*, U.S. Department of Education, Office of Special Education and Rehabilitative Services, Clearinghouse on the Handicapped, Publication E-88-22014, August 1988.

24. Berkowitz, *Disabled Policy*, 208; U.S. Commission on Civil Rights, *Accommodating the Spectrum of Individual Abilities*, Clearinghouse Publication 81, September 1983, 56.

25. U.S. Commission on Civil Rights, *Accommodating the Spectrum of Individual Abilities*, 61.

26. U.S. Commission on Civil Rights, *Accommodating the Spectrum of Individual Abilities*, 64, 71, citing *Mills v. Board of Education of D.C.*, 348 F Supp 866 (D.D.C. 1972) (the quote is on page 876).

27. U.S. Commission on Civil Rights, *Accommodating the Spectrum of Individual Abilities*, 64, citing *Wyatt v. Stickney*, 325 F. Supp. 381 (M.D. Ala. 1971).

28. David J. Rothman and Sheila M. Rothman, *The Willowbrook Wars* (New York, 1984).

29. Kim McQuaid, *The Anxious Years* (New York, 1989).

30. Economic data from David Koitz, Geoffrey Kollman, and Jennifer Neisner, *Status of the Disability Programs of the Social Security Administration* (Washington, D.C.: Congressional Research Service, 8 September 1992), 84.

31. Stephen Percy makes a similar argument in *Disability Rights Mandates*, 9.

32. Edward Berkowitz, "Professionals as Providers: Some Thoughts on Disability and Ideology," *Rehabilitation Psychology* 29 (Winter 1984): 211–16.

33. Richard K. Scotch, "Politics and Policy in the History of the Disability Rights Movement," *The Milbank Quarterly* 67, supp. 2, pt. 2, (1989): 390; Edward Berkowitz, "Domestic Politics and International Expertise in the History of American Disability Policy," *Milbank Memorial Quarterly* 67, supplement 2, pt. 1, (1989): 195–227.

34. Peter Holmes to HEW Secretary, 20 June 1975, Sarah Massengale Papers, Gerald Ford Library, Ann Arbor, Michigan.

35. Berkowitz, *Disabled Policy*, 211–21; Richard K. Scotch, *From Goodwill to Civil Rights* (Philadelphia, 1984); Frank Bowe, *Rehabilitating America: Toward Independence for Disabled and Elderly People* (New York, 1980); Bowe, *Handicapping America: Barriers to Disabled People* (New York, 1978).

36. I am indebted to Richard Scotch for teaching me this point, both in his writings (cited elsewhere in this article) and in private conversations.

37. On the influence of economists in the 1970s, see Berkowitz, *America's Welfare State*.

38. Martha Derthick, *Agency Under Stress: The Social Security Administration in American Government* (Washington, D.C., 1990); Hugh Davis Graham, "The Origins of Affirmative Action: Civil Rights and the Regulatory State," *Annals* 523 (September 1992): 50–62. Derthick and others have noted the enormous number of subcommittees involved in oversight activities in disability policy, an increase that took place largely during the 1970s.

39. I have drawn this paragraph almost directly from *Disabled Policy*, 223.

40. Reed's statement in the *Congressional Record* quoted in Berkowitz, "Disabled Policy: A Personal Postscript," 4.

41. On the numbers question, see Gerben DeJong, Andrew I. Batavia, and Robert Griss, "America's Neglected Health Minority: Working-age Persons with Disabilities," *The Milbank Quarterly* 67, supp. 2, pt. 2 (1989): 316; U.S. Department of Education, National Institute on Disability and Rehabilitation Research (NIDRR), "People with Disabilities in Basic Life Activities in the United States," *Disability Statistics Abstract*, no. 3, April 1992.

42. Quoted in Berkowitz, *Disabled Policy*, 186. I base my characterizations of the Republican disability-rights leaders on personal observation.

43. On Frieden, see Berkowitz, *Disabled Policy*, 195–96.

44. National Council on the Handicapped, *Toward Independence* (Washington, D.C., 1986), 18.

45. The National Council, "The Americans with Disabilities Act of 1988: Fact Sheet," privately obtained. The Act was introduced as S. 2345 and HR 4498.

46. Evan J. Kemp Jr., "Where Was George?" *Mainstream: Magazine of the Able-Disabled* 13 (September 1988): 13–14.

47. Edward M. Kennedy to Edward Berkowitz, 2 May 1989, privately held.

48. Nancy Lee Jones, "The Americans with Disabilities Act: An Overview of Major Provisions," 31 July 1990, Congressional Research Service Report, 90-366-A; Jane West, ed., *The Americans with Disabilities Act: From Policy to Practice* (New York, 1991).

49. "Americans with Disabilities Act of 1990," House of Representatives, *Report 101-485-Part 2*, 15 May 1990, 29; Berkowitz, *Disabled Policy*, 196–99. President Clinton thought enough of Heumann to appoint her to the assistant secretary of education job that Madeleine Will had held in the Reagan administration.

50. Edward Berkowitz and Richard Scotch, "One Comprehensive System? A Historical Perspective on Federal Disability Policy," *Journal of Disability Policy Studies* 1 (Fall 1990): 10–13.

51. Irving Kenneth Zola, "Toward the Necessary Universalizing of a Disability Policy," *Milbank Memorial Quarterly* 67, supp. 2, pt. 2 (1989): 404.

52. Quoted in Edward Berkowitz, "The Cost-Benefit Tradition in Vocational Rehabilitation," in Monroe Berkowitz, ed., *Measuring the Efficiency of Public Programs: Costs and Benefits in Vocational Rehabilitation* (Philadelphia, 1988), 23.

53. All quotations from House Report 101-485, pt. 2, 44–45.

54. I know this from my personal experience preparing testimony in favor of the bill. See testimony prepared for the Senate Committee on Labor and Public Welfare in consideration of the Americans with Disabilities Act, May 1989, reprinted in *Congressional Digest* 68 (December 1989): 304–12 [with David Dean].

55. Department of Health and Human Services, "The Social Security Disability Insurance Program: An Analysis," December 1992, mimeo.

56. Steven A. Holmes, "Sweeping U.S. Law to Help Disabled Goes into Effect," *New York Times,* 27 January 1992, A1, A12.

57. Section 2, Findings and Purposes, Public Law 101-336, 104 Stat. 327.

GÉRARD NOIRIEL

"Civil Rights" Policy in the United States and the Policy of "Integration" in Europe: Divergent Approaches to a Similar Issue

Comparing European and North American policies with respect to "civil rights" is a difficult exercise for two reasons. First, it is important to emphasize that Europe and the United States are not political entities of a same nature. Granted, the fact that the nations that today comprise Europe are heirs of common history explains in part the similarities in their political behavior and distinguishes them as a group from the "New World." Yet in the American case, despite the country's federalist struc-ture and the existence of fifty states within the Union, we are dealing with a single nation, endowed with a central government capable of generating policies that are valid throughout the territory. Such is not the case with Europe. As is well known, the European continent is divided into two sharply contrasted spheres. On the one hand, there is the East, thrown into confusion by the devastation of communism and mired in a profound economic crisis. On the other hand, there is the West, com-prised of nations that share a level of economic prosperity comparable to that of the United States but which do not form a single political entity. At present, the European Economic Community includes only twelve European states; the remaining countries, such as Switzerland, Sweden, and Austria, have yet to become members. In this essay, the question of "civil rights" will be examined specifically in light of those countries that already belong to the EEC. It must be recalled, however, that these nations do not form a coherent political entity as does the United States. While the Masstricht Treaty, currently in the process of ratification, is an essential step in that direction (with the establishment, in particular, of a single currency), the political sovereignty of member states has so far remained relatively intact. As a result, substantial differences continue to exist between their respective "civil rights" policies, which in some cases, such as Great Britain, bear greater resemblance to the American model than to other examples in continental Europe. Rather than imposing broad new measures, the crucial role of the European Community consists of promoting the convergence of national policies.

The second difficulty encountered by comparative research on the question of "civil rights" in Europe and the United States is that there is no real equivalent in Europe to what Americans refer to as "civil rights policy." In the United States the movement was generated in the 1960s by the struggle of blacks against racial segregation, and gradually it became extended to other groups such as women, ethnic minorities, and homosexuals.[1] While Europe also experienced struggles for "civil rights" in the 1960s, (in particular, feminist and regionalist movements), these movements had a much lesser impact than in the United States, given their absence of articulation with a broader cause comparable to that of black Americans. At the time, Europe was largely free of protesting racial or ethnic minorities. Only with the arrival of tens of millions of immigrants of primarily Third World origin in the 1980s did an "American-style" situation appear. This explains why the political issue of "ethnic minorities"[2] in contemporary Europe is associated, unlike in the United States, with the problem of immigration.

The Emergence of an Integration Policy for Immigrant Minorities in Europe

Until the 1960s, the European political scene was dominated by "social issues." To understand the political differences between Europe and the United States, the best source remains Alexis de Toqueville's *On Democracy in America.*[3] According to Tocqueville, these continents differed on two fundamental issues. First was the question of race. During his stay in America, Tocqueville was especially shocked by the antagonism among three racial groups: Indians, whites, and blacks. As an aristocrat profoundly influenced by the Enlightenment, he was of course appalled by the practice of slavery, which he regarded as "the most dangerous of all the afflictions which threaten the future of the United States."[4] But he also noted that "racial prejudice [was] stronger in the states which have abolished slavery than in those where slavery still exists."[5] Beyond slavery, what this French author could not understand was why the Americans attached such fundamental importance to the issue of race. The

various racial and ethnic groups that had settled in Europe from prehis-
toric times through the Middle Ages had gradually merged into a vast mix
that rendered physical differences barely noticeable. Thus in the period in
which Tocqueville wrote his essay, Europeans were much more sensitive
to the social distinctions between individuals than to racial differences.
This was especially true for the French, who in 1789 with the "Declaration of the Rights of Man and of the Citizen" had repudiated segregation
on the basis of ethnic origins, race, or creed. Philosophical traditions and
legal and administrative policies transmitted to later generations these
fundamental differences between North American and European visions
of social reality. These divergences are evident in the comparison of
French and American census classifications. American statistical categories were elaborated from the outset on the basis of racial cleavages (Indians, blacks, whites), whereas in France class (managers, workers, employees) and juridical criteria (nationality) have always been privileged by the
State.[6] This is not to say, of course, that discriminatory policies have
never been implemented in Europe. Quite the contrary. From the fif-
teenth and sixteenth centuries onward, the crowns in England, France,
and Spain carried out a policy of forced religious assimilation, illustrated
by the persecution of minority groups. Europe became, with the development of nationalism in the late nineteenth century and the triumph of
Nazism between the wars, the theater of ethnic and religious persecutions
of unprecedented scale and atrocity.

But in 1945, the dismantling of ethnic and religious persecution ush-
ered in a new era for Western Europe. In the early 1960s the question of
civil rights had therefore ceased to represent a major political issue, unlike
in the United States, where racial segregation was still widespread. Most
of Europe's former colonies obtained their independence in the same
period, gradually ending the anticolonial struggles of the 1950s (the Indo-
chinese and Algerian wars in the case of France), whereas the United
States was becoming increasingly involved in the conflict in Vietnam.

Tocqueville also underscored another difference between Europe and
the United States concerning the role of government in society: "A
European travelling through the United States," he observed, "is struck
by the absence of what we call government or administration" and by the
political weight of the "third power"—i.e., the court system.[7] This is
another difference that became deeper as time went on, particularly following the emergence of the welfare state in twentieth-century Europe.
Beginning in the nineteenth century, Europeans linked the development
of democracy to the growing incorporation of social groups into the
nation-state. This had three consequences for the subject discussed here.

First, citizens of the "old continent" turned to political parties rather than to judges and courthouses when it came to defending their interests, in the hope that once in power those parties would formulate policies that favored their constituencies.[8] European governments were thus compelled increasingly to intervene in social life, and the state became more and more involved in matters that were once the prerogative of religious communities and philanthropic associations. Finally, as a consequence of the broadening of social rights guaranteed by the state, a finer distinction was established between nationals and foreigners, with only the former being entitled to these advantages.

The strength of the civil rights movement in the United States can be attributed to the movement's objectives. Given the weakness of the American welfare state,[9] various dispossessed sectors of American society turned to civic demands as a means of resisting pauperization. In Europe in the 1960s, these demands were articulated by political parties, and they were defined not as "civil rights struggles" but as "social movements," pitting the representatives of capitalism (employers) against the representatives of the working class. The strength of the Communist party in France and Italy, that of the trade unions in Germany and Great Britain, and the considerable influence that Marxism enjoyed among intellectuals generated a movement of protest that aimed not at civil rights but at the seizure of state power. The goal of working-class emancipation was given priority, with the understanding that it would create the conditions for satisfying other demands (feminist, regionalist, etc.).

The Rise of Immigration in Europe

In the 1960s and 1970s, Europe became a world leader in immigration from the Third World. As a consequence, European societies have undergone considerable transformations, which explains why the question of "ethnic minorities" has become a political issue of foremost importance. According to official statistics, between 20 and 30 million foreigners entered Europe during the past twenty years (or 8 percent of the total population, compared with 6 percent in the United States).[10] The immigrants were attracted by the large automobile, chemical, mining, and building industries, which at the time suffered from an acute shortage of labor.[11] Each country tended to recruit immigrants from the regions of the world where it had formerly exerted political influence: Germany relied mostly on Turks, France on North Africans, Great Britain on Indians and Pakistanis, and the Netherlands on Surinamese. European governments clearly intended these immigrants to reside only temporarily on their soil. All of the immigration acts of the 1960s viewed immigrants as "guest-workers." In most countries, they were either referred to as "foreigners" (Germany and Switzerland) or as "immigrants" (France, Great Britain, and Belgium). Their status resulted from agreements negotiated between the countries of origin and those of settlement, and from international labor conventions. By and large, these immigrants enjoyed the same rights as native residents in terms of wages and social welfare. They suffered, however, from discriminatory regulations linked to their immigrant status. To reside in Europe, they had to obtain a residency permit, for which they were required to present a work contract (indicating the job they were to perform). They were prohibited from circulating freely and could not bring their families without official authorization. As foreigners, they were deprived of voting rights and excluded from public-service positions. They were also subjected to forms of "indirect" discrimination in that, for example, they were recruited to perform the most tedious, low-paying jobs, and the housing projects intended for them were often unfinished upon their arrival, among similar difficulties.

Although from the outset such expressions of discrimination met with strong opposition from progressive organizations throughout Europe, public opinion regarded the problems as temporary, since migrant workers were expected to return home within a few years of their arrival. But in the mid-1970s the world economic crisis reversed the situation completely. Before long, most European governments had put a stop to the recruitment of immigrants and adopted measures (such as the provision of financial aid) to encourage the return of foreign workers to their land of origin. The return policy, however, failed. By that time the majority of the immigrant population had been settled in Europe for at least ten years. Since they had become an irreplaceable resource for European economies, their departure was not particularly desired by the authorities. Moreover, a majority of the immigrants themselves were unwilling to return to their countries of origin, which had been hit even harder by the crisis. The result was that Europe became aware, at that moment, of its status as a "immigrant country," acknowledging the need for a policy to counter the effects of discrimination.

The adoption of civil rights protections seemed all the more necessary because the steps taken to halt immigration aggravated the situation of these workers. In certain countries, such as Great Britain, citizens of the former colonial empire were deprived of their freedom to move about. Everywhere police controls were tightened, and immigrants were increasingly frustrated in their efforts to see their families. The number of illegal immigrants (i.e., undocumented workers) soared. This description would be incomplete without some mention of the effects of the economic crisis itself. Foreign workers were the earliest victims of unemployment, not only because they occupied the most vulnerable positions but also because they were the targets of racism. During the era of economic prosperity, immigrants had remained virtually invisible to the public eye. They performed tasks that native workers were unwilling to accept. They resided in tenements or isolated camps for single men. More than ever, the rise in unemployment pitted foreign workers against native workers in the competition for available jobs. As their stay in the host countries became prolonged, immigrants gained visibility through the presence of their wives and children and by their tendency to converge in the poorest, most affordable neighborhoods. All over Europe, this increased visibility of immigrant groups generated a resurgence of the racism, often expressed openly by acts of violence against foreigners, which was thought to have been eliminated following World War II. It also took on more enduring forms, such as job discrimination, and the flight of native residents from neighborhoods and schools in which the presence of ethnic minorities was most noticeable. This in turn reinforced the tendency toward the emergence of ethnic ghettoes.

What European Policies of Integration Share in Common

In their efforts to end these forms of discrimination, European countries gradually formulated immigration policies that shared certain common characteristics.[12] First, a series of measures were taken to grant immigrants the same social rights as native residents. "Family regrouping" was practiced by all European governments as a means of providing single male immigrants with the opportunity to live normal family lives. Foreign workers eventually obtained the bulk of the social rights enjoyed by nationals such as family allowances, health insurance, and unemployment and retirement benefits. Measures in favor of housing for immigrant families and the education of their children in public schools were adopted in all countries They were also granted the right to vote and to run for some elective offices, even though their status as foreigners still prevented them from particpating fully in national political life. Second, in all European countries (although to varying degrees), specific steps were taken to compensate for the disadvantages encountered by immigrant workers. New institutions emerged for the sole purpose of facilitating their integration into the "host society" (such as the Commission for Racial Equality in

Great Britain, Fonds d'Action Sociale pour les travailleurs Immigrés and Secrétaire d'Etat à l'Immigration in France, and the Committee on Foreign Workers in Germany). Through various mechanisms adapted to each national context, most of these countries sought to reverse the tendency toward ethnic concentration in certain neighborhoods. In Germany, the government recommended that schools restrict the representation of immigrants in schools to 20 percent of the student body, while in Great Britain the limit was set at 30 percent. Many countries, such as the Netherlands, Great Britain, Germany, and especially France, reinforced sanctions against racist acts in their legislation. The indirecct expressions of racism were explored in order to be countered more effectively. Finally, European nations sought to promote the native cultures of immigrant groups. In Great Britain, Germany, and France in particular, the teaching of languages of origin in public schools was, as we shall see, introduced to varying extents. Exhibitions, television programs, and similar government initiatives strove to promote respect for other cultures and to struggle against the prevailing prejudice.

Different conceptions of citizenship in Europe are a major obstacle to establishing a common civil rights policy. On many levels, European nations confronted with the challenge of integrating immigrant minorities during the 1970s and 1980s reacted in similar fashion. Nonetheless, their opinions diverged on one fundamental question: the definition of citizenship. This significantly hampered the implementation of a coherent policy of equal rights. As we have seen, measures devised previously to reduce the discrimination experienced by immigrants failed to dissipate the legal barrier separating "nationals" from "foreigners." Despite having lived for decades in Europe, and often having been born there, several million individuals were deprived of the right to participate in national political life or to have access to public-service jobs. These injustices have, over the past few years, generated a vast debate in which two types of solutions are confronted: on the one hand, the broadening of the legal approach to nationality and, on the other, the extension of rights granted to ethnic communities.

One of the solutions most often raised in Europe to the problem of discrimination against immigrant minorities is to facilitate their access to citizenship and therefore to concomitant rights. France is the most adamant defender of this solution, whereas Great Britain and Germany are reluctant. If the French view nationality law as an instrument for the advancement of civil rights, it is because they see nationality and citizenship as being closely intertwined.[13] France has long enforced the strict legal equality of its citizens; to obtain civil rights, however, one must be juridically French. The establishment at the end of the nineteenth century of a legal framework for nationality, which to this day remains the most liberal in Europe (along with Sweden), has fostered the integration of millions of immigrants into French society.[14] Most foreigners who apply for naturalization achieve it, and through a combination of *jus soli* (children derive their citizenship from the land of their birth) and *jus sanguinis* (children derive their citizenship from the nationality of their parents) those children of immigrants who are born on French soil almost automatically become French upon reaching the age of adulthood.

The German approach to nationality is entirely different. As in France, nationality and citizenship are closely related, which explains why all citizens enjoy the same rights. But for historical reasons, the German concept of the nation is intimately linked to the notion of people, in the ethnic sense of the term *Volk*.[15] Hence the approach to nationality in German law, exclusively grounded in *jus sanguinis*, is today the most restrictive in Europe (with the exception of Switzerland). The descendants of individuals who left Germany in the nineteenth century, or even earlier, can easily obtain German citizenship if they prove their German ascendance, whereas millions of immigrants (mostly Turkish) who have resided in Germany for decades—as well as their children and grandchildren, even if they are born and raised in Germany—remain foreigners, deprived for the most part of civil rights on the grounds that they lack "German blood." Given this ethnic concept of the nation, most Germans find the French advocacy of liberalizing nationality law incomprehensible.

In Great Britain, unlike in France and Germany, nationality and citizenship bear little relation to one another.[16] A fundamental distinction exists between the status of "British subject" and that of "British citizen," which solely confers the right to residency. To prevent new arrivals of immigrants from these countries, however, nationality law has been gradually modified.[17] Citizens who come from the former colonies, known as "British Overseas Citizens" (or more familiarly, "British Blacks"), do not have British nationality. While they conserve political rights, they may not circulate freely from one country to another. Since the legal restriction of nationality is currently the cutting edge of the British policy of immigration control, the government evidently cannot accept French equal rights policy, which is completely foreign to the British logic.

The Problem of the Rights of Ethnic Communities

Today a number of European nations consider the best way to struggle against discrimination is to promote a policy of equality between different communities. This implies that ethnic communities should be allowed to become politically structured, to defend their language, traditions, and culture. Sweden was one of the first countries to choose that road. In the 1970s, Sweden proposed a policy of "partnership" that allowed minority groups to cooperate on an equal basis with the majority group. Minorities obtained the right to vote in local elections, and their children had the opportunity to receive schooling in their native language. Communities were granted important means to consolidate their ethnic identity and satisfy their specific demands. The mobilization of immigrant communities caused an awakening of ethnicity among such native minorities as the Lapps and the Finns, who were already well assimilated into the Swedish population. Their language, culture, and traditions are now officially recognized by the Swedish State.[18] The same evolution occurred in the Netherlands. Early in the 1980s, the Dutch government offically adopted a "multicultural" policy, which led to the term "ethnic minority" replacing the term "immigrants." Immigrant groups were thus given recognition of their official place within Dutch society on a level of equality with native Dutch minorities: Catholics, Protestants, and Jews. Besides obtaining the right to vote in local electons for individuals without Dutch citizenship, the ethnic communities were granted separate facilities to reinforce their identity in the areas of language, religion, and traditions.[19]

But it is in Great Britain that community solutions were implemented most systematically. At the electoral level, the British adopted the most liberal policy: most immigrants from the former colonies are voters and may be elected at all levels of political responsibility. As in the United States, the British privileged civic action to curb both political and social inequalities among individuals belonging to minority groups. But in the British case, since the 1960s the struggle against inequality was closely tied to the policy of restricting immigration.[20] While the British government installed legal discrimination between different categories of citizens to improve its control of access to its territory (reinforcing prejudice in public opinion against "British Blacks"), it simultaneously tried to mitigate this segregation by creating a large number of antiracist institutions, placed under the authority of the Interior Ministry. In 1965 the Race Relations Act prohibited discrimination in public areas. Two new institutions, the Race Relations Board and the Community Relations Commission (which had numerous local branches), were put in charge of overseeing the implementation of the law and taking violators to court. These measures were reinforced by a 1976 law that merged the two preceding organs into the Commission for Racial Equality, complemented by Race Relations Units established at the level of each municipality. The commission carried out surveys and issued reports on the problem of segregation. It employed several hundred people to work on improving race relations by informing communities of their legal options in the fight against discrimination and helping individuals initiate court action and otherwise protect their rights.

Eventually, the notion of "discrimination" was extended to encompass indirect forms of discrimination, most notably with respect to the rights to housing and employment. Following the riots that shook major British cities in the early 1980s, the social dimension of antidiscriminatory policies was accentuated. Along with actions intended to rehabilitate the most depressed neighborhoods (inner-city policy), measures similar to the American policy of affirmative action were taken to lessen the disadvantages faced by certain communities on the labor market. The new policy of equal opportunity stipulates that public-sector jobs must reflect the ethnic composition of society. Detailed studies on the racial composition of the workforce, as well as on gender and disability, revealed that ethnic minorities were underrepresented in the public sector and confined to less qualified positions. The idea that the number of jobs reserved for each community should be determined in proportion to their size has begun to make headway. Other studies show that in Birmingham, minority representation among employees adds up to only 6.9 percent of the city's workforce, when proportionally it should be 20 percent. In Manchester, the proportion is 2.8 percent, whereas ethnic minorities form 12.6 percent of the population. The same logic has established itself in the cultural realm. Languages and religions are officially recognized and receive public funding. Even though antidiscrimination policy is decided by the central government in Britain, its application is decentralized at the local level; numerous jobs created for the purpose of applying these measures are entrusted to members of the ethnic communities in question.[21]

Within Europe, the French stand out as radically refusing any community-inspired policy. Equal rights are perceived as unrelated to the struggle for civil rights, since all citizens already enjoy the same rights, but through the implementation of social policies directed at individuals (regardless of their ethnic origin) belonging to the same job category. this refusal to politicize the issue of ethnicity explains why the French government has not granted immigrants the right to vote in local elections, despite the fact that President François Mitterrand had promised to satisfy this demand before his election in 1981.[22] Since priority is given to social action, policies aimed at the promotion of equal opportunity and those directed at fighting racism are, in France, distinct. Traditionally, the Ministry of Social Affairs has played an essential role in the policy of assimilating immigrants. Over the past decade, specific forms of assistance to immigrant communities made their appearance in the realm of education (measures against backwardness in schools, promotion of literacy), housing (a percentage of public housing is reserved for immigrants), and employment (internships aimed at professional training). Most of these measures, however, are aimed at social groups, without distinction of ethnicity. Such is the case, for example, of the Minimum Insertion Wage (RMI—approximately $500 per month) paid by the state to the unemployed, who receive no benefits.[23]

The high proportion of immigrants among the poor in French society, however, makes them the prime beneficiaries of the policy. Moreover, in France the state controls this social policy from top to bottom, as a means of preventing the institutionalization of ethnic groups comparable to the United States and Great Britain. The French government has also created many jobs in its effort to promote the integration of marginalized groups, and these jobs are generally performed by members of ethnic minorities. Officially, however, they are attributed according to competence (knowledge of the area in question) rather than community membership, and occupants of such positions are placed under the authority of the French government rather than ethnic communities. The development of community-oriented mobilization is prevented because the representatives of these communities are not recognized as such by the authorities. Also, with the intention of avoiding the politicization of ethnic communities, the government is opposed to the formation of ghettoes. Since an important section of the immigrant population lives in public housing, the state can intervene to prevent the concentration of communities by implementing, building by building or even floor by floor, a careful balance between nationalities, professions, and size of families.

Of course, all ethnic groups have the possibility of practicing their religion and of defending their culture and traditions. French employers grant Muslims a day of rest during Ramadan. In school cafeterias, meals are prepared so as to respect the food restrictions applied by different religions. Thanks to government funding, the past decade has witnessed a growth in the number of associations committed to the defense of immigrant cultures and a concomitant increase in job opportunities for immigrant youth. According to the French conception, however, everything related to religion or ethnicity belongs to "private life" rather than to the public sphere. The government therefore refrains from intervening more directly in the struggle against discrimination. The antiracist struggle has primarily been waged in France not by political parties but by associations,[24] such as the Ligue des droits de l'homme (founded in the late nineteenth century during the Dreyfus Affair to combat anti-Semitism); the MRAP (created to combat fascism in the 1930s); or more recently, S.O.S.-Racisme (an association founded by young immigrant activists to counter the far right). Furthermore, in the French tradition, the struggle against discrimination is considered a fundamental aspect of the work of intellectuals: writers, philosophers, journalists. It is a key dimension of public life that cannot be confiscated by the administration.[25]

Different National Traditions in Europe

To understand the obstacles currently encountered by Europeans in their efforts to promote a common policy against discrimination, it must be emphasized that the differences outlined above are not restricted to the political level. They are embedded in much deeper oppositions, reflecting the different national histories to which citizens of each country are profoundly attached. Much of the misunderstanding is due to the fact that Europeans do not attribute the same meaning to the same words. For example, the French term for nationality designates membership within a people (*peuple*), a state, and a political community. The current meaning of the word "nation" originated during the French Revolution; it was conceived as a freely consented union of all citizens. Revolutionary references explain the importance the French attach to nationality law, the close relationship they establish between nationality and citizenship, and the concept of nationality law shared by a majority of citizens. For the Germans, in contrast, "nationality" has essentially ethnic connotations. Hence the notion that by a simple legal procedure an individual may join a new people is difficult for them to understand. Their attachment to "*Volk*" is attributable to the fact that for centuries, unlike the French, the Germans had neither a state nor stable territorial boundaries. Under these circumstances, only ethnic criteria allowed individuals to define themselves as Germans.[26] With the British, the misunderstandings stem from the fact that "nationality" is rarely employed in English, and that it refers in particular to an administrative formality: the ability to obtain a passport.[27] The history of Great Britain explains that what counts the most for the British is not their attachment to a nation but loyalty to the royal family. Hence the importance attributed to the notion of "British subjects" in the definition of citizenship.

The differences outlined above between French and British antidiscrimination policies cannot be understood unless we accept that each country applies its own concept of democracy to its ethnic minorities. Great Britain, consistent with "home rule" and "habeas corpus," encouraged tolerance, particularly with regard to religion, and the autonomy of communities. It modeled its policies toward ethnic groups upon its colonial experience, based on the consolidation of local authorities and the control of native leaders. This community-oriented concept of society was reinforced by the ascendancy of ethnic and religious criteria in political life. The new legislation on nationality led to the generalization within British society of the vocabulary of "race relations." Ethnic minorities themselves had appropriated the label "British Blacks," which had initially been used by the authorities to distinguish them from other citizens of the British empire. In 1991, when a census asked the entire population to indicate its ethnic origin, it became possible, in official statistics, to differentiate individuals according to their race and origin (whites, ethnic minorities, Africans, mixed).

This equal-rights policy, inspired by community-oriented principles, reinforced the structuring of British society along the same lines. For example, to implement the 1976 legislation against descrimination resulting from an individual's "racial group" (defined according to color, race, nationality, or ethnic origin), judges were compelled to adopt a logic that ultimately exacerbated these cleavages (often for the purpose of satisfying plaintiffs' claims). Hence Sikhs, Gypsies, and Rastas were newly defined as ethnic groups.[28] In a similar vein, the emergence of a labor market and political arena constructed around ethnicity led community representatives to stiffen such oppositions as a means of gaining legitimacy as spokesmen. Communities increasingly developed as autonomous entities competing to obtain specific advantages. British public policy as a whole became caught up in this logic. Everything is interpreted in community-specific terms, which leads to a spatial representation of society along ethnic lines, thereby enhancing the visibility of minorities. In London, Jamaicans tended to settle south of the Thames, while other West Indians settled to the north of the river. In certain British cities, such as Birmingham, nearly half the urban population may be composed of individuals belonging to one or another ethnic group.

The French conception of democracy inherited from the 1789 revolution is based on the primacy of the individual over the community and on the strict separation of matters regarded as private (faith and ethnicity) from those pertaining to the public sphere (political life and government policies). These are the principles applied to this day to encourage the assimilation of immigrants. Even if it were desired, an American-style "affirmative action" policy would be impossible because the instruments for its implementation do not exist. It has been prohibited by law for a century to inquire about the religion and racial, ethnic, or national background of individuals. An estimated one-third of the population living in France today is of immigrant origin (primarily from southern Europe, Eastern Europe, and Africa), but there is no way of knowing precisely. Neither is it possible to define the exact religious breakdown between Catholics, Protestants, Jews, Muslims, and others). The West Indian population in Paris may experience forms of discrimination, but French statistics provide no specific indication of this because people from the Antilles have French nationality and are included among other French citizens of the same social and professional categories. To implement a policy of positive discrimination would require surveys asking people to state their race, ethnic origin, and religion and then classifying them according to such criteria. In the eyes of the majority, such a practice would be regarded as racist and would resurrect memories of the persecution of Jews by the Vichy regime. Asked about this, an employee of the city of Roubaix (in northern France) replied: "I refuse to make people carry a yellow star."[29] No democrat in France would dare call the West Indians "French Blacks," for most citizens of the French overseas territories would regard it as an insult.[30]

French policy toward ethnic minorities is therefore strongly influenced by conceptions of society inherited from its historical past; conversely, its implementation contributes to the reinforcement of such conceptions. Hence, despite having been tempted by the Anglo-Saxon multi-ethnic model in the early 1980s, all political forces today agree that the "French model" of integration should be privileged in the formulation of policy.[31]

We can therefore conclude that European policies with respect to ethnic minorities have increasingly tended to diverge. Each society perceives in its neighbor the model that should be avoided. In France the latest report issued by the Haut Conseil à l'Intégration, responsible for overseeing the policies implemented in the immigrants' favor, strongly criticized the British model of the "right to difference," on the grounds that it encourages a "policy of minorities," which goes against the egalitarian ideal pursued by the French government.[32] John Major, on the other hand, justified his restrictive immigration policy in these terms: "I don't want to witness the development in Britain of the problems we see in Marseille. Therefore we will continue to apply our policy which consists of controlling migration flows and improving inter-racial relations."[33]

The Role of the European Convention on Human Rights

Given the helplessness of politicians, the development of a European legal framework may lay the groundwork for greater convergence. In this perspective, the most effective instrument available to the European community is the European Convention on Human Rights, as elaborated by the European Council and adopted in Rome in 1956 for the purpose of coordinating national legal frameworks in dealing with civil rights. Rather than limiting itself to a simple declaration, the Convetion establishes a full-fledged institutional mechanism for the protection of rights, which rests on three essential pillars:[34]

1. An agency for investigation and conciliation: the European Human Rights Commission
2. A political decision-making body: The Council of Ministers of the European Council
3. A legal decision-making body: the European Human Rights Court (comprised of independent judges elected to nine-year terms by the European Council Assembly)

The advocates of the rights of minorities have encountered a favorable tool in the principle of nondiscrimination, which is at the heart of the Convention.[35] The Supreme Court retained two criteria in defining the notion of discrimination: on the one hand, differences in treatment among a group of individuals entitled to a given right; on the other hand, the absence of objective and reasonable justification for a decision considered unjust by the individual in question. Given that Article 1 of the Convention stipulates its application to all persons residing in the member states, regardless of their nationality, immigrants can use it to defend themselves against certain forms of discrimination. For example, although the Convention does not guarantee the right to enter and establish oneself in any country, the jurisprudence of the European court has provided foreigners with a right to appeal in cases of expulsion. The discriminatory practices of certain cities (notably Paris) in the attribution of social welfare have been condemned, as well as discriminatory British legislation that bases entry and residency rights on the immigrants' gender. The European Human Rights Commission has condemned border controls based on ethnic identity.[36] That the results are still modest may be attributed to the fact that, unlike Americans, Europeans are not accustomed to consulting a judge as a means of defending their cause. But this situation should evolve rapidly in the years to come.

In conclusion, we are now in a position to assess the effectiveness of the two major political models of civil rights, defended in continental Europe and in the Anglo-Saxon world (Great Britain and the United States). What these models have in common is their pursuit of a shared ideal of liberty and justice. But they rest on diametrically opposed visions of the relationship between civil society and the state. In the continental European vision, the state should be present in all spheres of social life to impose egalitarian rules on its citizens. In the American conception, state policy, rather than substituting itself for communities, is based on their demands, and inequalities between individuals or groups may be corrected through the legal system. Even in those countries that are most inclined to support the logic of community, such as Sweden or the Netherlands, what Hugh Davis Graham has called the "first generation" of American civil rights has not yet been surpassed in Europe. Nor was the affirmative-action policy introduced under the Nixon administration in 1972 developed to its fullest extent in Great Britain, because of its negative appraisal by public opinion.

We have seen that Europeans insisted primarily on the social dimension of integration, whereas the Anglo-Saxon conception was fundamentally grounded in civil rights. Hence it is not surprising to observe that each political model obtained effective results in the sphere it chose to privilege. If we evaluate antisegregation policies on a social level, available results attest to the superiority, so far, of the continental European model. Studies have proven that in Switzerland, Sweden, and France, immigrants from the second generation onward enjoy the same degree of educational and professional success as their native counterparts in the same social category; and today, the deterioration of inner cities in Great Britain is worse than in French suburbs.[37] These observations are confirmed by the comparison of the South Side ghetto in Chicago and the Cité des Quatre Mille in la Courneuve (which is one of the most depressed zones and has one of the highest proportions of immigrants in the suburbs of Paris). State intervention (primarily in the attribution of housing) has preserved the coexistence of ethnic minorities and native French citizens (which still comprise 60 percent of the population) in the Paris community, whereas in Chicago, 92 percent of the population in the ghetto is black. The omnipresence of the welfare state and of the police have kept infant mortality and the crime rate in the Cité des Quatre Mille to average levels. In Chicago's South Side, due to the precariousness of welfare coverage, mortality among black children is three times higher than among whites, and 60 percent to 80 percent of families have a single parent (6 percent in la Courneuve).[38] Many studies have also shown that antidiscrimination policy in Chicago has failed to curb racism. Nathan Glazer has pointed out that the multiplication of legal actions encouraged by the adoption of civil rights laws led to the perpetual questioning of Americans as to their race, color, religion, and national origin, which in turn delineated the terms of identification and conditioned their representations of social life—even though the laws were originally intended to eliminate conflicts based on race, color, religion, or national origins.[39] Compared with France, the greater frequency and gravity of racist acts in Great Britain demonstrates that policies that politicize and accentuate the visibility of racial or ethnic differences are less effective than policies based on the separation between the activities of the state and those of the defense of human rights.[40] The aggravation of the social crisis among the poor in Anglo-Saxon societies and the failure of the struggle against racism explain why civil rights policies in the United States and Great Britain, which have generated a black bourgeoisie but have worsened the situation of the poor, are increasingly coming under fire. Hence the willingness to pay greater attention to the social dimension of these problems and less to their racial dimensions.[41]

In Europe, the continental model is also being questioned. While no one denies that on the social level its results are not as bad as in the United States, its political effects are the object of concern. In the United States, the revolution in civil rights was officially justified by the fact that the nation had a debt toward ethnic minorities, which for centuries had fallen victim to discrimination. It was felt that these communities should obtain compensation not only on social level but on a cultural one as well, by obtaining guarantees concerning their identity. In Europe, and especially in France, no such attempt was made. Although colonization also caused serious harm to the ethnic groups that have now become "immigrants,"[42] the notion of "moral debt" is nonexistent. Hence the low degree of legitimacy attributed by the French to the separate culture and history of these communities. In fact, the latter are constantly degraded, implicitly or explicitly, by a policy of integration that is defined completely in relation to the nationality and culture of citizens of the host countries.[43] This is undoubtedly one of the reasons organizations of the far right have been successful in the two countries where the models of assimilation are the most rigid (France and Germany), whereas their influence is negligible in the Anglo-Saxon countries.[44] These parties today threaten democracy, and democrats are at a loss as to how to check their development.

Ecole Normale Supérieure, Paris

Acknowledgment

This essay was translated from French by Geoffroy de Laforcade.

Notes

1. See Hugh Davis Graham, *The Civil Rights Era* (New York, 1990).

2. This expression is put in quotation marks because, as we shall see, some researchers deny the existence of such minorities.

3. Alexis de Tocqueville, *De la Démocratie en Amérique* (Paris, 1981), with an important preface by F. Furet: "Le système conceptual de la 'Démocratie en Amérique,' " 7–46.

4. Ibid., 454.

5. Ibid., 457.

6. This occurred even in the formal colonial empire, albeit in a context of extreme racial and ethnic diversity. On these differences between France and the United States, see Gérard Noiriel, *The French Crucible* (Minneapolis, 1994; French edition 1988).

7. Tocqueville, *Démocratie*, 134.

8. This explains why in all the European countries, participation in elections is stronger than in the United States, frequently attaining 70 percent to 80 percent of the electorate.

9. Social deductions vary between 40 percent and 50 percent of the GNP in Europe, which is much higher than in the United States or Japan.

10. These figures are not precise. On the one hand, they account for internal migrations within Europe (for example, in Germany a quarter of the foreign population comes from other EEC nations; and in France the Portuguese, European citizens, are the largest single immigrant community). On the other hand, the figures exclude African and Asian emigrants who remained citizens of the host country when the colonies proclaimed independence. (These national immigrants comprise a significant share of the total population in Great Britain and Holland.)

11. Stephen Castles and Godula Kosacks, *Immigrant Workers and Class Structure in Western Europe* (New York, 1973).

12. On this issue, see Thomas Hammar, ed., *European Immigration Policy: A Comparative Study* (Cambridge, 1985), and Dominique Schnapper, *L'Europe des immigrés* (Paris, 1992).

13. Dominique Schnapper, *L'Europe de l'intégretion: Sociologie de la nation* (Paris, 1991).

14. Unlike in other European nations, which have long been countries of emigration, France has been a country of immigration only since the nineteenth century.

15. On the differences between French and German definitions of citizenship, see Rogers Brubaker, *Citizenship and Nationhood in France and Germany* (Cambridge, Mass., 1992).

16. Ann Dummett and Andrew Nicol, *Subjects, Citizens, Aliens, and Others: Nationality and Immigration Law* (London, 1990).

17. Whereas until then nationality law had been, as in the United States, exclusively grounded in *jus soli*, in 1971 for the first time the government introduced *jus sanguinis* by adding the notion of "patrial" to British law. The 1981 British Nationality Act further reinforced these dispositions. Today, even the children of ethnic minorities have trouble becoming British citizens.

18. In Germany as well, although the situation varies from one *länder* to another, ethnic minorities were granted the right to vote in local elections (notably in Hamburg) and to a specific education. Muslim religion is taught in public schools in accordance with programs established by the University of Cairo; with Muslim educators paid by the

German state. Native minorities, such as Frisians and Danes, obtained recognition of their cultural identities.

19. Arend Lijphart, *The Politics of Accommodation: Pluralism and Democracy in the Netherlands* (Berkeley and Los Angeles, 1975).

20 Paul Sieghart, ed., *Human Rights in the United Kingdom* (London, 1988).

21. See Richard Jenkins and John Solomos, eds., *Racism and Equal Opportunity in the 1980s* (Cambridge, 1987), and John R. Edwards and Richard Batley, *The Politics of Positive Discrimination* (London, 1978).

22. In France as well, many immigrants from the former colonies enjoy full civil rights, but as French citizens. Such is the case, in particular, of residents from the Overseas Departments and Territories (the Antilles, French Polynesia, and the islands of Réunion). Citizens of the former colonies, however, legally became foreigners at the time of independence. In certain cases (such as Algeria), they could nonetheless choose between French nationality and that of their country of origin.

23. Didier Lapeyronnie and Marcin Fribes (with the collaboration of Kristin Cooper and Daniele Joly), *L'Intégration des minorités immigrées: Etude comparative France-Grande-Bretagne* (Paris, 1990).

24. Since 1901, associations in France had depended on private law; they are therefore juridically separate from state institutions.

25. See Cathie Lloyd, "Concepts, Models, and Anti-Racist Strategies in Britain and France," *New Community* 18 (October 1990): 63–73.

26. Only since reunification have the German people enjoyed territorial boundaries that pose no major political problems.

27. Patriotism is of course as pronounced in Great Britain as it is in France, but it is expressed through loyalty to the royal family rather than through nationality.

28. John Crowley, "Le Rôle de la Commission for Racial Equality dans la représentation des minorités ethniques britanniques," *Revue Européenne des Migrations Internationales* 6 (Fall 1990): 45–61.

29. Lapeyronnie and Fribes, *L'Intégration*.

30. The term "colored people" is also considered racist in France, considering that everyone, whites included, has a skin color. It must be recalled that the community of French citizens includes several million blacks (if immigrants are added to individuals residing in the Overseas Departments). Numerically, they are a larger group than those of North African origin.

31. To compare with the American model, see especially Donald Horowitz, "Immigration and Group Relations in France and America," in Donald Horowitz and Gérard Noiriel, *Immigrants in Two Democracies: The French and American Experience* (New York, 1992).

32. Quoted by John Crowley, "Le Modèle britannique d'intégration," *Migrations-Sociétés* 24 (November–December 1992): 37–45.

33. *Daily Express*, 8 April 1992, quoted by Alex Hargreaves, "Islam, education et politique," *Migrations-Sociétés* 24 (November–December 1992): 56–67.

34. See Frederic Sudre, *Droit international et européen des droits de l'homme* (Paris, 1989).

35. The restrictive nature of this convention for European governments is illustrated by the reticence many of them manifested prior to signing. France delayed ratification of the text for twenty-four years. While twenty-one countries of the European Council have signed the Convention, seventeen did so after expressing reservations on one or more articles they deemed unacceptable.

36. European institutions have been used to defend their civic demands, particularly those related to minority languages. In 1981, the European parliament voted to adopt a charter on linguistic and cultural rights for minorities. In 1982, a European bureau of the least widespread languages was created. And in 1988, the European Council Assembly adopted a project for a European charter of minority languages and cultures, which France was able to ratify only by amending the second article of its Constitution, which states that

"the language of the republic is French." See Henri Giordan, ed., *Les Minorités en Europe* (Paris, 1982).

37. This is also because Great Britain is today a poorer country than France (its GNP is 28 pecent lower).

38. Loïc J. D. Wacquant, "The Comparative Structure and Experience of Social Exclusion: 'Race,' Class, and Space in Chicago and Paris," in R. Lawson, C. McFate, and W. J. Wilson, eds., *Urban Marginality and Social Policy in America and Western Europe* (Newbury Park, Calif., forthcoming).

39. Nathan Glazer, *Affirmative Discrimination: Ethnic Inequality and Public Policy* (New York, 1975).

40. The greater gravity of racist acts in Great Britain can be attributed to the fact that they tend to be collective, whereas in France they are typically committed by isolated individuals. The problem raised here is clearly that of statistical recording. That the surveys are equally trustworthy and measure the same phenomena in both countries would have to be verified.

41. For the English case, see P. Gilroy, *There Ain't No Black in the Union Jack* (London, 1987). For the United States, see Alphonso Pinkney, *The Myth of Black Progress* (New York, 1984).

42. We know that in practice Americans reject the terms "immigrants" and "foreigners" to designate ethnic minorities because these terms are regarded as xenophobic.

43. Sami Naïr, *Le Regard des vainqueuers* (Paris, 1992).

44. In France the National Front, the leading party of the far right, now routinely obtains between 10 percent and 15 percent of the vote. On the issue of racism in France today, see P. A. Taguieff, ed., *Face au racisme* (Paris, 1992).

MARY ANN GLENDON

Rights in Twentieth-Century Constitutions: The Case of Welfare Rights

In the 1960s and 1970s, when the judicial rights revolution was in full swing in the United States, poverty lawyers and allied legal scholars urged the courts to add to the expanding catalog of constitutional rights certain social and economic rights—to housing, education, and a minimum decent subsistence. The advocates of welfare rights were not deterred by the absence of pertinent constitutional language. After all, if the Court could find a right to privacy in the "penumbra" of the Bill of Rights, who knew what else might be discovered there? Those efforts to constitutionalize what were historically matters of legislative discretion had only partial success. The Supreme Court did hold that, once government grants certain statutory entitlements such as welfare and disability benefits, the recipients have a constitutional right not to be deprived of those benefits without procedural due process.[1] The Court declined, however, to find that the entitlements themselves were constitutionally required.[2]

That result is hardly surprising in view of the fact that the welfare state was not even a twinkle in the eye of the Founding Fathers. It is worth speculating, though, about what a contrary holding in the 1960s and 1970s might have meant. The experience of other liberal democracies is illuminating in that connection, for most of their constitutions *do* contain welfare rights or solemn acknowledgments of collective responsibility to provide minimum decent subsistence to needy citizens.[3]

American Distinctiveness

The chief lesson to be learned from examining the way welfare is imagined in foreign legal systems is that, in this area as in so many others, the

United States is in a class by itself. The age of our Constitution is fore-most among the features that set the United States apart from other liberal democracies. The overwhelming majority of the world's constitu-tions have been adopted within the past thirty years.[4] The American regime of constitutional rights, however, was over a century old when the New Deal transformed the liberal night-watchman state into a liberal regulatory welfare state. In most of the nations with which we ordinarily compare ourselves, the sequence was just the reverse. In Canada, France, and Germany, for example, the foundations of the welfare system were in place well before the appearance there of regimes of judicially enforceable constitutional rights.[5]

A second distinguishing feature is that the American Constitution, unlike the constitutions of most other liberal democracies, contains no language establishing affirmative welfare rights or obligations. A third factor is the conspicuous unwillingness of American governments to ratify several important international human rights instruments to which all the other liberal democracies have acceded. And finally there is the unusual structure of our welfare state, which, much more than elsewhere, leaves pensions, health insurance, and other benefits to be organized privately, mainly through the workplace, rather than directly through the public sector. I will elaborate briefly upon the first three of these factors.

We Americans are justly proud of our long tradition of protecting individual rights, celebrated in this bicentennial decade of the Bill of Rights. We also take patriotic satisfaction in that, prior to 1945, we were one of very few countries that protected constitutional rights through judicial review. It is worth recalling, however, that American courts seldom exercised the power of judicial review claimed in *Marbury v. Madison* until the turn of the century, and then the courts deployed the power in a way that may well have impeded the development of the welfare state here for decades.[6] In the era of *Lochner* (1905), when the American Supreme Court routinely struck social legislation in defense of property rights, legislators in the rest of the industrialized world were busily constructing their infant welfare states on the basis of statutes broadly similar in spirit to those our Court was striking down.[7]

It was not until the active period of constitution-making following World War II that other nations widely adopted bills of rights and institu-tional mechanisms to enforce them.[8] At that time, the majority of liberal democratic countries opted for variants of a system developed in prewar Austria that has come to be known as the "European model" of constitu-tional control.[9] The principal feature that distinguishes the "European" from the "American" model is that, under the former, constitutional questions must be referred to a special tribunal that deals only or mainly with such matters. Constitutional adjudication is off-limits for other courts in such countries. It is only in the United States, and in the relatively small group of countries that have adopted the "American model," that ordinary courts have the power to rule on constitutional questions in ordinary lawsuits. Many nations that have adopted the European model are still further distanced from our system by the fact that constitutional questions may be presented to the constitutional tribunal only by other courts *sua sponte,* or by political authorities, but not by private litigants.[10]

Even among the handful of countries that have adopted a form of the American model of judicial review, such as Canada, Japan, and the Republic of Ireland, the United States remains unique. For in those nations, neither the supreme courts nor the lower courts thus far have exercised their powers of judicial review with such frequency and boldness as their American counterparts have exercised at both the state and federal levels. Indeed, to foreigners, the recent burgeoning of state court constitutionalism and the innovative use of injunctions by federal district courts beginning in the 1960s are two of the most remarkable features of the American legal system. Even if judicial activism in the Supreme Court has subsided somewhat in recent years,[11] the relative readiness of American judges at all levels of jurisdiction to deploy their powers of judicial review in the service of a variety of social aims has made the United States the model of a particularly adventurous form of judicial-rights protection.

What Counts as a Right?

A renowned European legal historian recently compiled a list he described as representing the "basic inventory" of rights that has been accepted by "most western countries" at the present time.[12] The list includes, first and foremost, human dignity, then personal freedom, fair procedures to protect against arbitrary governmental action, active political rights (especially the right to vote), equality before the law, and society's responsibility for the social and economic conditions of its members. An American reader of this list is apt to be struck both by the omission of property rights and by the inclusion of affirmative welfare obligations. Yet the list cannot be faulted as description of the law on the books of "most western countries." Welfare rights (or responsibilities) have become a staple feature of postwar international declarations[13] and have been accorded a place beside traditional political and civil liberties in the national constitutions of most liberal democracies.[14] It is the eighteenth-century American Constitution that, with the passage of time, has become anomalous in this respect.

As Gerhard Casper has pointed out, these differences regarding the rights that are accorded constitutional status in various countries are not merely a function of the age of the documents establishing those rights.[15] To a great extent, the differences are legal manifestations of divergent, and deeply rooted, cultural attitudes toward the state and its functions. Historically, even eighteenth- and nineteenth-century continental European constitutions and codes acknowledged state obligations to provide food, work, and financial aid to persons in need.[16] And continental Europeans today, whether of the right or the left, are much more likely than Americans to assume that governments have affirmative duties actively to promote the well-being of their citizens.[17] The leading European conservative parties, for example, accept the subsidization of child-raising families and the funding of health, employment, and old-age insurance at levels most Americans find scarcely credible.[18] By contrast, it is almost obligatory for American politicians of both the right and the left to profess mistrust of government.

These divergent attitudes toward the state have found constitutional expression in what are sometimes called "negative" and "positive" rights. The American Bill of Rights is frequently described as a charter of "negative" liberties, protecting certains areas of individual freedom from state interference.[19] Judge Richard Posner has succinctly stated the position: "The men who wrote the Bill of Rights were not concerned that the federal government might do too little for the people, but that it might do too much to them."[20] The Supreme Court, while willing to accord procedural due process protection to statutory welfare entitlements, has consistently declined to recognize constitutional welfare rights.[21] Chief Justice Rehnquist's opinion in *DeShaney v. Winnebago County Department of Social Services* reaffirmed that the Due Process Clause of the Fourteenth Amendment was "a limitation on the State's power to act, not . . . a guarantee of certain minimal levels of safety and security."[22]

These statements contrast markedly with the attitudes of the post–World War II European constitution-makers who supplemented traditional negative liberties with certain affirmative social and economic rights or obligations. The idea of government underlying the "positive rights" in European constitutions has a complex history. In part, it represents a transposition to the modern state of the feudal notion that an overlord owed certain protection to his dependents in exchange for their service and loyalty. More proximately, it reflects the programs of the major European political parties—one large group animated by Christian social thought, and another by socialist or social democratic principles. As Casper has observed, it was only natural that peoples accustomed to the notion of a state with affirmative responsibilities would carry that idea forward when they added bills of rights to their constitutions.[23]

In view of the long-standing American rights tradition, and the recent history of expansive judicial protection of a broad spectrum of individual and minority rights, the third aspect of American distinctiveness may at first glance seem puzzling. I refer to the dubious distinction of the United States as the only liberal democracy that has not ratified a number of important human rights instruments, notably the two United Nations Covenants on Civil and Political Rights, and on Economic, Social, and Cultural Rights.[24] This reticence, no doubt, is due in large part to our prudent unwillingness to submit to the jurisdiction of international organizations dominated by critics of the United States. But, particularly where economic and social rights are concerned, our reluctance is also attributable to our prevailing ideas about which sorts of needs, goods, interests, and values should be characterized as fundamental rights. Another likely reason is that the American civil litigation system is now well equipped to handle the potential consequences of characterizing a new set of interests as fundamental rights.

Welfare Rights and Welfare States

The reaction of many Americans to the foregoing contrasts might be that we have little to learn from other nations about welfare, and even less about rights. Other Americans, especially reformers who do not regard this American distinctiveness as a badge of honor, might be drawn in the opposite direction, toward viewing the rights or welfare arrangements in other countries as promising models for the United States to follow. Such reform-minded persons might ask: How have constitutional welfare rights worked out in practice? Do the "experiments" of other nations shed any light on what might have happened here had the Supreme Court in the late 1960s and early 1970s found a basis for welfare rights in the Fourteenth Amendment?[25] Though I will conclude that those questions lead almost to a dead end, it is instructive to examine why they do not open an especially fruitful line of inquiry.

As it happens, the contrast between the means of implementation of the American welfare system and other welfarist systems is less sharp than it initially appears. Though many countries have included welfare rights or obligations in their constitutions, no democratic country has placed social and economic rights on precisely the same legal footing as the familiar civil and political liberties. In most cases, the drafters have formulated the former somewhat differently than the latter.[26] In some countries, for example, the constitutional welfare language is so cryptic as to be meaningless without extensive legislative specification.[27] More common, the constitutions do specifically enumerate various social and economic rights, but present them merely as aspirational political principles or goals to guide the organs of government as they carry out their respective functions. For example, the Swedish Instrument of Government, in a section entitled "The Basic Princples of the Constitution," provides:

> Art. 2. . . . The personal, economic and cultural welfare of the individual shall be fundamental aims of the activities of the community. In particular, it shall be incumbent on the community to secure the right to work, to housing and to education and to promote social care and security as well as a favorable living environment.[28]

Continental lawyers call such rights "programmatic" to emphasize that they are not directly enforceable individual rights, but await implementation through legislative or executive action, and through budgetary appropriations. Programmatic rights figure prominently in the constitutions of the Nordic countries, as well as in the French, Greek, Italian, and Spanish constitutions.

The most interesting case in some ways is Japan, which accepted the American model of judicial review in 1947. In Japan, the catalog of constitutional rights (thanks to the New Dealers in the postwar occupational government) includes much of Franklin Roosevelt's "Second Bill of Rights,"[29] some of which are set forth in terms that are not, on their face, programmatic.[30] There is a right to decent minimum subsistence in Article 25, a right to receive an education in Article 26, and a right to work in Article 27.[31] In the drafting process, Article 25 was changed from a purely programmatic provision ("In all spheres of life, the State shall use its endeavors for the promotion and extension of social welfare and security, and of public health"), to a proclamation beginning with unvarnished American-style rights language ("All peole shall have the right to maintain the minimum standards of wholesome and cultured living").[32]

The adoption of the 1947 Constitution was quickly followed, however, by a Japanese Supreme Court decision holding that the right to a minimum standard of decent living in Article 25 was programmatic. The government's constitutional welfare obligations, according to that decision, "must, in the main, be carried out by the enactment and enforcement of social legislation. . . . [The] state does not bear such an obligation concretely and materially toward the people as individuals."[33] In the years that followed, the Japanese Supreme Court has maintained the view that the welfare rights in the Constitution are not judicially enforceable individual rights. In a leading case, *Asahi v. Japan*, decided in 1967, the Court held:

> [Article 25(1) merely proclaims that it is the duty of the state to administer national policy in such a manner as to enable all the people to enjoy at least the minimum standards of wholesome and cultured living, and it does not grant the people as individuals any concrete rights. A concrete right is secured only throught the provisions of the Livelihood Protection Law enacted to realize the objectives prescribed in the provisions of the Constitution.[34]

The *Asahi* decision went on to say that government officials would have to determine the minimum standard of living, subject to review for excess or abuse of power. In Japan, then, as in the countries where constitutional welfare rights are explicitly programmatic, and as in countries like our own without any constitutional welfare rights at all, the welfare state has been constructed through ordinary political processes.[35]

At this point, we might wonder whether the formal differences between the United States and other welfare states have any significance at all. After all, we too have a "program"—the New Deal statutes of the 1930s and 1940s, supplemented by the Great Society statutes of the 1960s—that comprises the cornerstone of our welfare state. Specifically, we have both aspiration and implementation in the Social Security Act of 1935, whose preamble declares that the statute is:

> To provide for the general welfare by establishing a system of Federal old-age benefits, and by enabling the several States to make more adequate provision for aged persons, blind persons, dependent and crippled children, maternal and child welfare, public health, and the administration of their unemployment compensation laws.[36]

Similarly the Housing Act of 1949 calls for "the realization as soon as feasible of the goal of a decent home and a suitable living environment for every American family."[37]

Should we conclude, then, that the provisions of modern constitutions which commit the state to affirmatively protecting certain economic and social rights have little or no practical consequence? That conclusion seems too strong, if only because such rights at least endow statutes implementing the constitutional "program" with a strong presumption of constitutionality.[38] Moreover, the constitutional status of social and economic rights seems likely to have synergistically reinforced welfare commitments by influencing the terms, the categories, and the one of public, judicial, and legislative deliberation about rights and welfare.[39] In countries with an already well-established welfare tradition, constitutional welfare commitments may well have been strengthened by that tradition, just as our Bill of Rights both emerged from and buttressed the Anglo-American rights tradition.

Nevertheless, there does not appear to be any strict correlation between the strength of constitutional welfare language and the generosity of welfare states, as measured by the proportion of national expenditures devoted to health, housing, social security, and social assistance.[40] For example, the United Kingdom, with no constitutional welfare rights, devotes proportionately more of its resources to social expenditures than its richer "neighbor" Denmark, where rights to work, education, and social assistance are constitutionally guaranteed. And analogous social expenditures consume considerably more of the budget of Germany, whose constitution merely announces that it is a "social" state, than they do in Sweden or Italy, whose constitutions spell out welfare rights in some detail.[41]

If there is a relationship between the constitutional states of welfare rights and the type of strength of a society's welfare commitment, it is only a loose relationship of consanguinity, with both the constitution and the welfare system influenced by such factors as the homogeneity or diversity of the population, the degree to which mistrust of government has figured in the country's political history, the vitality of political parties, the health of the legislative process, and the intensity of individualism in the culture. Such speculation leads only to the sort of conclusions that make sociology so unsatisfying to many people. It is difficult to become excited about the idea that a host of mutually conditioning factors, of which the constitutional status of welfare rights may be both cause and consequence, determines in numerous ways the shape of a given country's welfare state: its basic commitments, the priorities among those commitments, the spirit in which it is administered, the degree of support and approval it wins from taxpayers, and the extent to which it disables or empowers those who resort to it.

What If . . . ?

Still, a reform-minded American might consider the inconclusiveness of the foregoing analysis a source of encouragement. If the experience of other liberal democracies is any guide, the reformer might contend, according constitutional status to social and economic rights at least does not seem to cause any harm. At the margins, it may well exert a benign influence on the legislative process and on public deliberation by broadening the range of officially recognized social concerns, heightening their visibility, and underscoring their legitimacy. What a pity, the argument would go, that we have not bolstered the legal status of social and economic rights, either by recognizing them in our Constitution, as proposed to the Supreme Court in the 1960s and 1970s, or by ratifying the United Nations Covenant on Social, Economic, and Cultural Rights, as the Carter administration advocated in the 1970s.

It would be risky, in my view, however, to draw those inferences from the foreign experience, for reasons that reside, not in the foreign experience, but in distinctive American attitudes toward rights. Americans, for better or worse, take rights very seriously. It is not just the term but the very idea of "programmatic" rights that is unfamiliar and uncongenial to us. It is thus almost inconceivable that the constitutional welfare rights, had they appeared in the United States, would have been regarded by the public or treated by the legal community as purely aspirational. An American, hearing of a "right" that merely represents a goal or ideal, is apt to react as Mark Twain did when he learned that a preacher was condemning the Devil without giving the Devil the opportunity to confront the witnesses against him. "[It] is irregular," he said. "It is un-English; it is un-American; it is *French.*"[42] Most Americans, like Holmes and Llewellyn, believe that a right-holder should be able to call upon the courts to "smite" anyone who interferes with that right.[43] Furthermore, we take for granted that behind the courts' orders to respect that right are sheriffs, marshals, and the National Guard, if necessary.

As soon as we begin to imagine constitutional welfare rights that are other than programmatic, however, we start down a road that no other democratic country has traveled. That does not mean that we cannot make an educated guess about what consequences would be likely to follow if we made such a trip: recent history suggests that the most likely consequence of according constitutional status to social and economic rights would be something that has not occurred in the other liberal democracies—namely, a great increase in federal litigation.[44]

Still, comparing the United States to other countries does illuminate the problem. It demonstrates that we Americans place an unusual degree of reliance on our tort system (both ordinary personal injury litigation and constitutional tort actions) to perform certain social tasks that other advanced industrial nations handle with a more diversified range of techniques—for example, direct health and safety regulation and social insurance.[45] That reliance, in turn, suggests some further questions: Is our tort system well suited for all the jobs we at present ask it to do? Do our substantive tort law and our civil litigation system adequately assure timely, fair, and cost-efficient disposition of legitimate claims, while effectively discouraging frivolous ones? If a major reason for court-centered reform efforts in the United States has been "legislative paralysis,"[46] can American legislatures ever be induced to take an active role in improving public services in the areas of health, education, and welfare?

The Utility of Cross-National Comparisons

It may seem to follow from the discussion thus far that, contrary to what I asserted at the outset, Americans have little to gain from consulting other nations' experiences with rights and welfare. Certainly anyone who expects comparative studies to yield specific models for domestic law reform is bound to be disappointed,[47] for it is fairly clear that no other country has blazed a trail for the United States to follow. Nevertheless, the experiences of other countries may help us to find our own path by heightening our awareness of indigenous resources that we are inclined to overlook or underrate.

Beginning in the mid-1970s, economics became a constraint for all advanced welfare states. Even the Nordic countries (whose citizens are as proud of their famous cradle-to-grave welfare systems as we are of our Bill of Rights) began to sense that they had reached the limits of high taxation and direct public-sector provision of services. In that climate, policymakers abroad have gazed with interest at our relatively greater capacity for governmental and nongovernmental organizations to cooperate in the areas of health, education, and welfare, and at our ability, through our sort of federalism, to innovate and experiment with diverse approaches to stubborn social problems.

In some cases, tentative efforts at imitation have followed. In the area of industrial relations, for example, some countries have begun to experiment with American-style laws encouraging collective bargaining rather than the direct state regulation of the terms and conditions of employment that has been traditional in continental Europe.[48] Our innovative labor legislation of the 1930s—which has practically fallen into desuetude in the United States—has been seen in France and Germany as the prototype of "reflexive law" (legal norms that aim at facilitating and structuring private ordering, rather than imposing top-down state regulation).[49] And policymakers abroad have also begun to consider whether some types of social services can be delivered more efficiently and humanely by intermediate associations—churches, unions, community groups, and so on—than by the government. Our voluntary sector, shambles though it may appear to us, is still more vibrant than its counterparts in nations where excessive centralization has nearly extinguished nongovernmental initiatives in the areas of health, education, and welfare.[50]

Ironically, these American institutions and experiences are attracting interest abroad just when they are showing the effects of long neglect at home. The United States represents a rare working example, albeit an imperfect one, of what European writers call the principle of "subsidiarity": the notion that no social task should be allocated to a body larger than the smallest one that can effectively do the job.[51] The legal apparatus that promotes and facilitates the subsidiarity principle includes federalism, relfexive legal norms that foster private ordering, and programs that use the mediating structures of civil society, such as churches and workplace associations, to help deliver social services.

These aspects of American law are attracting increased attention because every country in the democratic world is experiencing a tension between two ideals—a regime of rights and a welfare state. Every country is grappling with a set of problems that are in a general way similar: how to provide needed social aid without undermining personal responsibility; how to achieve the optimal mix of markets and central planning in a mixed economy; and how to preserve a just balance among individual freedom, equality, and social solidarity under constantly changing circumstances. The problem of constitutional rights in the welfare state is nothing less than the great dilemma of how to hold together the two halves of the divided soul of liberalism—our love of individual liberty and our sense of a community for which we accept a common responsibility.

Below the surface of that dilemma lies a more serious one. Neither a strong commitment to individual and minority rights nor even a modest welfare commitment like the American one can long be sustained without the active support of a citizenry that is willing to respect the rights of others; that is prepared to accept some responsibility for the poorest and most vulnerable members of society; and that is prepared to accept responsibility, so far as possible, for themselves and for their dependents. We should make no mistake about the fact that liberal democratic welfare states around the world are now demanding certain kinds of excellence in their citizens to a nearly unprecedented degree. They are asking men and women to practice certain virtues that, even under the best of conditions, are not easy to acquire—respect for the dignity and worth of one's fellow human beings, self-restraint, self-reliance, and compassion.

The questions that seldom get asked, however, are these: Where do such qualities come from? Where do people acquire an internalized willingness to view others with genuine regard for their dignity and concern for their well-being, rather than as objects, means, or obstacles? These qualities do not arise spontaneously in homo sapiens. Nor can governments instill them by fear and force. Perhaps there are alternative seedbeds of civic virtue besides families, neighborhoods, religious groups, and other communities of memory and mutual aid. If there are, however, history provides scant evidence of them. It is hard to avoid the conclusion that both our welfare state and our experiment in democratic government rest upon habits and practices formed within fragile social structures— structures being asked to bear great weight just when they are not in peak condition. The question then becomes: What, if anything, can the government do to create and maintain (or at least to avoid undermining or destroying) social conditions that foster the peculiar combination of qualities required to sustain our commitments to the rule of law, individual freedom, and a compassionate welfare state?

In a large, heterogeneous nation such as the United States, this question about the underpinnings of civic virtue is particularly urgent. It has been constantly repeated since Tocqueville said in the 1830s that America was especially well endowed with moral and cultural resources—with vital local governments, and with a variety of associations that stood between citizens and the state.[52] As with our natural resources, however, we have taken our social resources for granted, consuming inherited capital at a faster rate than we are replenishing it. Indeed, like an athlete who develops the muscles in his upper body but lets his legs grow weak, we have nurtured our strong rights tradition while neglecting the social foundation upon which that tradition rests.

We Americans, with our great emphasis in recent years on certain personal and civil rights, have too easily overlooked the fact that all rights depend on conserving the social resources that induce people to accept and respect the rights of others. Perhaps it is time, therefore, to take a fresh look at our constitutional framework, and to recall not only that the Bill of Rights is part of a larger constitutional structure, but that its own structure includes more than a catalog of negatively formulated political and civil liberties. As Akhil Reed Amar has pointed out, scholars, litigators, and judges who concentrated singlemindedly in the 1960s and 1970s on judicial protection of individual and minority rights permitted other important parts of our constitutional tradition to fall into obscurity.[53] As it happens, those parts of the tradition that have been in the shadows—federalism, the legislative branch, and the ideal of government by the people—have an important bearing on maintaining the social capital upon which all rights ultimately depend.

And so, by a long and circuitous route, a cross-national approach to rights and the welfare state points back toward the American Constitution and toward the "Madisonian understanding that individual liberty and strong local institutions need not be at cross-purposes with one another."[54] If America's endangered social environments do indeed hold the key to maintaing simultaneously a liberal regime of rights and a compassionate welfare state, then we must start thinking about how both rights and welfare, as currently conceived, affect those social environments. Reflecting upon our own tradition, moreover, should give us pause before indulging the disdain for politics that underlies so much current thinking about legal and social policy. One of the most important lessons of 1789 the world learned anew in 1989: that politics is not only a way to advance self-interest, but a way to transcend it. That transformative potential of the art through which we order our lives in the polity is our best hope for living up to our rights ideals and our welfare aspirations in the coming years.

Harvard Law School

Notes

1. *Goldberg v. Kelly,* 397 U.S. 254 (1970) (welfare entitlements); *Mathews v. Eldridge,* 424 U.S. 319 (1976) (social security disability payments).

2. E.g., *Lindsey v. Normet,* 405 U.S. 56 (1972) (no constitutional right to housing); *San Antonio Independent School District v. Rodriguez,* 411 U.S. 1 (1973) (no constitutional right to education).

3. Louis Favoreu, "La Protection des droits economiques et sociaux dans les constitutions," in *Conflict and Integration: Comparative Law in the World Today* (1988), 691–92.

4. Three-quarters of the approximately 160 single-document constitutions in the world have adopted since 1965. Lis Wiehl, "Constitution, Anyone? A New Cottage Industry," *New York Times,* 2 February 1990, B6 (citing Professor Albert P. Blaustein of the Rutgers Law School).

5. Expanded suffrage in the French Third Republic and fear of militant socialism in Bismarck's Germany in the late nineteenth century led those countries to adopt factory legislation, rudimentary social welfare laws, and statutes regulating commerce and public utilities. France adopted a limited form of constitutional control only in 1958, and judicial

review was established in Canada only in 1982. In Germany, though some courts in the Weimar Republic had claimed the power to rule on the constitutionality of laws, constitutional review did not become a significant feature of the legal order until 1951, when the Federal Constitutional Court was established in what was then West Germany. Donald Kommers, *The Constitutional Jurisprudence of the Federal Republic of Germany* (Durham, N.C., 1989), 6–11.

6. As James Q. Wilson has noted. In the first seventy-five years of this country's history, only two federal laws were held unconstitutional; in the next seventy-five years, seventy-one were. Of the roughly nine hundred state laws held to be in conflict with the federal Constitution since 1789, about eight hundred were overturned after 1870. In one decade alone—the 1880s—five federal and forty-eight state laws were declared unconstitutional. James Q. Wilson, *American Government: Institutions and Policies,* 3d ed. (Lexington, Mass., 1986), 83.

7. See, for France, Leon Duguit, *Law in the Modern State* (London, 1919), 32–67 (translated by Frida and Harold Laski); and for England, A. V. Dicey, *Lectures on the Relation Between Law and Public Opinion in England During the Nineteenth Century* (London, 1914), 259–302. See, generally, Alexander Alvarez, "Dominant Legal Influences of the Second Half of the Century", in *The Progress of Continental Law in the Nineteenth Century,* 11 Continental Legal History Series 31 (Boston, 1918), 52–56.

8. For a concise survey of the development of judicial review, see Louis Favoreau, "American and European Models of Constitutional Justice," in David S. Clark, ed., *Comparative and Private International Law: Essays in Honor of John Henry Merryman* (Berlin, 1990), 105–11.

9. For a discussion of why the American model was widely regarded as unsuitable for transplant, see Mauro Cappelletti, *Judicial Review in the Contemporary World* (New York, 1971), 53–66.

10. Favoreau, "American and European Models, 112–13. But Germany is an exception. There the bulk of the caseload of the Constitutional Court consists of constitutional complaints by private citizens. Kommers, *Constitutional Jurisprudence,* 32–33.

11. I use the word "somewhat" advisedly. See, for example, *Missouri v. Jenkins,* 110 S Ct 1651 (1990), in which the Supreme Court *in dicta* authorized a lower federal court, as part of a desegregation plan, to direct a local school district to levy taxes for capital improvements to schools, even without the normal requirement that the voters approve.

12. Franz Wieacker, *Foundations of European Legal Culture,* 37 *American Journal of Comparative Law* 1, 29 (1989).

13. See, for example, the *United Nations Universal Declaration of Human Rights,* adopted by the General Assembly on 10 December 1948:

Article 22
Everyone, as a member of society, has the right to social security and is entitled to realization, through national effort and international cooperation and in accordance with the organization and resources of each State, of the economic, social, and cultural rights indispensable for his dignity and the free development of his personality.
Article 25
Everyone has the right to a standard of living adequate for the health and well-being of himself and his family, including food, clothing, housing and medical care and necessary social services, and the right to security in the event of unemployment, sickness, disability, widowhood, old age or other lack of livelihood in circumstances beyond his control.

The *United Nations Covenant on Economic, Social and Cultural Rights* was opened for signature in December 1966 and came into force a decade later after being ratified by nearly ninety countries, but not, so far, by the United States. The United States did, however, sign the Universal Declaration and the *Helsinki Final Act of 1975* (which, like the *Universal Declaration,* calls for a nonbinding commitment to stated human rights). See, generally,

Richard B. Lillich, *United States Ratification of the United Nationas Covenants*, 20 *Georgia Journal of International and Comparative Law* 279 (1990); Louis B. Sohn, "United States Attitudes Toward Ratification of Human Rights Instruments," 20 *Georgia Journal of International and Comparative Law* 255 (1990).

14. The formulations vary from the bare recitation in the Geman Basic Law of 1949 that the Federal Republic of Germany is a "social" state (Article 20), to detailed lists of specific social and economic rights such as those contained in the constitutions of France, Italy, Japan, Spain, and the Nordic countries.

15. Gerhard Casper, *Changing Concepts of Constitutionalism: Eighteenth to Twentieth Century*, 1989 *Supreme Court Review* 311, 318–19 (the Continental concept of the "state" is closer to the Anglo-American notion of the "welfare state" or the "administrative state"). See also Leonard Krieger, *The German Idea of Freedom: History of a Political Tradition* (Boston, 1957).

16. See Casper, 1989 *Supreme Court Review*, 319–21. Early constitutions used the language of obligation rather than of rights: for example, "It is incumbent on the authorities of the State to create conditions which make it possible for every person who is able to work to earn his living by his work." Norwegian Constitution of 1814, 110, reprinted in Gisbert H. Flanz, *Norway*, in Albert P. Blaustein and Gisbert H. Flanz, eds. *Constitutions of the Countries of the World* (Dobbs Ferry, N.Y., 1976).

17. "[The state achieves legitimacy] not so much through its constitution as through the active, welfare-providing administration." Casper, 1989 S Ct Rev, 325 and n. 69 (quoting a treatise by a former constitutional law professor now serving on the German Constitutional Court).

18. See William Pfaf, *Barbarian Sentiments: How the American Century Ends* (New York, 1989), 25.

19. See David P. Currie, *Positive and Negative Constitutional Rights*, 53 *University of Chicago Law Review* 864 (1986), which includes discussion of instances in which the U.S. Supreme Court has found "duties that can in some sense be described as positive" in negatively phrased provisions of the Constitution.

20. *Jackson v. City of Joliet*, 715 F2d 1200, 1203 (7th Cir 1983).

21. The Court did, however, extend procedural due process protection to certain forms of "new property." See, for example, *Goldberg v. Kelly*, 397 US 254 (1970) (welfare entitlements); *Mathews v. Eldridge*, 424 US 319 (1976) (social security disability benefits).

22. 489 US 189, 195 (1989).

23. Casper, 1989 *Supreme Court Review*, 331.

24. Alfred de Zayas, "The Potential for the United States Joining the Covenant Family," *Georgia Journal of International and Comparative Law* 299 (1990); Lillich, *United States Ratification of the United Nations Covenants*, 20.

25. See, for example, Frank I. Michelman, *The Supreme Court 1986 Term-Foreword: On Protecting the Poor Through the Fourteenth Amendment*, 83 *Harvard Law Review* 7 (1969).

26. "[T]here are two categories of fundamental rights: immutable and absolute rights that exist whatever the epoch or the reigning ideology; and other rights, known as economic and social rights, that 'carry a certain coefficient of contingency and relatively' and whose recognition is a function of the state of society and its evolution." Favoreau, *La Protection des droits economiques*, 701.

27. For example, the German republic is a "social" state. German Basic Law of 1949, Art 20. The treaty of German reunification, however, obliges the legislature to consider adding a list of affirmative "goals of the state" to the traditional political and civil rights at present enumerated in the Basic Law. Fred L. Morrison, "Constitutional Mergers and Acquisitions: The Federal Republic of Germany," 8 *Constitutional Commentary*.

28. Gisbert H. Flanz, *Sweden*, in Blaustein and Flanz, eds., *Constitutions*, 9–11.

29. The "Second Bill of Rights," which Roosevelt urged in his 1944 State of the Union message, included the following:

The right to a useful and remunerative job in the industries or shops or farms or mines of the nation;

The right to earn enough to provide adequate food and clothing and recreation;

The right of every family to a decent home;

The right to adequate medical care and the opportunity to achieve and enjoy good health;

The right to adequate protection from the economic fears of old age, sickness, accident, and unemployment;

The right to a good education.

See Cass R. Sunstein, "Constitutionalism After the New Deal," 101 *Harvard Law Review* 421, 423 (1987) (quoting Roosevelt's "Second Bill of Rights"). See also Cass R. Sunstein, *After the Rights Revolution: Reconceiving the Regulatory State* (Cambridge, Mass., 1990), 21–22.

30. See Akira Osuka, "Welfare Rights," 53 *Law and Contemporary Problems* 13 (1990). See also Nobushige Ukai, "The Signifance of the Reception of American Constitutional Institutions and Ideas in Japan," in Lawrence Ward Beer, ed., *Constitutionalism in Asia: Asian Views of the American Influence* (Berkeley and Los Angeles, 1979), 114–27.

31. Property as such is not among the rights protected. It supposedly was excluded in order to conform the Japanese procedural guarantees to the American Due Process Clause as it stood *de facto* after the U.S. Supreme Court accepted "the necessity of direct state intervention in social and economic processes." Osuka, 53 *Law and Contemporary Problems*, 15–16. According to Osuka, the Japanese Constitution "substantially incorporat[ed] the fruits of the New Deal," Id at 16. The Japanese Constitution of 1947 is set forth in Hiroshi Itoh and Lawrence Ward Beer, eds., *The Constitutional Case Law of Japan: Selected Supreme Court Decisions, 1961–70* (Seattle, 1978), 256–69.

32. The original programmatic draft proposal was retained as Article 25(2), preceded by the right to a minimum standard of living in Article 25(1). Osuka, 53 *Law and Contemporary Problems*, 15.

33. Ibid., 21.

34. *Asahi v. Japan*, translated and reprinted in Itoh and Beer, eds., *The Constitutional Case Law of Japan*, 130, 134.

35. Shortly after adopting the 1947 Constitution, Japan supplemented its prewar social legislation with a series of important statutes in the areas of unemployment relief, social security, and child welfare. Osuka, 53 *Law and Contemporary Problems*, 16 n. 5.

36. Preamble, Social Security Act, 49 Stat 620 (1935), codified at 42 USC 301 et seq (1988).

37. Housing Act of 1949, 63 Stat 413 (1949), codified at 42 USC 1441 et seq (1988).

38. See Osuka, 53 *Law and Contemporary Problems*, 17–18.

39. For an example of how the constitutional principle of the social welfare state has affected the interpretation of the equality principle in Germany, see the German Constitutional Court decision which held that medical schools could not impose numerical limits on admissions unless they had class-size restraints. Numerus Clausus Case I, 33 BVerfGE303 (1973), excerpted in Kommers, *Constitutional Jurisprudence*, 295–302. The Court explicitly stated: "Any constitutional obligation [of the legislature] that may exist does not include the duty to supply a desired place of education at any time to any applicant." Of the constitutional right to education, the Court also said: "[We] need not decide whether . . . an individual citizen can use this constitutional mandate as the basis for an enforceable claim [against the state] to create opportunities for higher study."

40. Percentages of central government expenditure devoted in 1988 to health, housing, social security, and welfare in selected countries with "high-income economies" are as follows:

Federal Republic of Germany	67.6%
Sweden	55.3

Norway	46.8
Italy	45.8
United Kingdom	44.5
United States	44.0
Canada	43.2
Ireland	42.7
Denmark	42.4

World Development Report 1990, table 11 (Central Government Expenditure) (New York, 1990), 198–99.

41. Ibid. One cannot fit the United States readily into such comparisons because of the unique structure of our welfare state. But sophisticated analyses consistently rate us poorly, especially in assisting child-raising families. See Alfred J. Kahn and Sheila B. Kamerman, *Income Transfers for Families with Children: An Eight-Country Study* (Philadelphia, 1983), 182–95; Samuel H. Preston, "Children and the Elderly in the U.S.," *Scientific American* 44 (December 1984), 251; Timothy M. Smeeding and Barbara Boyd Torrey, "Poor Children in Rich Countries," *Science* 873 (November 1988), 242.

42. Mark Twain, *Concerning the Jews, in The Writings of Mark Twain: Literary Essays* (New York, 1899), 263, 265.

43. Oliver Wendell Holmes, Jr., *The Path of the Law*, 10 Harvard Law Review 457, 460–61 (1897); Karl Llewellyn, *The Bramble Bush* (Dobbs Ferry, N.Y., 1960), 85.

44. For example, since the 1960s, Section 1983 has been the second most heavily litigated section of the United States Code. Peter H. Schuck, *Suing Government: Citizen Remedies for Official Wrongs* (New Haven, 1983), 199.

45. Basil S. Markesinis, "Litigation-Mania in England, Germany, and the USA: Are We So Very Different?" 49 *Cambridge Law Journal* 233, 243–44 (1990).

46. Ibid., 242.

47. For a critique of the use of comparative law as a source of "models," see Rodolfo Sacco, "Legal Formats: A Dynamic Approach to Comparative Law," 39 *American Journal of Comparative Law*.

48. See Mary Ann Glendon, "French Labor Law Reform 1982–83: The Struggle for Collective Bargaining," 32 *American Journal of Comparative Law* 449, 485–91 (1984).

49. "Reflexive law" is an expression used by some legal sociologists to designate an alternative to direct regulation, in which legal norms shape procedures to coordinate interaction among social subsystems, rather than prescribe outcomes. See Gunther Teubner, "Substantive and Reflexive Elements in Modern Law," 17 Law and Society Review 239, 276 (1983).

50. For a comparison of nongovernmental service organizations in the Netherlands, England, Israel, and the United States, see Ralph M. Kramer, *Voluntary Agencies in the Welfare State* (Berkeley and Los Angeles, 1981).

51. Markus Heintzen, "Subsidaritatsprinzip and Europaische Gemeinschaft," 46 Juristenzeitung 317 (1991).

52. Alexis de Tocqueville, *Democracy in America* (New York, 1953), 126–33.

53. Akhil Reed Amar, "The Bill of Rights as a Constitution," 100 Yale Law Journal 1131, 1133–37 (1991).

54. Ibid., 1136.

Contributors

HUGH DAVIS GRAHAM is Holland N. McTyeire professor of American history at Vanderbilt University. His recent publications include *The Civil Rights Era* (Oxford, 1990) and *Civil Rights and the Presidency* (Oxford, 1992).

JANE SHERRON DE HART is Professor of History at the University of California at Santa Barbara. Her most recent publications include her prize-winning study (with Donald G. Mathews), *Sex, Gender, and the Politics of ERA* (1990); (with Linda Kerber) *Women's America: Refocusing the Past* (1991); "Gender on the Rights: Meanings Behind the Existential Scream," *Gender and History* 3 (1991); and "Oral Sources and Contemporary History," *Journal of American History* 79 (1993).

PETER SKERRY is Director of Washington Programs at UCLA's Center for American Politics and Public Policy and has been a fellow at the American Enterprise Institute and the Brookings Institution. He has a Ph.D. in political science from Harvard and has written for numerous publications, including *The New Republic, Commentary,* the *New York Times,* the *Wall Street Journal,* and *The Public Interest.*

EDWARD D. BERKOWITZ, Professor and Chairman, Department of History, George Washington University, writes on social welfare policy. His publications include *Disability Policy* (1987), *America's Welfare State* (1991), and, most recently, *Social Security and Medicare: A Policy Primer* (1993). An associate editor of the *Journal of Disability Policy Studies,* Berkowitz is a participant in a continuing Milbank Foundation project on the implementation of the Americans with Disabilities Act.

GÉRARD NOIRIEL is Professor of Social History at the Ecole Normale Supérieure in Paris. He has published extensively on labor and immigration history, focusing most recently on issues of national identity. He has authored *The French Crucible: A History of Immigration in France, 19th–20th Centuries* (forthcoming, University of Minnesota Press) and *La Tyrannie du National* (Calmann-Lévy, 1991) and co-edited *Immigrants in Two Democracies: French and American Experience* (New York University Press, 1992).

MARY ANN GLENDON is the Learned Hand Professor of Law at Harvard Law School. Her recent books include *Rights Talk* (1991), *The Transformation of Family Law* (1989), and *Abortion and Divorce in Western Law* (1987).